ADVANCED
EXPERT
COURSEBOOK

Jan Bell and Roger Gower

Contents

Contents

Exam overview

➤ See pages 167–172 for more detailed information and task strategies.

Cambridge *Certificate in Advanced English* has four papers. Paper 1 receives 40% of the total marks and the other three papers have 20% each. The pass mark is based on an overall mark (you do not need to pass every paper to pass the exam). There are three pass grades (A, B and C) and two fail grades (D and E).

Paper	Task type	Task description
Paper 1: Reading and Use of English 1 hour 30 minutes Eight parts 56 questions in total	**Part 1:** multiple-choice cloze (8 questions) **Part 2:** open cloze (8 gaps) **Part 3:** word formation (8 gaps) **Part 4:** key word transformation (6 questions) **Part 5:** multiple choice (6 questions) **Part 6:** cross-text multiple matching (4 questions) **Part 7:** gapped text (6 questions) **Part 8:** multiple matching (10 questions)	**Part 1:** Choosing a word or phrase from four options to fill in gaps in a text. **Part 2:** Filling in gaps in a text with an appropriate word. **Part 3:** Changing the form of a given word to make it fit the gaps in a text. **Part 4:** Using a given word to complete a sentence so that it means the same as a previous sentence. **Part 5:** Answering four-option multiple-choice questions on a text. **Part 6:** Matching a prompt to the relevant part of one of four texts. **Part 7:** Completing a gapped text with paragraphs which have been removed and placed in jumbled order. **Part 8:** Matching information to 4–6 different texts (or different parts of a text).
Paper 2: Writing 1 hour 30 minutes Two tasks (one compulsory, the other a choice out of three options) 220–260 words each	**Part 1:** essay (compulsory) **Part 2:** one writing task: the choice may include a letter, a proposal, a review or a report	**Part 1:** An essay based on two points in the input text. **Part 2:** Carrying out a writing task, using an appropriate format and style. There are three task types to choose from.
Paper 3: Listening Approximately 40 minutes Four parts 30 questions in total	**Part 1:** multiple choice (6 questions) **Part 2:** sentence completion (8 questions) **Part 3:** multiple choice (6 questions) **Part 4:** multiple matching (10 questions)	**Part 1:** Three short unrelated extracts of around 1 minute each; each extract has two three-option multiple-choice questions. **Part 2:** A 3–4-minute monologue with eight sentence completion questions. **Part 3:** A 4-minute interview or discussion with six four-option multiple-choice questions. **Part 4:** Five short related monologues of around 30 seconds each. There are two tasks of five questions each, which must be selected from a list of eight options.
Paper 4: Speaking Approximately 15 minutes Four parts	**Part 1:** conversation, giving personal information (2 minutes) **Part 2:** 'long turn', giving information and expressing opinions (1 minute each candidate) **Part 3:** collaborative task, exchanging information and ideas (3–4 minutes) **Part 4:** discussion, developing the topic from Part 3 (5 minutes)	**Part 1:** The interlocutor asks each candidate questions about themselves. **Part 2:** Each candidate, individually, compares two out of the three photos given (1 minute) and comments briefly on the other candidate's photos (30 seconds). **Part 3:** Each candidate works with a partner for 2 minutes to discuss a task based on a diagram. They then try to reach a decision in 1 minute. **Part 4:** The interlocutor leads a discussion between the two candidates, developing the topics related to Part 3.

1 Success

Lead-in

1 Look at the photographs. What did these people have to do to achieve success?

2a How important are the following factors in becoming successful? Put them in order of importance for each photo (1 = the most important, 10 = not important at all).

| ability to take risks | a supportive family | clear focus | determination | financial security |
| hard work | innate ability | luck | ruthlessness | self-confidence |

b Compare your answers and discuss, giving examples from your experience.

c What differences would there be for a successful sportsperson?

3 How important is success to you? Is it more important than friends and family?

Reading (Paper 1 Part 8)

Before you read

1 a Read the title, introduction and text headings. Which jobs do you think are the most and least prestigious?

b What qualifications, personal qualities, work experience, etc. would you need in order to get one of these jobs? What might hold you back from achieving your aim?

Scanning

2 a Read the questions first, highlighting the key points that are reported. This will help you find the information you are looking for in the text. The first one is done for you.

b Read each extract quickly and highlight information which answers the questions.

Multiple matching

3 Read the strategy, then do the task. Use the Help notes for support with certain items.

EXPERT STRATEGY

Scan the sections to find ideas or information which answer the questions, but make sure the meaning is exactly the same. See page 169 for a full list of strategies.

➤ **HELP**

1 More than one person had financial problems, but who was quite poor at one stage of his/her life?

3 Look for an expression that means *confirm somebody's good character or ability* in the text.

5 Look for a phrase which means *knowing influential people*.

---

*For questions **1–10**, choose from the people (**A–D**). The people may be chosen more than once.*

Which person

overcame a financially disadvantaged background to become successful?	1
was rewarded for all the effort put into a work placement?	2
believes that personal recommendation was the main factor in obtaining a job?	3
appreciated being offered encouragement and expertise as a student?	4
is aware that knowing influential people would have been a career benefit?	5
used to feel depressed by the lack of job opportunities?	6
finds the prospect of having to pay back a student loan daunting?	7
had a couple of false career starts?	8
is unsure about future career prospects?	9
had a strong preference about what kind of place to study at?	10

Discussion

4 What do all these successful people seem to have in common?

5 Check the meaning of these key words from the text.

EXPERT WORD CHECK

against the odds   CV   foresee   half-hearted   master's degree
networking   portfolio   scrape through   shadow (*v*)   vital

---

The secret of my success

Four high-flying graduates talk about what it takes to land a top job in one of the elite professions.

A The barrister

At the age of nine, without a word of English, Hashi was sent from Kenya to live in Britain, where he was raised exclusively on state benefits, with very little to live on. 'I attended badly performing schools and was always moving around between different relatives.' Despite this, Hashi managed to scrape through his exams and get into university to study law. Much later, having done a master's degree, he was inspired to become a barrister so that he could represent people in court. 'But first you have to do a work placement where you shadow a barrister. Unfortunately, it took me 18 months before I was accepted because I didn't have any contacts in the profession. It isn't fair, but there is no point trying to pick a fight with a system.' Now a junior barrister at a top firm, Hashi attributes this outstanding achievement against the odds to a combination of the people who believed in him, the scholarships and loans which enabled him to afford the course, strong self-discipline and a lot of hard work.

B The fashion designer

Having set her heart from childhood on a career in costume design, Lilly worked in the theatre straight after school, only to realise that this job wasn't for her. Literature, which she tried next, bored her. 'So I sent some drawings off and was accepted for an art degree, which I loved because I had tutors who knew what they were talking about. But it was the head of the course on my master's degree in fashion who really helped me to develop my confidence and individual style. Every summer, I was taken on for a three-month work placement, organised by the college. I took these really seriously – I can't understand people who are half-hearted about them. In my second year I was making prints 16 hours a day for a famous designer and some of them got used in his fashion collection.' However, though Lilly did work for a number of well-known designers, there were also discouragingly long periods of unemployment before she finally got a permanent job.

C The banker

While still at the London School of Economics (LSE), Wen Du got some work experience in banking. 'LSE helps you to find these work placements but it's still quite tough, so I had to do loads of networking. When you are eventually looking for a job, you need certain academic qualifications so companies will be interested in interviewing you. But, after that, it's more about how much you know about banking, so experience while you are still at university is vital. I was working 12–13 hours a day during my placements but you take long hours in your stride provided you are learning. After I finished university, I was offered a job at one of my work placements. However, I had the opportunity to do a master's degree in finance, so I did that first. For me, salary isn't the main priority in a first job; it's about how much you can learn and how much responsibility your line manager will give you. I want to do well, but because there are so many uncertainties in our field, I can't foresee where I'll be in five years.'

D The architect

Having eventually settled on architecture as a career, Amandine came to London from the USA and started building a portfolio of her work by attending local college courses. This got her onto a university foundation art course and then into the highly competitive Architectural Association (AA) school. 'I picked the AA because it has such a close-knit family atmosphere, which for me is essential. But I knew I couldn't go there unless I got a scholarship because the fees are so high, especially given that the course takes seven years. Even though I had two-thirds of it paid for me, I still owe a fortune; the debt is a huge weight on your shoulders at my age. I now have a job in a company that has always interested me, thanks to friends that worked here and could vouch for me. It's great to have an impressive CV but even better to have a good character reference.'

Vocabulary

Collocations: adjectives + nouns

1a Complete each sentence with an adjective from A and a noun from B.

A

close-knit	heavy	high	main	tight	wide

B

community   deadlines   priority   salary   variety
workload

1 How much does finding a job with a ____ ____ matter to you?
2 What is the ____ ____ for you when looking for a job?
3 Are you good at meeting ____ ____ ?
4 Would you be willing to take on a ____ ____ ?
5 Would you enjoy being part of a ____ ____ at work?
6 How important is it for you to have a ____ ____ of work to do?

b Ask and answer the questions in Exercise 1a about your attitude to jobs.

Verbs + nouns

2a Underline one word/expression in each set that does not normally collocate with the word(s) in bold.

1 **take something** *personally / severely / seriously*
2 **make** *the best of something / time for something / the opportunity for something*
3 **take** *a list / no for an answer / the time to do something*
4 **hand in** *your resignation / your business / your essay*
5 **do** *a course / law / a good impression*
6 **have** *a speech / a career / an impact*

b Tell each other two true things about your own life and one untrue thing, using the expressions in Exercise 2a. Ask your partner to guess which one is untrue.

Phrasal verbs and expressions with *take*

3a Circle the correct prepositions in 1–8. Then replace the phrases in *italics* in sentences a–h with one of these expressions in the correct form.

1 take something *in / at* your stride
2 be taken aback *with / by* someone
3 take no notice *at / of* something
4 take pleasure *of / in* something
5 take pity *on / at* someone
6 take advantage *of / with* something or someone
7 take exception *with / to* something
8 take pride *in / of* something/someone.

a Have you ever *used a particular situation to get what you want from* something/someone?
b What things do you *ignore*?
c What do you *enjoy doing*?
d Have you ever *been very surprised or shocked by* someone's behaviour?
e Which difficult things do you *do without effort*?
f Have you ever helped someone that you *felt sorry for*?
g Which of your achievements do you *feel a great sense of self-respect about*?
h Have you ever *been angry or upset by* anything someone has said?

b Ask each other the questions in Exercise 3a, using the expressions with *take*. Did anything surprise you?

4a Complete the text with words from Exercises 1–3.

My (1)____ priority after leaving university was to try and pay off some of my student loan. I applied for jobs, but the interesting ones had all been **snapped up**. I ended up at a burger bar and decided to (2)____ the best of it.

I was a bit taken (3)____ at first by the (4)____ workload, but I took it all in my (5)____ and learnt things which **have stood me in good stead** later in life. Dealing with a (6)____ variety of people **from all walks of life** was **part and parcel** of the job and I use these skills to help me with problems which **crop up** nearly every day in my present job as a journalist.

b Look at the idiomatic expressions in bold and discuss possible meanings.

Discussion

5 At what age do people normally start working in your country? How important is it to have a work placement to get experience before you are offered a permanent job?

Use of English 1 (Paper 1 Part 3)

Word formation

1 Look at the title and guess what the article will be about.

2 Read the article and work out which part of speech (e.g. adjective) fits in each space.

3a Read the strategy, then do the task. Use the Help notes for support with certain items.

EXPERT STRATEGY

Read the whole sentence, not just the line, to work out your answers. See page 167 for a full list of strategies.

➤ **HELP**

1 What suffix do you need to add to make this abstract noun?

3 This word needs two changes – a prefix to make the opposite of the adjective, and a suffix to make an adverb.

4 Is this singular or plural?

*For questions 1–8, read the text below. Use the words given in capitals at the end of some of the lines to form a word that fits in the gap **in the same line**. There is an example at the beginning (0).*

The office as a playground

Having set up an IT server company when he was only 19, entrepreneur Daniel Foster's next project was to create an environment which would bring a feeling of (0) *playfulness* into the workplace and help avoid stress. He believes that, for young people growing up with technology, there is no real (1)_____ these days between work and home. Although his company's offices look dreary from the outside, appearances can be (2)_____ . Inside the building, amongst the games consoles, football tables and floor cushions, workers are barefoot and (3)_____ dressed in shorts, rather than in more conventional suits and ties. Work still goes on though. Daniel's (4)_____ regard fun as a reward rather than an excuse not to work and he justifies the (5)_____ cost by pointing out that happy relaxed staff tend to be more (6)_____ in their work. He also believes that a pleasant atmosphere helps with the (7)_____ of staff. Workers from one of his main (8)_____ are often amongst the first to apply for any job vacancies.

PLAY

DIVIDE

DECEIVE

FORMAL

EMPLOY

ADD
PRODUCE

RECRUIT
COMPETE

b Make a note of the new words you created in Exercise 3a and other parts of speech connected to them. Underline the stressed syllable in each word.

Discussion

4 How important is the environment you work or study in? Give reasons.

Listening 1   Developing skills

Before you listen

1   You will hear a business manager called David Thomas telling a group of university students how to make a good impression at job interviews. What do you think he will say? Make a list of *Dos* and *Don'ts*.

2   🎧 01   Listen to the introduction. How will his talk be organised?

Using discourse markers: separating main points from details

3   🎧 02   Listen and number David's main points in the order he talks about them. Notice how discourse markers (e.g. *OK*), pauses and changes in tone of voice show that he is moving on to the next point. Write down any discourse markers you hear.

Main points		Tips
a Get together your paperwork __	→	Investing in a **(1)**____ will help you to organise it.
b Use relaxation techniques __	→	Imagine you're a **(2)**____ even before the interview begins.
c Look your best _1_	→	Ensure that your clothes are both **(3)**____ and comfortable.
d Check out the route __	→	A **(4)**____ beforehand is recommended.
e Do your homework __	→	Time spent on **(5)**____ is never wasted.

Listening for specific information

4a   Look at David's tips. Think of the type of word which will go in each gap. Use the exact words if you can remember them.

b   🎧 03   Listen again and complete the tips with 1–3 words or check your answers. The speaker will not say the sentences in exactly the way that they appear on the page, but the words you need to write down are always in the audioscript.

c   Discuss your answers.

Sentence completion (Part 2)

5a   Read information from the second part of the talk below and predict what kinds of word are missing.

b   🎧 04   You will hear part of an interview in which business manager David Thomas is talking about how to make a good impression at interviews. For questions **1–4**, complete the sentences with a word or short phrase. (Note: in the exam there will be 8 questions.)

> Making a good impression at interviews
>
> David says that it's important for interviewees to smile and establish **(1)**____ when first meeting the interview panel.
>
> David recommends that interviewees focus on their **(2)**____ when seated.
>
> David advises interviewees not to speak in excess of **(3)**____ when answering a question.
>
> In David's opinion, if interviewees lack **(4)**____ when they speak, then interviewers will start to lose interest in what candidates are saying.

c   Compare your answers and check you have spelt the words correctly.

6   Which of David's advice did you find useful? Is there anything you disagree with?

> **EXPERT WORD CHECK**
>
> favourable   feasible   fidget (*v*)   long-winded   moderate
> mumble (*v*)   pay off (*v*)   ramble (*v*)   safety margin   slouch

Language development 1

➤ EXPERT GRAMMAR page 173

Mixed verb forms: present and past (simple, perfect and continuous)

1a Read the extract. Would you like an experience like this? What does the title mean?

◉ **Browsing blogs**

Time out, not time off

A few years ago, I **(1) had** six months free between finishing law school and starting as a trainee solicitor. I **(2) was feeling** restless and wanted to do something exciting, but I didn't have much money.

Then I met someone at a party who **(3) had just got back** from the USA, where **(4) she'd been working** as a guide in one of their national parks. I immediately applied to the same organisation and was offered a job in Hawaii.

When you arrive, you **(5) get** a crash course in plant biology, history and geology so that you can lecture on the volcanic history of the islands to tourists. At first I used to have very little confidence but as I got used to it, I'd improvise and even make some jokes.

(6) I've been working as a solicitor for a few years now, so **(7) I'm earning** a reasonable amount. But **(8) I've** still **never been** anywhere that I've liked more than Hawaii.

b Name the verb forms in bold. Underline other examples of the same verb forms.

c Explain why one verb form is used rather than another. Then check your answers in Expert grammar on page 173.

d Which two verb forms (not in bold) in the text can be used to talk about habit in the past? Are they interchangeable in this context?

Perfect and simple forms

2 Circle the most appropriate form of the verbs in *italics*.

1 Hawaii *is / has been* the most exotic place I *have ever been / ever went* to.
2 I *am / have been* with this firm for years. I *joined / have joined* it when I got back from my gap year.
3 Lucy *had / has had* much more money since she *got / has got* promoted recently.
4 I *stopped / had stopped* feeling nervous by the time I *was called / being called* for interview.
5 I *have / have had* a company Audi for a year now and before that I *owned / had owned* a second-hand Fiat.
6 Tom *sent / has sent* off CVs to around 50 companies before he *got / has got* an interview.

Continuous forms

3 Tick the simple and continuous forms that are used correctly. Correct those which aren't. There may be more than one possible answer.

After her boss **(1)** *was sacking* her from her secretary's job because she **(2)** *had been daydreaming*, J K Rowling **(3)** *was starting* to write the first Harry Potter novel. However, 12 publishers **(4)** *rejected* it before Bloomsbury **(5)** *were giving* her a contract. She has now **(6)** *sold* well over a million copies.

Mixed verb forms

4a Complete the text with the present, past or past perfect of the verbs in brackets. Use either the simple or continuous form. There may be more than one possibility.

The Beatles' famous audition for Decca records **(1)_____** (take place) in London in 1962. Decca's representative, Smith, **(2)_____** (already/see) the band perform and arranged a recording session at Decca's London studio. After driving down from Liverpool on 1st January, the band **(3)_____** (arrive) just before their audition was due to take place because it **(4)_____** (snow) heavily all the way down the motorway. To make matters worse, Smith then **(5)_____** (turn up) late because he **(6)_____** (celebrate) New Year's Eve the night before.

After the Beatles **(7)_____** (record) around 15 songs, Decca rejected them on the grounds that 'guitar groups are on their way out.' The Beatles then **(8)_____** (go on) to become the most popular group in history and 50 years later, people **(9)_____** (still/buy) their music.

b Write a few sentences about a band or author you like, using simple, perfect and continuous forms.

Writing 1 Using an appropriate register

1a Read this extract from a letter and answer the questions.

 1 What is the writer's reason for writing? What does he/she hope to achieve?

 2 Who is the writer writing to? How does this affect the style?

However, the principal reason for writing (1) *on this occasion / this time* is to (2) *say how fed up I am / express my dissatisfaction* with the inadequate parking facilities in place at your college. The (3) *rationale for encouraging / main reason why we encourage* our young people to get a driving licence as soon as they are legally entitled to do so is (4) *so that they can / to enable them* to transport themselves to college without having to (5) *be reliant / rely* on their parents. As you (6) *must realise, / are doubtless aware,* the local town council has recently (7) *imposed / put in place* parking restrictions (8) *just near / in the immediate vicinity* of the college, and therefore, (9) *I must urge you to / please could you consider* finding a (10) *way round / solution* to this problem as soon as possible.

b Circle the correct alternatives to complete the extract, and give reasons. The choice will depend on how formal you want to be.

2 Read this informal email (A) and then work with a partner to complete a similar email, in a semi-formal style (B). The first letter of each missing word is given and there is sometimes more than one possibility.

A

Subject: travelling funds

Hi Judi,

Thought I'd drop you a line and ask if I could take you up on your offer to lend me some money.

The thing is that I've just finished my university course and I'm really keen to use this time to do some volunteering overseas – and pick up another language while I'm at it. But I won't be able to do this unless I can get some cash to pay for my flight and living expenses!

I REALLY don't want to put you under any pressure, but we have loads of friends in common who'll tell you I can be trusted to pay you back!

Please get in touch – you have my mobile number.

Hope to hear from you soon.

Cheers,

Chloe

B

Subject: travel grant

Dear Mr Turner,

I am writing (0) regarding the advertisement for a travel grant which I saw online.

Having just (1) c_____ my three-year university course, I am anxious to do some volunteering overseas, which means I'll also be able to (2) a_____ another language.

However, I will be (3) u_____ to do this unless I (4) r_____ some kind of financial (5) a_____ which will (6) e_____ me to pay for my flight and living expenses.

I know a (7) n_____ of people who would be able to (8) v_____ for my character, should you wish to (9) c_____ them.

I look forward to your (10) r_____ .

Yours sincerely,

Tom Wilmott

3 Look back at texts A and B in Exercise 2. Find an example of each of these stylistic features in the emails. Write formal (*F*) or informal (*I*) in the list below.

 __ phrasal verbs
 __ contracted forms
 __ complex structures
 __ idiomatic expressions
 __ dramatic punctuation
 __ linking words
 __ missing pronouns

4a You have just finished a holiday job in an English-speaking country. Unfortunately, you were not happy with *one* aspect of the job. Work in pairs to decide what the job could be and what problems might have come up.

b Write a polite letter to your ex-employer to express your disappointment.

Listening 2 (Paper 3 Part 2)

Before you listen

1 Discuss these questions.

What problems can some young children have when they start school in a foreign country? What can be done to help them?

2 Read this extract from a talk by a teacher.

> 'When I first started teaching there before we had our impressive hi-tech buildings with their wonderfully light and airy classrooms and interactive whiteboards, all our premises looked run-down. But the lessons were fun, partly because nearly all the children were born in the village and grew up there.'

1 Complete the sentence with a word or short phrase from the text. You must use the exact words (maximum three).
Louise uses the word (1)_____ *to describe the building where she first taught.*

2 Which word(s) or idea in the text could distract you into giving the wrong answer?

Sentence completion

3 🎧 05 Look at the task below. Read the questions and the strategy carefully, then listen and do the task. Use the Help notes for support with certain items.

EXPERT STRATEGY

In Paper 3 Part 2, you are listening for concrete pieces of information. Your answers will follow the same order as the information in the text. See page 171 for a full list of strategies.

➤ HELP

2 Is your answer about Louise or another teacher?

3 You are listening for a medium of communication.

6 Which subject were all the students together for?

You will hear a teacher called Louise Rosberg talking about the integration of migrant children into the primary school where she works. For questions 1–8, complete the sentences with a word or short phrase.

MIGRANT CHILDREN AT PRIMARY SCHOOL

Louise uses the word (1)_____ to describe the building where she first taught.

When migrant children first came into the school, Louise tried using a (2)_____ to engage the interest of the other students.

The school once asked migrant children to prepare a (3)_____ about their own countries.

Louise gives the example of (4)_____ as a subject which the migrant children found particularly challenging.

When funds were provided to help migrant children, (5)_____ made decisions about how to spend them.

Currently, the only subject in which migrant pupils are fully integrated into lessons is (6)_____ .

On occasions, (7)_____ are employed to help improve migrant children's behaviour.

Louise mentions that migrant children get guidance on (8)_____ from specialists when they go on to secondary school.

Discussion

4 What are the advantages of having migrant children in schools?

EXPERT WORD CHECK

affluent   allocate   an initiative   assimilate   grasp (*n*)   liaise
mainstream   master (*v*)   mutual respect   stretch (*v*)

What are the advantages of these ways of learning?

A

B

Speaking (Paper 4 Part 2)

Vocabulary: feelings

1a Sentences 1–8 express how some of the learners in the pictures might be feeling. Ignore the gaps at this stage and match them to pictures A, B and C.

1 It's difficult not to feel ____ with information. There's just too much of it.

2 I rarely feel ____ into working at weekends. I don't have to if I don't want to.

3 My instructor's very friendly. I never feel ____ by him.

4 When you work on your own it's easy to get ____ and look out the window.

5 I was very ____ about how I would feel about being the only one, but once we got started, it was great.

6 They all look as though they want to work hard. They seem such a ____ group.

7 I'm lucky. I'm a ____ student because I have a caring instructor there to help me.

8 At last! I was so ____ when he stopped talking. I was finding it hard to concentrate.

b Underline the stress on these words. Use a dictionary if necessary. Then complete the sentences in Exercise 1a using these words.

apprehensive   directionless   disillusioned
distracted   engaged   inspired   intimidated
motivated   muddled   overwhelmed   passive
pressurised   relieved   self-conscious
well-supported

c Make sentences for some of the other words in the box to show you know their meaning. Use a dictionary if necessary.

d 🎧 06 Group the adjectives according to how many syllables there are in the word. Say each word, then listen to check.

2a Complete each sentence about one of the pictures. Use the words in Exercise 1 and any other words you know.

1 It's easy to get bored because …
2 You get far more involved in what you're learning when …
3 You can get discouraged when …
4 So as not to feel too overwhelmed, it's best to …
5 Unless you're self-disciplined, …
6 If the communication is two-way, …
7 When you get positive feedback, …

> How might the learners be feeling?

b Think of a learning situation you have been in (e.g. a driving lesson, a sport). Tell your partner about it using the headings below to say what the experience was like, but don't say what it is you learnt.

1 the teaching approach
2 what you liked best/found most satisfying
3 the most difficult aspect
4 whether you would like to have learnt it in a different way

c Try and guess what your partner learnt and then ask more about the situation.

3a Read the strategy.

EXPERT STRATEGY

In Paper 4 Part 2, you should not simply describe the pictures – your response should include hypothesis or speculation from the start.
See page 172 for a full list of strategies.

b 🎧 07 Look at the photos again. Listen to the interlocutor's instructions and answer the questions.

1 What TWO things does the task involve?
2 How long does the candidate have to do it?

c 🎧 08 Listen to Simon doing the task. Which learning situations did he talk about? Do you agree with the points he made about each one?

Useful language: comparing, contrasting and speculating

4a 🎧 09 Listen again to the sample answer in Exercise 3c and complete these sentences about the pictures, using your own ideas or Simon's.

1 These situations are similar because ____ .
2 The most obvious difference between the situations is that ____ whereas ____ .
3 Unlike the students in the first picture, who ____ , the person ____ .
4 They're bound to be a bit ____ .
5 I expect she's feeling ____ because ____ .
6 It looks as if ____ . There seems to be ____ . It must be ____ . (*Choose one*)

b In the recording, what three expressions did the student use in place of *I think*?

Long turn

5 Work in pairs. Turn to page 203. Take turns to do the task in Exercise 3b. Each of you should use a different combination of photos. The person who is not doing the task should time the other one (about one minute).

Task analysis

6 Did you complete both parts of the task and speak for a full minute? If not, what problems did you have?

Language development 2

The passive

1 Look at these sentences. When is the passive used?

1 I was made to feel very welcome by the others.
2 The students seemed overwhelmed by all the data being thrown at them.

➤ EXPERT GRAMMAR page 174

2a Rewrite the sentences with the passive. Begin with the words given.

1 We must give all students an identity card.
   All students _____ .
2 Someone's starting the fires deliberately and they're spreading very quickly.
   The fires _____ .
3 They say he is the greatest drummer alive.
   He _____ .
4 They'll send out the results in six weeks.
   The results _____ .
5 We can't do anything about it without a receipt.
   Nothing _____ .
6 We've decided that we'll interview three students.
   It _____ .
7 My grandmother has just given me that chair.
   That chair _____ .

b Compare the active and passive alternatives in questions 1 and 2 in Exercise 2a. When would the passive be more natural? When would the active be more natural?

3a Complete the text with the correct form of the verbs in brackets.

⊚ **Browsing blogs**

Good-quality feedback is important to the development of learners, but too often a tutor's response **(1)____** (perceive) as demoralising and unhelpful. As a way of improving the process, some trainers now use screen-capture software, which **(2)____** (allow) their computer screen and voice **(3)____** (record) at the same time. First, a web link **(4)____** (email) to the student and, on **(5)____** (open), a video clip **(6)____** (start) to play, showing the homework that the student **(7)____** (submit) earlier. A section of the text **(8)____** (highlight), and the tutor's voice **(9)____** (can/hear) making comments. Students **(10)____** (remark) that, when teachers **(11)____** (give) video feedback, they **(12)____** (tend) to elaborate on the good points more and, if suggestions for improvement need **(13)____** (give), they **(14)____** (explain) more fully.

b How do you feel when you are given written feedback on work you have done? Which ideas in the text in Exercise 3a do you agree with and why?

4 Complete the sentences with your own ideas, using the passive form of the verbs in brackets.

1 I remember once I _____ . (give)
2 If you come to my country you _____ . (allow)
3 In my view too much money _____ . (spend)
4 Children always hate _____ . (make)
5 I can't imagine I _____ . (invite)

Register

5a Find an example of a formal sentence in the text in Exercise 3a.

b Complete the second sentence so that it has a similar meaning to the first sentence, using the words given. Make the second sentence more formal than the first. There may be more than one possible answer.

0 We'll soon have the study tours details ready.
   AVAILABLE, NEAR
   Details of the study tours *will be (made) available in the near* future.
1 We've looked at the programme again and decided we should cut back a bit on the number of places we go to.
   DESTINATIONS, SLIGHTLY
   Having reviewed _____ reduced.
2 All the same, I expect there'll be a lot more replies to our advert this year.
   ANTICIPATED, INCREASE, RESPONSE
   Nevertheless, it _____ to our advertisement.
3 At the moment, the marketing department is working on the brochure.
   CURRENTLY, DEVELOPED
   The brochure _____ the marketing department.
4 This year, they've picked Liverpool as the Capital of Culture, so it's important that we still go there.
   SELECTED, REMAINS
   Having been _____ key destinations.
5 We suggest you book soon if you don't want to be disappointed.
   RESERVATIONS, RECOMMENDED
   Early_____ disappointment.

Use of English 2 (Paper 1 Part 2)

Simón Bolívar Youth Orchestra

Lead-in 1 Look at the photos above and discuss the questions.

1 What are the advantages of teaching children to play musical instruments? Are there any disadvantages?
2 What is the best age to teach children a musical instrument?

Open cloze 2a Read the title and the text below quickly and answer these questions. (Ignore the gaps at this stage.)

1 Why was the Simón Bolívar Youth Orchestra set up?
2 Why did it make such an impact when it first arrived in Britain?
3 What change has been made recently and why?

b Read the instructions. What do you have to do?

c Read the strategy, then complete the task. Use the Help notes for support with certain items.

EXPERT STRATEGY

Look at the words around each gap. What kind of word (e.g. preposition, adverb) is needed to fit the context and the grammar? See page 167 for a full list of strategies.

➤ **HELP**

2 You need a preposition to complete the expression.

6 Think of a word to complete a linking expression.

7 A positive or a negative word?

*For questions 1–8, read the text below and think of the word which best fits each gap. Use only **one** word in each gap. There is an example at the beginning (0).*

The Simón Bolívar Youth Orchestra

The Simón Bolivar Youth Orchestra was named **(0)** _after_ Venezuela's national hero. It is the product of a radical education system, which promotes social change by encouraging communities regarded **(1)____** the most deprived in the country to get involved in communal music making.

The orchestra arrived in Britain in 2007, **(2)____** the musical direction of Gustavo Dudamel. They amazed everyone with their sheer brilliance and exuberance.

Nothing quite **(3)____** it had ever been seen in the concert halls of Britain before and for a **(4)____** years they swept all before them as praise was lavished **(5)____** the young virtuosos. In **(6)____** , Dudamel's star continued to rise in the years which followed and he was appointed music director of the Los Angeles Philharmonic. Now, nearly two decades later, the 'Youth' of the name has been dropped as many of the players are youthful **(7)____** longer. However, when this inspirational orchestra returned to Britain this year, critics were beside **(8)____** with delight that their brilliance and force still shone through.

Discussion 3 What should be the role of music in education? Which school subjects get priority and more respect than others and why?

19

Writing 2 (Paper 2 Part 2: Letter of request)

Lead-in **1** Discuss these questions.

1 When do people write letters of request? (e.g. at work, when studying) Have you ever written one? Was it effective?
2 What tips would you give to someone wanting to write a letter of request?

Understand the task **2** Read the task below and answer these questions.

1 WHO are 'you'? WHO are you writing to?
2 What is the PURPOSE of your piece of writing? What EFFECT do you want to have on the reader?
3 What POINTS do you have to include? Which information do you have to INVENT?
4 What STYLE will you use: formal? neutral? informal and friendly?
5 What will make the reader feel it is a WELL-WRITTEN letter?

> *You are an international student in New Zealand and your course is about to finish. You have been offered a job with a local company, which you accepted, but are no longer available on the start date you agreed with the company. Write a letter to the company to:*
> * *explain the reason you are not available*
> * *reassure them of your commitment*
> * *propose a solution.*
> *Write your **letter** in 220–260 words.*

Plan your letter **3a** Look at these jumbled notes and match them to the topic areas given in the task. Ignore any notes that don't fit and add any others you wish.

* could spend a few days with present engineer before I leave (unpaid)

* won't happen again

* very tightly knit family

* father has had an accident

* need to go back shortly and arrange home care

* no need to readvertise

* sister returning home (great!) from university course abroad

* father wants to be independent

* really keen to make role as assistant systems analyst into career with company

b Decide which points you will definitely use and make a paragraph plan. Omit any points you choose not to use. (For example, any points which are less relevant or could be misinterpreted.) Where will you add your reason for writing?

Paragraph 1: Saying who you are
Paragraph 2: _____
Paragraph 3: _____
Paragraph 4: _____
Paragraph 5: Closing comments
Remember you only have 220–260 words.

Language and content

4a Circle the correct word or phrase.

1 My father lives *by his own / on his own* and has *had recently / recently had* an accident.

2 He's *quite an independent / quite independent* person.

3 He's determined that I *might / would / should / could* further my career abroad.

4 I cannot be *absolutely / totally / fully* absent at *a such / such a* difficult time.

5 I know the current engineer is leaving *shortly afterwards / soon after* 1st March.

6 I hope you will understand my *awkward situation / predicament / trouble* and will accept my suggested *remedy / answer / solution*.

b Rewrite the sentences in a style more appropriate for a formal letter. Begin with the prompts given.

1 You offered me the job of assistant systems engineer.
(*I was a successful ...*)

2 Sorry, but can you let me start two weeks later?
(*It is with ... that I must ...*)

3 The accident has put him out of action, so I've got to go back.
(*The unfortunate incident ...*)

4 He's very worried because he doesn't want to hold me back.
(*He is extremely ...*)

5 Obviously, you might think that this is going to happen time and time again.
(*It would be only natural ...*)

6 I had to start at the beginning of March – you made a big point of that.
(*You were very ...*)

7 Given the state of play, I'd be glad to come in before I go.
(*In the ...*)

8 Give us a call if you wish to talk about it.
(*Should you ...*)

c Complete these sentences.

1 I was delighted when I heard that I _____ .

2 However, since then _____ .

3 My dilemma is that _____ .

4 Please let me assure you that _____ .

5 Whatever you decide, _____ .

Write your letter

5 Now read the strategy and write your letter in 220–260 words, using some of the language from the exercises above.

> **EXPERT STRATEGY**
>
> Make sure each paragraph focuses on a different topic, and there is a clear linking of ideas between sentences and paragraphs. Avoid one-sentence paragraphs, except sometimes at the beginning or end. See page 170 for a full list of strategies.

Check your answer

6 Edit your work using the Expert writing checklist on page 190.

Review

1 Choose the correct word to complete the sentences.

1 His CV obviously __ an excellent impression on the interviewers.
  A made   B gave   C did   D got
2 Very few interviewees demonstrated such a __ variety of skills as Alice.
  A high   B wide   C broad   D long
3 I should warn you that this project will have very __ deadlines.
  A tight   B severe   C reduced   D restricted
4 Her relaxed body language __ a positive impact on everyone who met her.
  A provided   B gave   C allowed   D had
5 It's debatable whether he will be able to __ his ideas into practice.
  A place   B use   C leave   D put
6 I was impressed by how he __ the interview in his stride.
  A did   B saw   C took   D made

2 Complete the text with the missing prepositions.

When I first started secondary school, I felt intimidated (1)____ a group of older kids, who used to take great pleasure (2)____ making fun of my hairstyle and the clothes I wore. Although they didn't do or say anything too bad, I was always apprehensive (3)____ walking to school. My friends told them to grow up but the gang took absolutely no notice (4)____ them whatsoever.

My response to this unwanted attention was to try to make the best (5)____ a bad situation. I tried not to stand out in any way. I also felt pressurised (6)____ wearing exactly the same brands of shoes and clothes as my tormentors.

Eventually, they appeared to take pity (7)____ me and decided to leave me alone, but they had probably just got distracted (8)____ having another student to talk about.

3 Circle the correct words to complete the sentences.

1 Julia was taken *aback / over* by the amount of homework she was given.
2 Problems with clients appear to *jump / crop* up all the time at work.
3 Doing work experience has *supported / stood* me in good stead.
4 Unfortunately, all the holiday jobs I wanted had been *eaten / snapped* up.
5 If you can take all the pressure in your *stride / step*, the experience will be worthwhile.
6 She was totally *overwhelmed / overpowered* by the amount of choice she was offered.

4 Complete the sentences with the active or passive form of the verbs in brackets.

1 By the time the work is finished, the junior school ____ (close) for over three months.
2 Apparently, all the classrooms ____ (repaint) at the moment.
3 The building ____ (expect) to have been finished last month.
4 The teachers ____ (hope) to move back since January.
5 Parents ____ (invite) to go on a tour of the classrooms as soon as they are finished.
6 In the meantime, plans of the new premises ____ (can/see) online.
7 The main priority during the last few weeks ____ (be) to keep everyday life for the pupils as normal as possible.
8 Rumours ____ (circulate) for some time about who has donated the funds for the refurbishment.

5 Complete the text with the missing words. Use the active or passive form of a verb in the box.

be	carry	hide	never/find	never/leave	offer
run away	tie	want	work		

Isla MacKinnon (1)____ as a private investigator since she (2)____ the job at the age of 19. The idea was to do it for a year before going to university, but that (3)____ six years ago. Her first job was looking for a child who (4)____ from home. He (5)____ , but she says you just have to move on and remember the reasons why you originally (6)____ to do the job.

She always (7)____ a small rucksack. On the strap, there is a little button, which connects to a camera that (8)____ inside the bag.

She told me that she (9)____ on her own at any time. A colleague always monitors her. If she feels she is in any danger, she (10)____ her hair up as a distress signal to those who are watching.

2A

> **Reading and Use of English:** Multiple choice (Part 5); Multiple-choice cloze (Part 1)
> **Vocabulary:** Adjectives: describing attitudes; Fixed expressions: describing characteristics; Phrasal verbs and collocations
> **Listening:** Developing skills (listening for gist, identifying attitudes and opinions); Multiple choice (Part 3)
> **Language development:** Review of relative clauses; Relative pronouns with prepositions; Reduced relative clauses; Combining sentences
> **Writing:** Planning and organising (Part 2)

2B

> **Listening:** Multiple choice (Part 3)
> **Speaking:** Social interaction (Part 1)
> **Language development:** Use of articles; Singular and plural nouns and verb agreement; Determiners and pronouns
> **Reading and Use of English:** Open cloze (Part 2)
> **Writing:** Report (Part 2)

Lead-in

1   What effect do you think these events will have on the person's life? Will the effects be positive or negative? Could they sometimes be both? Give examples.

2a Think of a context and a short dialogue for each of these expressions.

| chop and change | for a change | get changed | spare change | That makes a change! |

b   What is meant by these sayings? Which do you most agree with and why?
    • A leopard can't change its spots.
    • You can't teach an old dog new tricks.
    • A change is as good as a rest.

3   Are you the kind of person who gets excited or frightened by change? Give examples.

4   What major life changes do you expect to make (e.g. leaving home, starting university/ work)? What effect will they have on your life? Give reasons.

Reading (Paper 1 Part 5)

Before you read

1 Read the introduction to the article. What possible answer might there be to the question?

Skimming

2 Read the article quickly. What impact did the teachers at each of the writer's schools have upon his life?

Multiple choice

3a Read question 1 and follow this procedure. The first two stages are done for you for question 1.

　1 Highlight the key words in the stem.
　2 Highlight the part of the text which gives you the information.
　3 Complete the stem in your own words.
　4 Read the options. Which was the nearest to your answer?
　5 Read the highlighted text closely to check it has the same meaning.

　b Do the rest of the task. Use the Help notes for support with certain items.

➤ EXPERT STRATEGIES page 168

➤ HELP

2 Find another expression meaning *left*. Look for the reasons he did this.

4 Look at the phrase *Suddenly, it works*. What does *it* refer to and how is this different to what they are used to?

5 Look carefully at the first sentence of the fifth paragraph.

Task analysis

4 Discuss your answers, explaining why you chose each option.

Discussion

5 Discuss the following questions.

　1 Who has influenced you most – family or friends?
　2 Which famous people are positive role models for young people?

For questions 1–6 choose the answer (A, B, C or D) which you think fits best according to the text.

1　In the first paragraph, the writer mentions the *Dream School* experiment on TV because
　A he has experienced the type of incoherent teaching techniques shown in it.
　B he can identify with the attitude of the students who took part in it.
　C he once participated in a similar research project himself.
　D he is convinced that the idea will fail.

2　The writer left his first secondary school because
　A his parents did not recognise the value of education.
　B he had already set his heart on a specific job.
　C he resented the way he was treated there.
　D his teachers believed he had no academic potential.

3　The writer's experience at the next school he attended was more successful because
　A he had already made up his mind to adopt a co-operative attitude.
　B he was inspired to fulfil his potential.
　C he felt the timetable provided more flexibility.
　D he realised the need to focus on a future career.

4　The writer believes the students at the *Dream School* did not initially respond to the experiment because
　A it took time for them to accept the discipline.
　B none of them would admit that they needed help.
　C they were made to feel unworthy of attention.
　D the subjects were taught badly.

5　The writer's purpose in describing the Raleigh project is to illustrate that
　A the number of law-breakers in an area is related to the academic success of its schools.
　B students should be responsible for monitoring each other's behaviour.
　C children will achieve more academically if they are given more individual help.
　D limiting the number of disadvantaged students in schools can achieve good results.

6　In the writer's view, schools should try to
　A help difficult children by ensuring there is a caring adult available for them to talk to.
　B make sure the same education is available for both rich and poor alike.
　C ensure that all students have a voice by providing smaller classes.
　D put pressure on the government to fund voluntary social projects where needed.

Only connect

Every year, hundreds of thousands of sixteen year olds in the UK leave school with few or no qualifications. What, if anything, can be done to stop schools failing young people?

I left school at the age of 16 and lost my sense of direction. Fifteen years later, this memory was triggered by a TV experiment called *Dream School* in which a celebrity gathers together 20 kids who hate school and asks some of Britain's smartest people – none of whom are trained teachers – to teach and inspire them. And in the faces of the kids – alternately bad-tempered, unable to listen and desperate to change – I can see my younger self. There are half a million such kids in Britain, and during this rough and ready attempt to turn a few of them round, some of the so-called 'teachers' try aggressive discipline, others try sympathetic indulgence, and beneath this pedagogical chaos the ideal solution becomes clear.

On the first day at my first secondary school, I remember thinking, 'How dare they tell me what I'll be doing every day?' I loved to learn – I was always reading – but my reaction to being ordered to do it made me come across as hostile. The teachers responded to me scornfully, which led to mutual hatred. So I was always skiving off school without permission, always on the brink of being expelled, until I dropped out as soon as I legally could. Although distressed by my behaviour, my parents were unable to convince me to stay on to do my 'Advanced' level exams. Since they had left school at 16 too, they didn't really have a leg to stand on. Anyway, I spent a year playing video games and having fantasies of being 'discovered'. (For some reason, I thought I was going to be an actor, even though I am utterly incapable of acting, in the same way that today's kids dream of achieving fame through reality shows like *The X Factor*.)

Finally, I was persuaded to try out another school, although I didn't have high expectations. But something happened that I had never found in the education system before; there were teachers there who took the time to figure out why I was so resistant to their praise and to find a way of teaching that would nurture me. Outwardly indifferent and unimpressed, I was inwardly astonished. My sense of self began to change and I began to think, for the first time, that I might have ability. It was their encouragement and caring that turned my life around. Some were strict and some were soft, but it was the emotional connection that mattered.

You can see the same process happening in *Dream School*. These kids associate education with being told they are useless. One of the 'teachers' tells them, in effect, to pull themselves together. But being looked down on sends them back into a same-old spiral of shame and rage. The 'teacher' then shifts strategy, instinctively sensing the need to get to know them individually. Suddenly, it works and the kids begin to react. There can be discipline – indeed, the kids want it, deep down – but first there has to be a bond. It's there when one of the 'teachers' tells a kid that his photo is brilliant and when another tells a boy he's great at maths. They then begin to work – like plants finally given water and sunshine. But can a principle like this be introduced into our education system?

Recently, the US city of Raleigh passed a law to restrict the number of underachieving students in each school so that those who needed most help wouldn't all be lumped together. The idea was that if there are one or two disaffected young people in the class, the others create a group dynamic that discourages bad behaviour, and if that doesn't work the school can give the troublemakers personal attention. If they make up the majority, it's impossible. Within a decade, Raleigh went from being one of the worst-performing districts to one of the best, with the added benefit that crime in the neighbourhood also fell substantially.

However, my first school wasn't crammed full of chaotic students and yet it still let me down. What do you do then? The rap artist, Plan B, has talked about how his educational misery only ended when his school set up a Pupil Referral Unit – a calm place where he could be given one-to-one attention by sympathetic and consistent teachers. When a child is seriously misbehaving, it should be a flashing light that they need to establish a relationship with someone. Until the government is prepared to invest money in schemes like this, the principles uncovered in the experiment will be just that – dreams.

EXPERT WORD CHECK

crammed   figure out   nurture   pull yourself together
rough and ready   scheme (*n*)   shift (*v*)   skive   substantial   trigger (*v*)

Vocabulary

Adjectives: describing
attitudes

1a Replace the adjectives in *italics* with one of the words/expressions below. Add a preposition if necessary.

deliberately unfriendly   despise   fed up   threatening
uninterested   upset

1 Have you ever had a teacher or boss who was *aggressive with* you?
2 Have you ever been *hostile* towards somebody you met?
3 Is there a politician whose ideas or opinions you *feel scornful about*?
4 Are there any national issues that you get *distressed by*?
5 Are there any world issues that you are *indifferent to*?
6 What things have you been *disaffected by* at college or work?

b Ask and answer the questions, giving reasons.

Fixed expressions:
describing characteristics

2a Match the sentence beginnings 1–6 with their endings a–f.

1 I have never *seen eye to eye*
2 I never *did as I was told*
3 I like to *get my own way*
4 I prefer to *keep myself to myself*,
5 I sometimes *rub people up the wrong way*
6 I frequently do things *on a whim*,

a because I have a slightly aggressive tone at times.
b with my father on politics.
c all the time because I'm obstinate.
d at school, which used to get me into a lot of trouble.
e rather than tell people everything.
f which is the complete opposite of my parents, who plan everything.

b Discuss which of these sentences are true for you.

Phrasal verbs and
collocations

3 Circle the correct words or phrases to complete the text. Discuss your answers with a partner.

When I was young, I always used to look (1) *over / up* to my uncle and we became quite (2) *close / near* when I was a teenager. To some people, he came (3) *round / across* as a little eccentric but from my perspective, he was really (4) *good / big* fun. He also had a very dry sense of humour. I like to think I take (5) *up / after* him. From a very early age, I had my heart (6) *set / placed* on art school, although art doesn't really (7) *follow / run* in the family. But he supported me in whatever I did and always had (8) *large / high* expectations for me. I have many reasons to be grateful to him.

4 Work in pairs. Choose some of the expressions from Exercises 1–3 and use them to talk about your immediate or extended family.

Use of English 1 (Paper 1 Part 1)

Lead-in

1 To what extent are grandparents valued in your culture? Has this changed much over the last 20 years?

Multiple-choice cloze

2 a Read the text quickly for general understanding.

1 Give two reasons why grandparents are still important today.
2 What is a potential source of tension in families?

b Read the strategy on page 167, then do the task. Use the Help notes for support with certain items.

➤ EXPERT STRATEGIES page 167

Task analysis

3 Which of the gapped words in each set of options form part of a collocation?

Discussion

4 Discuss these questions.

1 Which members of your family do you have the closest ties with? Why?
2 Do you agree that there is a basic human need for an extended family? Give reasons.

Writing

5 Write a short paragraph describing the role that grandparents or other close relatives have played in your upbringing. It could be in the form of a story or diary extract.

For questions 1–8, read the text below and decide which answer (A, B, C or D) best fits each gap. There is an example at the beginning (0).

The extended family

The need for a family in which (0) __A__ relatives provide care and continuity is a very basic one. Psychologists believe that grandparents (1)__ a key role in the development of early societies, and there is evidence that children whose grandmothers were still alive (2)__ a much better chance of surviving into adulthood. In modern times, parents continue to (3)__ on grandparents for practical support. For example, they are often the (4)__ emergency contact for schools if a child's parents are working or (5)__ unavailable. Although aunts and uncles may also help, it is widely (6)__ that the emotional bond and stability provided by grandparents facilitates a child's emotional adjustment. This is (7)__ important during times of stress, although tensions can also emerge at such times which put family unity at (8)__ . For example, if a husband's parents do not have a good relationship with their daughter-in-law, the close bond between grandparents and grandchildren may be threatened.

0	A close	B nuclear	C immediate	D near
1	A held	B played	C made	D acted
2	A sought	B took	C stood	D won
3	A trust	B resort	C swear	D rely
4	A alternative	B variable	C divergent	D modified
5	A meanwhile	B otherwise	C whereas	D therefore
6	A consented	B permitted	C accepted	D judged
7	A particularly	B principally	C specifically	D exactly
8	A menace	B danger	C risk	D peril

➤ **HELP**

1 Which verb collocates with *a key role*, to mean *have a very important part*?

6 This verb goes with *widely* and means *people believe*.

8 All these words mean the same thing but only one collocates with *at*.

Listening 1 Developing skills

Before you listen

1 Discuss these questions.

1 What social media do you use?

2 Do you think social media has had a positive or negative effect on people's relationships? Give reasons.

Listening for gist

2 🎧 10 Listen to Laura talking about her boyfriend's marriage proposal. What was unusual about it?

Identifying attitudes and opinions

3a 🎧 11 Listen again. Choose from these adjectives to answer questions 1–4.

amused   delighted   flattered   irritated
self-conscious   taken aback   tolerant

How does or did Laura feel … *← Taken aback*
1 when she received a message from Dan? *delighted*
2 just after Dan proposed to her? *self conscious*
3 when she thought about it later? *flattered*
4 about Dan's obsession with technology? *tolerant*

b Compare and give reasons for your answers.

4a 🎧 12 Listen to the second part of Laura's anecdote and choose the best option to complete this sentence.

When talking about her wedding day, Laura admits that

A she resented the way that Dan got distracted by technology.

B she forgave Dan for breaking the rules they'd agreed on.

C she regretted not allowing Dan to video with his mobile phone.

D she compromised by letting Dan record two wedding videos.

b Which option(s)

1 reflect(s) something that was said in the text but doesn't/don't answer the question?

2 is/are not an accurate reflection of the text?

3 answer(s) the question and paraphrase(s) the language in the interview?

Multiple choice (Paper 3 Part 3)

5a 🎧 13 Read questions 1–3 and then do the task.

*You will hear part of an interview with a psychologist called Carolyn Adams, who is talking about her research into the impact of social networking. For questions **1–3**, choose the answer (**A, B, C** or **D**) which fits best according to what you hear. (Note: in the exam you will answer 6 questions.)*

1 What possible effect of social networking is beginning to concern Carolyn?

A people being disadvantaged by not meeting face-to-face

B people behaving rudely in the company of others

C people finding it hard to express their emotions

D people developing an addiction to it

2 What has surprised Carolyn most about the impact of social networking?

A the way in which people use it to document a new relationship

B the value it has as a means of confirming a romantic commitment

C the pressure put on people to share every detail of daily life

D the tendency for people to behave in an uncharacteristic way online

3 How does Carolyn feel about the future of social networking?

A sure that there will soon be an alternative

B convinced that the benefits outweigh the problems

C worried that psychological problems might increase

D confident that the rules of online behaviour will be resolved over time

b Compare your answers and say what made you choose them.

c How easy was it to identify which question related to which part of the recording? What helped you to do this?

Discussion

6 Do you agree with Carolyn? Are we better or worse off by using social networking? Give reasons.

EXPERT WORD CHECK

accountable   astounded (*adj*)   awkward
catch unawares   cotton on   glued to
go over old ground   liable   lurk   sneak (*v*)

Language development 1

Review of relative clauses

> EXPERT GRAMMAR page 174

1 Read sentences A–D, then answer questions 1–4.

A The restaurant *that* Laura went to was a special one for her and Dan.

B Laura got a text message from Dan, *who* was waiting outside.

C Dan, *whose* friend was hiding behind a tree, had the proposal videoed.

D Everyone *who* I meet asks if I was thrilled.

Which sentence/sentences

1 contain(s) non-defining relative clauses? (i.e. non-essential information)

2 has/have relative pronouns which refer to the object of the verb in the relative clause?

3 could replace the relative pronoun with *which*?

4 contain(s) relative pronouns which can be left out?

2a Complete the sentences using relative pronouns. Which sentences need additional punctuation?

1 I have a friend _____ cousin is an actor.

2 Ella's colleague _____ you met last week has invited me for a meal.

3 Lee has step-sisters and brothers _____ is quite common these days.

4 Have you been to that new restaurant _____ is near the railway station?

5 I haven't finished reading that book _____ you gave me last week.

6 It's a beautiful area _____ some of the best beaches in the world are to be found.

b Compare your answers. Can any pronouns be left out?

Relative pronouns with prepositions

3a Underline the correct words to complete the text.

Romeo and Juliet is a play **(1)** *by which / in which* the lovers fall in love at first sight. Juliet's cousin is killed by Romeo, **(2)** *as a result of which / in which case* Romeo is exiled. The lovers go to see Friar Lawrence, **(3)** *without his help / without whose help* they would be unable to marry.

Romeo and Juliet make many plans for their future, **(4)** *most of them / all of which* go wrong. Juliet is forced to marry someone else, **(5)** *at which point / by when* she takes a sleeping draught to pretend she has died. A lot of young actors, **(6)** *many of whom / any of these* have been unknown, have taken on the roles.

b Take turns to read the sentences in Exercise 3a aloud, replacing the relative pronouns with expressions more typical of spoken language.

Reduced relative clauses

4 In the following sentences, the relative clauses have been 'reduced' using a present or past participle clause or an infinitive with *to*. Say them in a different way, using relative clauses.

1 Henry VIII, *born* in 1491, married his sister-in-law Catherine of Aragon when his brother died.

2 Twenty years later he divorced Catherine, *believed* to be too old to give him the son *he* desperately wanted.

3 He had also fallen in love with a woman *living* at court, Anne Boleyn, *later executed*.

4 The only woman *to give* him a son was his next wife, *called Jane Seymour*.

5 However, Jane Seymour, *said* to be Henry VIII's favourite, died during childbirth.

Combining sentences

5a Read the following story of the relationship between Elizabeth Taylor and Richard Burton. Then combine the groups of sentences using relative and reduced relative clauses.

1 Elizabeth Taylor was a well-known Hollywood actress. She made many films with the Welsh actor Richard Burton. The most famous film was probably *Who's Afraid of Virginia Woolf.*

2 In 1961, they made their first film together. It was based on the story of Cleopatra. Elizabeth played the Queen in it.

3 The couple fell in love on the set. They were already married to other people. They attracted huge publicity.

4 The couple married in 1964. They went on to live a very lavish lifestyle. As a result of this, they became even more famous.

5 Richard bought Elizabeth a huge diamond. It was the largest, most expensive in the world. It was engraved with the message, 'Eternal Love till Death'.

6 They got divorced in 1974. They met up again later. They remarried a year later.

b Work in pairs and take turns to feed back on your answers. Make sure that you pause to add the extra information when there are non-defining relative clauses.

Writing 1 Planning and organising

1 Work in pairs. Decide the order in which you would do the following when writing. Give reasons.

   a Make a note of useful expressions you can use. ___
   b Write a neat version of your draft. ___
   c Write notes of your ideas and then decide on the best order. ___
   d Check for correct spelling and punctuation. ___
   e Group your ideas into a plan for different paragraphs. ___
   f Cross out any irrelevant points and expand any important points. ___

2a In which of these texts would you often expect to find an introduction, supporting paragraphs and a conclusion?

   1 a magazine article
   2 a report for an organisation
   3 a personal note
   4 a review
   5 a set of directions
   6 an informal letter

   b Discuss your answers.

3a Read this task. How many paragraphs do you think will be needed?

Write a review of a film, DVD or a book that you really enjoyed. Give a brief outline of the plot, saying what you thought of it and why you'd recommend it.

b Look at the notes made by a student. Why are two points crossed out?

• 'Pride and Prejudice' – have seen lots of different versions
• Keira Knightley and Matthew Macfadyen – ~~great young actors. Macfadyen unknown then~~
• I always watch Jane Austen films
• interesting new version of well-known story
• main focus on family dynamics and two main characters
• ~~wonderful photography~~, film locations, costumes
• released on DVD
• better for young people
• love story
• a man and a woman from different backgrounds are prejudiced about each other, eventually fall in love

c Decide on the best order for these paragraph topics.

   ___ recommendation
   ___ plot summary
   ___ opinion in detail: acting, direction, music
   ___ title/type of film
   ___ overall impression

d Complete this paragraph plan using the topic headings and notes above.

   Paragraph 1: _____
   Paragraph 2: _____
   Paragraph 3: _____
   Paragraph 4: _____
   Paragraph 5: _____

4a Work in pairs. Discuss a film or a story you have both seen or read.

b Plan and write a review of it together but don't give it a title. Make sure you organise it carefully and use cohesive devices to link topics together.

c Read the reviews written by other students in the class. Guess what the film or book is. Which sounds like the one you would most/least like to see or read? Give reasons.

Listening 2 (Paper 3 Part 3)

Before you listen

1 Discuss your views on these questions.

1 Which crimes are the biggest problem in the region where you live? What punishment should be given for them?

2 In what ways can committing a crime affect a young person's life?

3 Do you think criminals are let off too easily by the courts? Give reasons.

2 Read the multiple-choice questions 1–6 below and mark the key words.

Multiple choice

3 🎧 14 Read the task below and the strategy on page 171. Use the Help notes for support with certain items.

> *You will hear an interview with a dance teacher called Lucy Chapman, who works with young offenders, and Dylan Baker, who is one of her students. For questions 1–6, choose the answer (**A**, **B**, **C** or **D**) which fits best according to what you hear.*

1 Lucy says the main aim of the project with young offenders is to
   A encourage them to be less violent.
   B ensure that they get a qualification.
   C keep them away from other people.
   D provide them with an alternative to prison.

2 What motivated Lucy to take part in the project?
   A a wish to give young criminals a purpose
   B her dream of staging a dance production
   C a belief that she could make the participants famous
   D the challenge of putting on a very demanding course

3 What led Dylan to become a teacher on the course?
   A He wanted to prove something to his parents.
   B He had no choice in the matter.
   C He was encouraged by his tutor.
   D He was successful in motivating his classmates.

4 Lucy says the young offenders make sudden progress when
   A they pass on what they've learnt to children.
   B they start to get up early and improve their eating habits.
   C they try to do what they'd thought was impossible.
   D they learn from their mistakes on stage.

5 Lucy says the most demanding aspect of her work is
   A persuading officials to come and see what the offenders can do.
   B making sure offenders commit fewer crimes.
   C teaching offenders to read and write.
   D convincing offenders that their new skills might help them get a job.

6 Lucy says the most satisfying aspect of her job is
   A building up a reputation for the project.
   B making a difference to people's lives.
   C doing something unexpected but exciting.
   D producing good dancers.

➤ HELP

1 Listen for when Lucy says something would be 'pointless'. What is she referring to?

3 Listen for the interviewer's question to Dylan about how he became a dance teacher. What was it that changed his attitude?

5 Listen to Lucy's response to the interviewer's comment about a real challenge. The answer comes at the end of her turn. Why are the other answers wrong?

EXPERT WORD CHECK

be woven into   constructive
impose limitations   peer (*n*)
radical   rave notice   reluctant
rigorous   steer (*v*)   transferable

Discussion

4 Do you think that the programme is a good idea? Why/why not? Can you think of alternative ideas for a rehabilitation programme?

Speaking (Paper 4 Part 1)

Interacting socially

1a What questions do you think the interlocutor asks Candidate A and Candidate B?

1 Interlocutor: _____
   Candidate A: I work in an office.
   Interlocutor: _____
   Candidate A: I've been studying English for six years.

2 Interlocutor: _____
   Candidate B: Well, actually it was quite recently. When I left college, I was lucky enough to be invited to stay on a ranch in the USA, and it really opened my eyes to a very different way of life. The people were so relaxed and hospitable – it was wonderful.
   Interlocutor: _____
   Candidate B: Oh, lots of things, I hope. I've met this fantastic person at work and we're seeing a lot of each other. I'm hoping we might be married by then, although I don't feel quite ready for it yet. I'm also looking for a nicer flat. In five years' time, I'd like to be living somewhere a bit bigger.

b 🎧 15 Listen and check.

c Which candidate repeats the words of the question? Why are Candidate B's answers better examples of social interaction? Underline useful phrases in Exercise 1a.

d How could you expand on these answers?

1 I'm still a student.

2 I prefer to get my news on the internet.

3 It's very important to speak more than one language.

4 The people were very friendly in our village.

5 I wouldn't want to be rich and famous.

6 Facebook is the best way of keeping in touch with friends.

2a Match the questions and pairs of answers below with the topics. Choose which answer in each pair is better.

communication   imaginary situations   relationships   work and study
your background

1 What do you enjoy most about learning English? _____
   A: I think what I appreciate most is the opportunity to communicate with people from different cultures.
   B: I enjoy studying grammar, reading, listening, vocabulary and speaking.

2 Who has had the most influence on your life – your friends or your family? Why? _____
   A: I don't know who has had the most influence. My parents probably.
   B: If I'm honest, the person who's meant most to me in my life is my elder sister. She's a great achiever and has been a role model to me in all sorts of ways.

3 What do you think is the best way to keep in touch with friends and family? _____
   A: Internet telephone calls. They're great. I couldn't be without them.
   B: That's a tricky question because there are so many different ways these days and I like to use all of them. Facebook is good for all sorts of things but you can't beat an internet telephone call where you can see the face of the other person talking.

4 What did you like most about the area where you grew up?
_____
   A: Well, I suppose the thing that most people liked about it is that everyone was very friendly and there was a great community spirit, but I myself really enjoyed the beautiful countryside. We were surrounded by hills and I loved to go for early morning walks.
   B: Everyone said it was a great village. We all knew each other, but there weren't many shops and there wasn't much to do in the evenings.

5 Do you ever wish you were rich and famous? _____
   A: Everyone wants to be famous these days. All the TV programmes are about fame. We live in a celebrity culture.
   B: Actually, I've never really wanted to be famous because I value my privacy too much and I don't think I could cope with all the media attention I would get. However, a little more money would be helpful!

EXPERT STRATEGY

Invent opinions if necessary, but react naturally. Show enthusiasm and keep talking, using linking expressions where possible to expand on your answers.
For a complete list of task strategies see page 172.

b Read the strategy, then take turns at asking and answering the questions yourselves, using some of the phrases below. Pay attention to the words you stress and your intonation.

Opinions
As a matter of fact ... (for me ... the thing that)
What I really love about ... (is that ...)
Well, personally (personally speaking) I'd say (by far the most ...)
Mainly,/Most of the things ... (I liked ...)

Surprise
Believe it or not ... (I've never)

Hesitation
Let me think./I'm not sure.
I've never given it a lot of thought. (Probably ...)

Prediction
I'm pretty certain that ... (I'll never ...)

Sample answer

3a 🎧 16 You will hear two students doing Part 1 of the test. There are two parts. Listen to the first part, in which the interlocutor asks the candidates some questions. Why are Paola's answers better than Frédéric's?

b 🎧 17 Listen to the final part, in which the interlocutor asks some more questions.
   1 What expressions does Paola use to give herself 'thinking time'? Can you think of others?
   2 What should Frédéric have done when he was unable to think of an answer?

Social interaction

4a Work in groups of four and choose a role.
   Interlocutor: Ask the questions on page 203. Stop the discussion after two minutes.
   Candidates A and B: Respond to the interlocutor.
   Assessor: Listen and evaluate the candidates' performance.

b Change roles so that everyone has a turn at answering the questions.

Language development 2

Use of articles

1a Which alternative is correct and why?

1 *Biology / The biology* is *study / the study / a study* of *living organisms / the living organisms.*
2 I heard that *the murderers / murderers* were charged and sent *to prison / to the prison.*

> EXPERT GRAMMAR page 175

b Complete this text using the best article for each space: *a*, *an*, *the* or *ø* (no article).

I am **(1)**____ forensic scientist based in **(2)**____ UK, specialising in **(3)**____ examination of **(4)**____ footprints and glass. My job is to use **(5)**____ science to help identify **(6)**____ criminals and recreate **(7)**____ order of events in accidents. It's not **(8)**____ easy job because you often see **(9)**____ darkest side of **(10)**____ humanity but I enjoy **(11)**____ variety in **(12)**____ work I do. One day I might be working on **(13)**____ motoring offence, **(14)**____ next day **(15)**____ murder, and it can be satisfying knowing that you have helped **(16)**____ court to understand **(17)**____ complicated scientific issue.

c Would you like to be a forensic scientist? Give your reasons.

Singular and plural nouns and verb agreement

2a Are these words followed by a verb in the singular, plural or either?

a majority of (+ noun/pronoun)   genetics
the government   the police

b Read the grammar reference on pages 175–176 and correct the mistakes. There may be more than one mistake in each sentence.

1 People agrees that a number of things needs to be done to improve detection rates.
2 Is there an evidence which suggest that she was at the scene of the crime?
3 On the flight home, one of his luggages came open and one of his belongings was missing.
4 The number of private investigators have risen year on year.
5 Four days are a long time to wait for an appointment.
6 Two percent are a small pay rise. They say 80 percent of the staff is going on strike.
7 We were making no progresses until he gave us a good advice.

Determiners and pronouns

3a Determiners are often used to talk about quantities and amounts. Circle the correct alternative. Why is the other alternative wrong?

1 I've got *little / a little* sympathy with the rioters. They should be sent to prison.
2 It's inevitable that *the most / most* of them come from poor backgrounds.
3 *Many / Much* people got caught up in the violence.
4 I've seen *each / every* single piece of news coverage.
5 *A great deal of / Many* damage was caused to property.
6 *An awful lot / A large amount* of people suffered.
7 I saw one poor woman. *All / Both* her hands were burnt.
8 *Hardly any / Very little* of the rioters were convicted.

b What are the main causes of civil disturbance in modern society?

4a Do you like crime stories? Give reasons.

b Complete this extract from a blog with the quantifiers below.

both   either   neither   no   none   not   one
the whole

◎ Browsing blogs

Last month, I bought some Scandinavian crime novels, **(1)**____ of which I'd ever read before. **(2)**____ one of them had any humour, and **(3)**____ amount of persuasion will convince me that they make pleasant reading. Although I haven't been to **(4)**____ country, **(5)**____ Denmark and Norway are said to be two of the most peaceful countries in the world. **(6)**____ reason critics give for the success of the writers Henning Mankell and Stieg Larsson is that they explore the effect of violence on **(7)**____ social fabric of their country. **(8)**____ of them is much interested in the solving of puzzles.

Use of English 2 (Paper 1 Part 2)

Lead-in 1 What do you imagine are the biggest problems for someone coming out of prison?

Open cloze 2a Read the title and the text below quickly and answer these questions. (Ignore the gaps at this stage.)

1 What is the answer to question 1 above?
2 What is Sir Richard Branson's ambition?
3 Why was he nearly sent to prison himself?

b Read the instructions and find out what you have to do.

c Read the strategy on page 167, then do the task. Use the Help notes for support with certain items.

*For questions **1–8**, read the text below and think of the word which best fits each gap. Use only **one** word in each gap. There is an example at the beginning (**0**).*

A SECOND CHANCE

Sir Richard Branson, **(0)** *one* of the UK's most high-profile businessmen, has contacted managers in the various businesses he owns to suggest they should employ ex-prisoners. '**(1)**____ deserves a second chance,' he says. 'After all, **(2)**____ of us is perfect'. He was in trouble himself when he was younger: on one occasion for tax reasons, on the other for protesting **(3)**____ American policy during the Vietnam War. On **(4)**____ occasion was he innocent and he could have ended up in prison.

'Being a prisoner affects your whole life. Very **(5)**____ even manage to get a job interview after they're released,' he says. Branson is also working with a charity called Working Chance, which has successfully placed nearly 200 female ex-prisoners **(6)**____ work. He was impressed by the fact that many of those helped by the charity do not return to a life of crime. Re-offending tends to be the norm amongst adults released from prison, most of **(7)**____ are reconvicted within two years of **(8)**____ released.

> **HELP**

1 A pronoun. Positive or negative? What form is the verb which follows?
4 How many occasions? Positive or negative?
7 A relative pronoun.

Task analysis 3 Discuss this question.

Which of the strategies on page 167 did you use to do the task?

Discussion 4 Do you think employers should recruit ex-prisoners whenever possible? Do you agree that anti-discrimination laws should protect ex-prisoners? Give reasons.

Writing 2 (Paper 2 Part 2: Report)

Lead-in

1 Discuss these questions.

   1 In most countries there are charities (for example, to help children, the poor, improve health, help animals, etc.). How do they raise their money? What do you think is the most effective way of raising money for charity?

   2 When do people write reports? When might someone write a report for a charity?

Understand the task

2 Read the task below and answer these questions.

   1 How many parts are there to the question? Mark each part.

   2 Use the strategy to analyse the question.

   3 What will make the reader think it is a well-written report?

You are part of a research group which has asked young offenders, as part of their community service, to help raise money for charity. You have been asked to write a report about the project.

You should include:
- *information about the purpose of the project*
- *techniques used for raising money*
- *what happened as a consequence of the project.*

Add a conclusion.

*Write your **report** in 220–260 words.*

EXPERT STRATEGY

For any piece of writing you need to consider:
- WHO you are and WHO you are writing to (target reader)
- WHY you are writing (purpose)
- What STYLE will be appropriate, e.g. formal, neutral (register)
- How many PARAGRAPHS you will have (length)
- How you should PRESENT the information/argument (layout).

See page 170 for a full list of strategies.

Plan your report

3a Choose the best headings for your report from these alternatives and add them to the paragraph plan below. What is the aim of each paragraph?

Conclusion/Proposals/Suggestions
Foreword/Prologue/Introduction
Overview/Aims of the project/General impression
Raising money/Methods of fundraising/
How the money was raised
What I felt/Suggestions/Results

Paragraph 1: Introduction
Paragraph 2: _____
Paragraph 3: _____
Paragraph 4: _____
Paragraph 5: _____

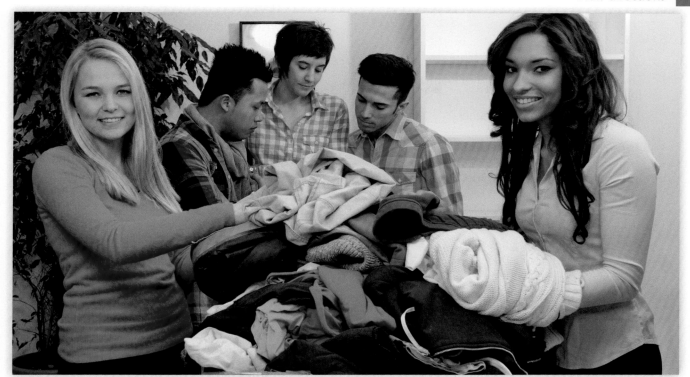

b Match these notes to the headings.

- help organise jumble sale
- provides important life skills (e.g. learning to be part of society)
- £200 raised
- worked hard to do something positive; some had picked up litter before – this far more rewarding
- interviewed young offenders/officer responsible/ charity rep.
- charity collections (under supervision)
- useful paid work in community
- can help them understand impact of offending behaviour
- can help change behaviour
- collection boxes → local businesses

c Decide which points in the notes you will definitely use and add them to the plan. Add any further points you would like to use. Remember you only have 220–260 words.

d Think of a suitable title for the whole report.

Language and content

4a Read the phrases below. Why is the passive often used in reports?

Introduction
The main purpose/principal aim of (this report) is to …
(This report) is intended to …
*(This report) describes/discusses/provides/outlines/
   deals with …*
As preparation for (this report), …
In order to prepare for (this report), …
This report is based on …
I interviewed (one of …) who …
I conducted …

Generalising
*In the main, …/In general, …/On the whole, …/
   It seems that everyone …*

Talking about specifics
It was decided that …
(Collections) were carried out …
(The total raised) exceeded …
(An appeal) was launched (to) …
The largest part of (the sum raised came from) …
(A large amount of money) was raised by …
(Many) said that …

Concluding
To sum up, … /To summarise, …
In short, …/In conclusion, …
In my view, this experience shows that …

b Write an opening sentence for each of the paragraphs in your plan, using some of the phrases in Exercise 4a. You can change the words in brackets if you wish.

Write your report

5 Now write your report in 220–260 words, using some of the language above. Make sure you organise your report carefully. Divide it into sections with clear headings.

Check your answer

6 Edit your work using the writing checklist on page 190. Pay particular attention to grammar, spelling and punctuation. Are there any errors that might cause comprehension difficulties?

Review

1 Use the word in CAPITALS to form a word that fits in the gap.

1 My friends were initially rather ____ about my career change. **SCORN**
2 There is no evidence our dog would ever be ____ towards other dogs. **AGGRESSION**
3 Bad working conditions often result in ____ workers. **AFFECT**
4 Ben is not an ideal flatmate but he's ____ and fairly tidy. **RELY**
5 Lucy's motivation comes from having very high ____ for her future. **EXPECT**
6 It's very ____ to hear the news coming out of the war zone. **DISTRESS**
7 Most of my friends appear totally ____ to what is going on in the world. **DIFFER**
8 There is a lot of ____ towards anyone not supporting the strike. **HOSTILE**

2 Complete the sentences with the correct form of the verbs below.

accept   come   get   keep   look   rub   run
see   set   stand

1 I ____ my heart on becoming an actor when I was about five.
2 I tended to ____ up to my sister because she was six years older than me.
3 Julia always ____ across as being rather arrogant, but she probably isn't.
4 You don't ____ a chance of finishing on time if you chop and change all the time.
5 It is widely ____ that having children is life-changing.
6 Do you think sporting ability ____ in families?
7 Conor is quiet and prefers to ____ himself to himself.
8 My father always manages to ____ people up the wrong way.
9 I have never really ____ eye to eye with any of my colleagues.
10 My younger brother always seems to manage to ____ his own way.

3 Rewrite the clauses in bold to make them more formal. Use *whose*, *which*, *where* or *whom*. You may need to add a preposition and change the punctuation.

1 Crime writing is the genre **that he's best known for**.
2 I was introduced to lots of people **but I hadn't met any of them before**.
3 I forgot to contact her, **which meant that, as a result, I missed an important meeting**.
4 The company had a series of setbacks **and never really recovered from them**.
5 There were two flights available, **but I couldn't get on either of them**.
6 I went to the lecture, **and just about understood most of it**.
7 The club has very generous supporters, **whose financial support they rely on**.
8 The electricity may go off, **and in this case, press this switch**.

4 Complete this article about Bastoy prison with one word in each gap where necessary. Write ø where no word is needed.

Bastoy Prison

Recently, I had to write (1)____ article on what has been called (2)____ world's first 'human ecological prison', located on (3)____ small island of Bastoy. Most of (4)____ 115 prisoners there have (5)____ beautiful views of (6)____ ocean from their red-painted wooden houses. They are provided with their own keys, and each person (7)____ given a job in which they learn a variety of different skills.

The prisoners seem happy there. The vast majority (8)____ already served in a high-security jail before coming to Bastoy, and shown a desire to change.

The experiment appears to have been (9)____ huge success, showing a much lower reoffending rate than most open prisons.

There has been a lot of criticism of Bastoy, which some people (10)____ described as a 'holiday camp'. But although they enjoy being there, very (11)____ of the prisoners would want to stay. All of them say that (12)____ freedom is what matters most to them.

3 Leisure time

Lead-in

1 Compare the photos. What makes people do these activities in their leisure time?

2a Do you think it's important to have at least one leisure activity which is creative?

 b What do you think makes some people more creative than others? Think about:
   • aspects of their personality (e.g. *independence, persistence*)
   • the genes they inherit
   • childhood experiences
   • being prepared to make mistakes
   • how much encouragement they receive.

3 Read this quote. Do you think you can learn and be entertained at the same time?

> *'I would rather entertain and hope that people learnt something than educate people and hope they were entertained.'* (Walt Disney)

Reading (Paper 1 Part 7)

Before you read   **1**   Look at the photo, the title of the article and the introduction.

    1   What is happening in the photo?
    2   What do you think the article will be about?

2   🎧 18   Listen to these sounds. What are they supposed to be? What could Foley artists use to create these sounds?

Skimming   **3**   Read the main text to see if you guessed correctly in Exercise 1.2. Ignore the missing paragraphs at this stage. What does a Foley artist do?

Heard any good films lately?

Foley artists can recreate any sound, from the crunch of footsteps on snow to the rustle of a book. Named after Jack Foley, the first person to turn a silent movie into a musical, these specialists make an art of sound.

5   When directors shoot a film, they're worried about capturing the action and the actor's voice. Nothing else. Not hearing a sword scraping against a tree or a court shoe tiptoeing across a marble floor. Well, the sword is probably made of plastic and the 'marble' floor is probably painted plywood. So when 10 it comes to the edit, things don't come across as they're supposed to.

1

During this process, known as 'the Foley', the artists are responsible for making the background noise sound as real as the dialogue. When done well, these effects are integrated to 15 the extent that they go unnoticed by the audience. It helps to create a sense of reality in a scene, whether the noise is meant to come from inside or outside.

2

Foley can also be used to rectify a continuity problem. If an actor is holding something, but forgets to bring it back into 20 the shot, the sound of the object being put away off camera can be inserted later. It can fill in blanks, too. Foley artist Paul Hanks remembers a TV series in which they forgot to film a horse. So they used sound to create the impression there was one there. However, they don't stop at just creating sounds!

3

25   Things have moved on a long way since 1927, when the art of sound began in films. In those early days, microphones could only pick up dialogue, so Jack Foley had to add in the other sounds later. He projected the film onto a screen and recorded the footsteps and the movement all in one track. At that time, 30 the sound had to match exactly what was going on. Digital technology has meant the sounds can be manipulated to fit.

4

It is dreamed up at *Universal Sound* – the only studio in Britain to specialize solely in Foley. From the outside, it could be an expensive home. There's a swimming pool, where the 35 sounds for the *Harry Potter* computer games were recorded. But the heart of the operation is in the middle of the house, where there are three studios with thick walls. The main studio, where Hanks and mixer Simon Trundle are working, resembles a student bedsit.

5

40   Right now, he's struggling with the sounds of table football. If this were a different project, with a different budget, he would have rented a table. Instead he's slamming the handle of a broom into the spring mechanism of a toaster. 'Too tinny,' says Trundle.

6

45   Alex Joseph, in the studio next door, has been responsible for the Foley on a wide range of films and television. What he likes about Foley is that it's absolutely unique in every film. And, maybe because of his training as a psychologist, he is interested in subliminal messaging, using sounds rather than 50 visuals. 'You can really play with people's heads,' he says. 'I set up characters before they even appear. It's a bit of a dark art.'

Gapped text   **4**   Follow this procedure for question 1.

1 Read the text before and after the first gap in the article and guess what information is missing. Use the highlighted words to help you.
2 Look at the highlighted words in option C below. In what way do the words link? (topically? linguistically? logically?)
3 Complete the rest of the task. Read the strategy on page 168 and use the Help notes for support with certain items.

➤ EXPERT STRATEGIES page 168

*Six paragraphs have been removed from the article. Choose from the paragraphs **A–G** the one which fits each gap (1–6). There is one extra paragraph which you do not need to use.*

A   But although the science has continued to develop, Foley is still all about the 'performance'. A footstep is not just a footstep; it can be angry, happy, sad, confused, clumsy, swaggering, light, heavy. And that performance – which conveys the meaning to the viewers – could only ever come from the human imagination.

B   The action they're recording culminates in a car pulling up at speed. As a protagonist runs away, Hanks reaches for his box of 'surfaces', which contains everything from sand to gravel. He runs his suede gloves across tarmac to recreate the sound of tyres and roots around in a box of shoes for 'running'.

C   Which is why everyday sounds like these have to be added in post-production in order to enhance the quality of audio for TV, radio and video games as well as films. Any sound can be created, from the swishing of clothing and footsteps to squeaky doors and breaking glass.

D   For example, in the absence of a bird, they might recreate the sound of flapping wings by blowing up a pair of kitchen gloves, and then slapping them together in time with the action on screen.

E   The entire opening of the film involves the hero, James Bond, chasing a villain. This high-energy sequence is from *Casino Royale* and it is the work that the Foley artists are most proud of.

F   Running along the side of one wall, a Canadian mini-series is playing out in stop-start chunks. There's no brief from the director so it's up to them to decide what needs to be recorded. Hanks watches and listens, picking out the important sounds before recording the Foley.

G   There is yet another way in which Foley art is the director's friend. Often more than 80% of film dialogue isn't recorded 'clean'. Maybe there was noise in the distance – a car for instance. Foley can cover it up.

➤ **HELP**

2 The first sentence of the following paragraph makes it clear that the missing information will relate to more examples of Foley work.

4 Look at the first sentence of the next paragraph. What is dreamed up at *Universal Sound*?

5 Look for a description of the room. Which pronoun links to Hanks and Trundle? *He*, in the paragraph following the gap, will also link back to one of these names.

Task analysis   **5**   Compare your answers. Discuss the kind of links you found between the options and the rest of the text.

Discussion   **6**   Which of these jobs connected to film do you think is the most creative? Why? Which would you be best at? Give reasons.

- actor
- casting director
- computer graphic designer
- costume designer
- director

- location scout
- producer
- props maker
- screenwriter
- sound engineer

EXPERT WORD CHECK

brief (*n*)   chunk (*n*)   marble   protagonist   squeak (*v*)
subliminal   surface (*n*)   swaggering (*adj*)   swish (*n*)   tarmac

Vocabulary Extending lexical range

Near synonyms

1 Look back at the text on pages 40–41 and underline these verbs. Use a less formal word or phrase to express the same meanings in the context.

1 *capturing* the action (lines 5–6)
2 *rectify* a continuity problem (line 18)
3 (the sound) can be *inserted* later (lines 20–21)
4 *resembles* a student bedsit (line 39)
5 *conveys* the meaning (option A)
6 The action *culminates* in (option B)
7 in order to *enhance* the quality (option C)

Phrasal verbs

2 Replace the words in italics with one of the phrasal verbs from the box in the correct form. The phrasal verbs all appear in the text.

cover up   move on   pick out   pull up
root around in   set up

1 I *searched* my handbag but couldn't find my purse.
2 It's important to *establish an identity for* your characters as early as possible in the story.
3 I *stopped my car* outside the restaurant.
4 The government tried to *prevent people discovering* the scandal.
5 Last week I had to *identify* a possible burglar in a line-up.
6 Technology has *developed* considerably since you bought this computer.

Verbs to describe sounds or actions

3a The verbs in A are all used in the text. Match them with nouns in B which they commonly collocate with. Which ones refer to sounds?

A	B
1 scrape	a a door
2 rustle	b an apple
3 crunch	c your arms around
4 slap	d mud off your boots
5 slam	e a newspaper
6 flap	f someone on the back

b Complete the sentences with one of the verbs from Exercise 3a in the correct form.

1 I ____ my foot on the brake as the cat ran in front of the car.
2 The flag on top of the building was ____ in the wind.
3 As the car pulled up, the tyres ____ on the gravel drive.
4 I love the sound of the leaves ____ in the wind.
5 He lost his temper and ____ his brother.
6 Would you mind ____ the ice off the windscreen so I can see out?

Metaphors

4a Match 1–6 with their endings a–f to make sentences. Explain what the metaphors in *italics* mean, using a dictionary if necessary.

1 Amanda only just managed to *scrape through*
2 I'll just see if I can *rustle up*
3 When it *comes to the crunch,*
4 It's pointless *getting into a flap*
5 He's always *ramming his opinions down our throats*
6 We were both *rooted to the spot*

a until we know exactly what's happened.
b even though it's obvious we're not interested.
c we will probably have to sell the house to survive.
d after we heard the news of the accident.
e her exams, as usual.
f a meal with what I have left in the fridge.

b Work in pairs. Tell each other about a time you

1 got into a flap about something.
2 only just scraped through a test.
3 were rooted to the spot.
4 had somebody's opinions rammed down your throat.
5 rustled up a wonderful meal.

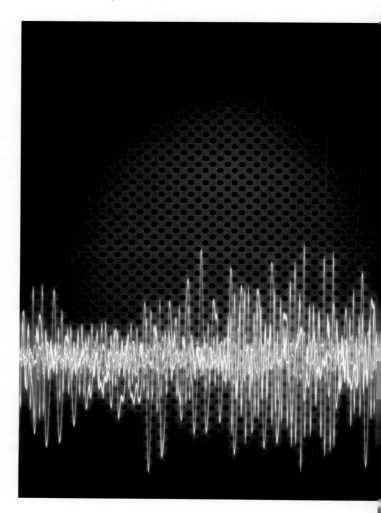

Use of English 1 (Paper 1 Part 1)

Lead-in

1 Compare traditional toys or activities with modern electronic games. What are the advantages and disadvantages of each type?

Multiple-choice cloze

2a Read the text below quickly. In what ways did Miyamoto transform the concept of electronic games?

> EXPERT STRATEGIES page 167

b Read the strategy on page 167, then do the task. Use the Help notes for support with certain items.

*For questions 1–8, read the text below and decide which answer (**A**, **B**, **C** or **D**) best fits each gap. There is an example at the beginning (0).*

The man who invented playtime

Shigeru Miyamoto is probably the most influential man of the last twenty years in **(0)** C of the number of people who play his electronic games – *Mario Bros, Wii Fit* and **(1)**__ others. It is due to him that Nintendo, at $85 billion, is now one of the most highly **(2)**__ companies in Japan.

The **(3)**__ majority of video games are created by engineers but Miyamoto is an artist, playful and endlessly creative. Hired by Nintendo to reinvent an arcade game, he broke through the **(4)**__ which had previously pitched these games only at adults. To capture the American market, Miyamoto **(5)**__ with *Donkey Kong* – its family-friendly style in sharp contrast to the violent games which had previously **(6)**__ the industry. Then, in 1983, his arcade hit *Mario Bros* became the biggest game franchise in the world. **(7)**__ Miyamoto's great success in entertainment, though, his next phase of game design – the DS and the Wii – focused on self-improvement, as well as making games interactive and creative. It also **(8)**__ Nintendo, already a big player, into a giant on the world stage.

0	A regards	B concerns	C terms	D relations
1	A numerous	B limitless	C infinite	D immeasurable
2	A estimated	B evaluated	C priced	D valued
3	A enormous	B vast	C massive	D extensive
4	A fence	B barrier	C boundary	D wall
5	A put up	B came up	C took up	D turned up
6	A dominated	B commanded	C governed	D oversaw
7	A Nonetheless	B Albeit	C Despite	D While
8	A swapped	B switched	C turned	D formed

> **HELP**

5 This phrasal verb means *had the idea for*.
8 The word you need goes with *into* to make a phrasal verb meaning *became something different*.

Task analysis

3a Which linking word has a similar meaning to the answer for number 7? What changes would you need to make to the structure of the sentence?

b Make a note of collocations (including phrasal verbs), set phrases, dependent prepositions and linking words which are new to you. Add examples.

Discussion

4 Can electronic games encourage people to become more intelligent? What influence, if any, do you think they have on health and crime?

Listening 1 Developing skills

Before you listen

1 Look at the pictures.

1 What might the most and least enjoyable aspects of these activities be?
2 What words and expressions are related to the activities?

Listening for the main idea

2a 🎧 19 Listen to a woman talking about her hobby and answer the questions.

1 What is her hobby?
2 What does she enjoy about it?
3 What went wrong at first?

b What other information did you hear which is not relevant to the questions?

3 What words and expressions did you hear which told you how the speaker felt about her hobby?

Multiple matching (Paper 3 Part 4)

4 🎧 20 Listen and complete both Tasks One and Two. You will hear the extracts twice.

➤ EXPERT STRATEGIES page 171

You will hear the extract you heard in Exercise 2a and two more short extracts in which people are talking about their hobbies. (In the exam, there will be five speakers and eight options in each task.)

TASK ONE
*For questions **1–3**, choose from the list (**A–F**) what each speaker enjoys about their hobby.*

TASK TWO
*For questions **4–6**, choose from the list (**A–F**) the problem each speaker has had with their hobby.*

While you listen you must complete both tasks.

A the excuse to unwind	A finding it time-consuming
B the personal challenge	B lacking original ideas
C the creative outlet	C being too self-critical
D the financial benefits	D being over-ambitious initially
E the potential career prospects	E having insufficient energy
F the contact with like-minded people	F failing to fulfil people's expectations

Speaker 1 [1]
Speaker 2 [2]
Speaker 3 [3]

Speaker 1 [4]
Speaker 2 [5]
Speaker 3 [6]

Discussion

5 Which creative activity would you most like to try, and why?

EXPERT WORD CHECK

curl up   fussy   get a buzz   in common   initially   innovative
in the same boat   intimidating   issue (n)   underestimate

Language development 1

Review of future forms

1a Underline the most appropriate verb form in *italics*. In some cases both are possible.

Subject: photography course

I've just remembered the photography course I told you about (1) *starts / will start* next Monday. I (2) *'m going to / will* sign up for one term initially because I really don't know if I (3) *'ll / am going to* be any good. Apparently, in the first term we'll (4) *be learning / learn* all about the techniques of photography and I've been told the teacher (5) *gives / is giving* us lots of practical demonstrations. Hopefully, by the end of the term, (6) *we'll have taken / we're taking* some photos ourselves. As soon as I (7) *have had / will have had* my first lesson, I'll email with all the news. I hope I won't (8) *make / be making* a fool of myself!

b Discuss your answers, explaining your choices. If both are possible, explain the difference in meaning and what it shows about the context.

➤ EXPERT GRAMMAR page 177

Expressions with future meaning

2a Rewrite these sentences, replacing the words in *italics* with a suitable expression from the box. There is sometimes more than one possibility.

be (not) + infinitive   be due + infinitive
be bound/sure + infinitive   be (un)likely + infinitive
expect (sb) + infinitive   be on the point/verge of + -ing
be about + infinitive

1 I think the government *is definitely going to* try and cut subsidies for the arts.
2 The measure *probably won't* come into effect until next year.
3 The government *is going to* announce its decision any minute now.
4 The opposition says that many people *will* lose their jobs if the plans go ahead.
5 The government *will* meet at 2 p.m. today.
6 The prime minister *will* visit Japan as part of his overseas tour.

b Discuss these questions.
1 What places are you most likely to visit in the next year or so?
2 What are you unlikely to be doing in the foreseeable future?
3 What kind of occupation do/did people expect you to have?
4 What are you about to do in the next few hours?

Future in the past

3a Complete these sentences, using *would be, was/were going to, was/were to have, would have, was/were about to, was/were due to.*

1 Can it wait until tomorrow? I ____ just ____ leave.
2 We ____ meet up for lunch, but there's been a train strike.
3 I was hoping we ____ made a profit by now, but we haven't.
4 The meeting ____ start at 3 p.m. but it's been delayed.
5 I thought this holiday job ____ really tedious but I've enjoyed it.
6 The latest sales figures ____ been published today, but there's been a hitch.

b Work in pairs and take turns at reading out sentences 1–6. Focus on the weak forms of *was* /wəz/ and *were* /wə(r)/ and the words which have most stress.

c Work in pairs. What changes of plans have you had recently? Write two true sentences and one false sentence about your plans, using the future in the past. See if your partner can guess which is the false one.

4 Complete the second sentence so that it has a similar meaning to the first sentence, using the word given. You must use between three and six words, including the word given.

1 There's a strong likelihood that they will cancel the concert.
   HIGHLY
   It _____ the concert will be cancelled.
2 Thomas was just going to phone you to apologise.
   POINT
   Thomas was just _____ you to apologise.
3 It's our parents' 25th wedding anniversary next year.
   MARRIED
   Next year, our parents _____ 25 years.
4 The train should have arrived at six.
   DUE
   The train _____ at six.
5 Everyone assumes Tom will pass his driving test this time.
   EXPECTED
   Tom _____ fail his driving test this time.

Writing 1 Coherence

> **EXPERT WRITING**
>
> In the exam you are assessed on your ability to produce well-organised pieces of writing with a logical sequence of ideas.
> Make sure
> - your introduction states the topic clearly
> - each new paragraph has one main idea, stated in a topic sentence
> - the main idea is supported by relevant details
> - the details are presented in a logical sequence
> - the details are connected by linking words and punctuation.

1 Compare these two paragraphs. Which paragraph fulfils the requirements listed in Expert Writing?

A People used to think that great artists such as Leonardo da Vinci, Mozart or Shakespeare had artistic gifts which were bestowed on them by the gods. These days, creativity is beginning to be better understood by psychologists. Highly creative people tend to want to create from a sense of dissatisfaction: they often had an unhappy childhood. Many were unwell, or unpopular and lonely because of their introverted, antisocial or workaholic personalities. One advantage of being unpopular, though, is that it would leave them with more time to cultivate their talent, and this appears to be the crucial factor.

B To be creative you need to take risks. If I wanted to become creative, I would decide which area I would be creative in. Creativity can sometimes make you rich or famous. I would tell myself I had to be confident and never give up. Creativity is something which everyone can aspire to. The worst enemy of creativity is trying to be a perfectionist. It doesn't require intelligence. You need curiosity and adaptability. A lot of people are afraid of criticism. You have to be able to make mistakes.

2 Read the information about ways of organising details in a paragraph. Decide how Paragraph A in Exercise 1 is organised.

Methods of organising the supporting points
1 Example: provide a list of examples or an illustration to support the main idea.
2 Time: describe the events in the order they happened.
3 Comparison/contrast: show how things are similar or different.
4 Emphasis: list supporting information so that the most important is last. The reader is most likely to remember the last thing read.

3 Work with a partner and rewrite Paragraph B.
1 Choose one of the sentences as the topic sentence or write your own.
2 Cross out any irrelevant details.
3 Decide on a logical order for the supporting points.
4 Use appropriate linking words and punctuation to connect your ideas.

4a Plan and write your answer to this task.

Write a short paragraph from an essay in which you describe an artist (e.g. painter, writer, musician) that you admire, explaining why you admire him/her.

b Exchange your answer with a partner. Is your partner's answer well organised? Are the ideas linked together?

➤ EXPERT WRITING page 191

➤ EXPERT STRATEGIES page 169

Listening 2 (Paper 3 Part 4)

Before you listen

1 Discuss these questions.

1 Are you or have you ever been a fan of a particular entertainer or sportsperson? How devoted were you? What things did you do?
2 Why do people become fans? Do you think it is possible to be too fanatical?

Multiple matching

2a Read the tasks below and mark the key words in the questions.

b 🎧 21 Read the strategy on page 171, then do the tasks. Use the Help notes for support with certain items.

You will hear five short extracts in which people are talking about being a fan of a famous singer.

TASK ONE	**TASK TWO**
For questions 1–5, choose from the list (A–H) the reason each speaker became a fan.	*For questions 6–10, choose from the list (A–H) what each speaker finds most difficult about being a fan.*

While you listen you must complete both tasks.

A I loved his speaking voice.		A the expense
B I shared his sense of humour.		B how time consuming it is
C I identified with his feelings.	Speaker 1 [1]	C having no room to store collected items
D I thought his appearance was unusual.	Speaker 2 [2]	D the mess it creates
	Speaker 3 [3]	E the negative effect on others of being over-organised
E I saw him as a role model.	Speaker 4 [4]	F the amount of travel involved
F I liked his sense of independence.	Speaker 5 [5]	G unkind comments from strangers
G I was attracted by his looks.		H living with an embarrassing reminder of it
H I found his performance very exciting.		

Speaker 1	[6]
Speaker 2	[7]
Speaker 3	[8]
Speaker 4	[9]
Speaker 6	[10]

➤ **HELP**

Speaker 1 Listen for the phrase 'The lyrics were so full of sadness'. What he says next gives his reaction. (Task One)
Speaker 2 Listen to what she says about 'the fan club thing'. This tells you the answer. (Task Two)
Speaker 4 How does she feel about her tattoos now she's a bit older?

Discussion

3 Have you followed a celebrity on Twitter or Facebook? Do celebrities have too much influence? Give reasons.

Task analysis

4 Compare your answers.

1 What did you focus on the first time you listened? Why? Did you find any answers?
2 What did you do the second time you listened?
3 What was the hardest part of the whole exercise? Why?

EXPERT WORD CHECK

accommodating (*adj*)   caption (*v*)   clutter (*n*)   cuddle up
exasperated   hoarder   inventory   loft   merchandise
string of passions

Speaking (Paper 4 Part 3)

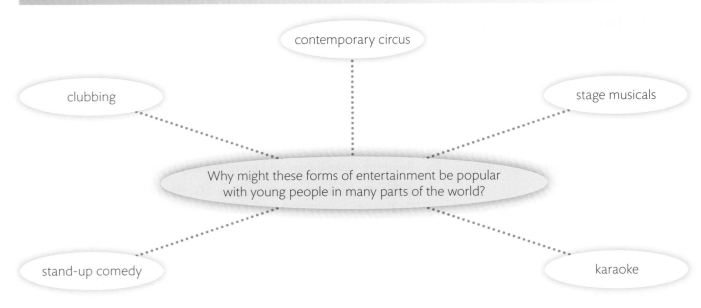

clubbing

contemporary circus

stage musicals

Why might these forms of entertainment be popular
with young people in many parts of the world?

stand-up comedy

karaoke

Vocabulary: entertainment

1a Most of these phrases are from the Listening tasks on page 47.
Can you match them with one or more of the activities in the
spidergram above?

it costs a fortune   it has me in fits   it inspires you   it's very moving
it's best to see them live   it's only a craze   you're totally blown away

b Circle the correct preposition.

1 pack a lot *with / into* it
2 perform *in / on* stage
3 play *in front of / towards* a live audience
4 put *in / on* a fantastic show
5 sing *into / at* a microphone
6 sit *in / at* the front row
7 take part *in / of* the show

c Choose the correct word to complete the phrasal verb.

1 The show has really __ off. It's packed out every night.
   A got   B taken   C held   D pulled
2 The performers __ so much into it. They were exhausted by the end.
   A placed   B gave   C stuck   D put
3 Some people go just to __ up the atmosphere. It's very relaxed and
   intimate.
   A soak   B drink   C look   D give
4 The beautiful songs really __ you out of yourself and make you
   forget your troubles.
   A pick   B take   C push   D work
5 You just pick your favourite song and __ it out as best you can!
   A perform   B hang   C sing   D belt
6 We couldn't keep going all night. We had to __ out every so often.
   A chill   B cool   C relax   D pass

2 Answer these questions. Use expressions from Exercises 1a, 1b
and 1c.

1 Which is the most/the least enjoyable of the activities in the
   spidergram? Give reasons.
2 What sort of people go to them? Why do they go?
3 Which of these forms of entertainment will still be popular in
   20 years' time and why?

Sample answer

EXPERT STRATEGY

Give your opinion but take care not to dominate, making sure you use a wide range of structures and vocabulary. Invite your partner to give his/her opinion and develop what he/she says.
For a full list of strategies see page 172.

3a Read the strategy.

b 🎧 22 Listen to the interlocutor's instructions for the first part of the task and answer the questions.
1 What do you have to do?
2 How long have you got to do it?

c 🎧 23 Listen to two people doing the task. Do you agree with their opinions?

d 🎧 24 Now listen to the interlocutor's instructions for the second part of the task and the candidates' discussion. Do you agree with their conclusion?

EXPERT STRATEGY

Don't come to your conclusion too soon.

e Read the Speaking assessment criteria on page 171. How successfully did the candidates carry out the task? Did they follow the advice in the task strategies?

Useful language: exchanging ideas

4a 🎧 25 Listen to the sample answer again and answer the questions.

Which of the phrases in the box below is used to:
1 state your opinion?
2 qualify something you or someone else has just said?
3 give yourself thinking time?
4 involve your partner?
5 add something?
6 introduce disagreement?
7 change the subject?
8 reach a conclusion?

Anyhow, they're …   Certainly not … but …   I know what you mean but …
Let's go for …   Let's move on, shall we?   Mind you …
Oh, that's a difficult one.   Well, personally …   Well, actually …
Wouldn't you agree?

---

b Can you think of other phrases for each heading?

c Read the conversation. One expression in each set can't be used in the context. Cross it out.

A: Have you seen how many gigs he's got lined up in the next few weeks? It's ridiculous.
B: Yes. Nobody can do all that and be at their best every night.
(1) *Anyway, / Mind you, / Having said that,* people always say that when he's on tour and he always seems to get rave reviews.
A: True. But won't he be burnt out by the time he reaches 30?
(2) *Besides that, / Not only that, / Having said that,* if he gets this kind of exposure we'll all get fed up with him.
B: You're right. It could kill his career in the long run.
A: (3) *Mind you, / Actually, / Having said that,* he must be earning a fortune. We should be so lucky!

Collaborative task

5a Work in groups of three and do the tasks in Exercises 3b and 3d. One student should time the exchange and check that the strategies are followed and that the criteria stated in the Speaking assessment (e.g. turn-taking) are met.

b Tell the class briefly which activities you have chosen and why.

Language development 2

Modals and semi-modals (Part 1)

1a What is the modal in this sentence and what does it express? How would you say the sentence in the past?

Karaoke may be great fun but it's not to everyone's taste.

b Underline the modal and semi-modal verbs and match them to the functions below.

1 Stage musicals must have got something right. They're so popular.
2 You might have told me that Adele had a new album out!
3 These days you don't need to dress up when you go to the opera.
4 She can't have finished her stand-up routine already!
5 Phone the box office. They should be open now.

---

criticism   disbelief   expectation
making an assumption   necessity

---

c Correct the student mistakes in these sentences and say what grammatical rules the students have broken.

1 We couldn't to get into the gig.
2 You'll need find someone with a spare ticket
3 I walked away because he can't give me a sensible price.
4 You should avoided the ticket touts. It's lucky you weren't ripped off.
5 They're so loud. I'm sure you can hear them from outside when they start!

➤ EXPERT GRAMMAR page 178

Necessity, prohibition, advice, criticism, permission

2a Express these sentences in another way using *can, should, must, need (to), have to* or *ought to* in the positive or negative.

1 He's a great stand-up comedian. It's essential that we book tickets.
2 No, it's not essential to get tickets before we go.
3 You're not allowed to turn up without a ticket.
4 I think the best thing for you to do is to phone and find out.
5 They say it's too late to buy them now, so why didn't you buy them before?

b Complete the second sentence using a modal so that it means the same as the first. Note that some are in the past.

1 You can't interview Gwyneth until I've spoken to her agent.
   I _____ to Gwyneth's agent before you can interview her.
2 I expected the agent to call me back yesterday.
   The agent _____ yesterday.
3 I can give you the information you want even if you don't get an interview.
   You _____ to get the information you want.
4 If you come next week, I'll let you see her straightaway.
   Come next week and you _____ wait to see her.
5 The only way I could get an interview was to camp outside her dressing room.
   I _____ in order to get an interview.
6 Her agent called security, even though it wasn't necessary.
   Her agent _____ security, but he did anyway.

Ability, possibility/probability, deduction

3a Circle the correct words to complete the text.

My uncle says that in the old days, when you missed a film at the cinema you thought you'd missed it forever. This **(1)** *must be / must have been / had to be* very frustrating as you **(2)** *can't have / couldn't have / mightn't have* seen it any other way. He says that a film which **(3)** *might be / might have been / must have been* hugely popular when it came out would disappear forever.

That's not true now. Last week, not only **(4)** *was I able to / could I / did I succeed* buy an obscure silent movie somebody told me about, but I **(5)** *could / managed to / can* download a fantastic new movie I'd missed when it came out a short time ago as well. Many films which **(6)** *would have been / must have been / can be* forgotten now have a new life. According to some analysts, a film **(7)** *might / must / can't* make as much as 50 percent of its total revenue from DVD rights.

b Tell each other about something difficult that you managed to do and something you'd like to be able to do.

➤ See Module 10 on page 162 for Modals and semi-modals (Part 2).

Use of English 2 (Paper 1 Part 4)

Key word transformations

1a Read these task instructions and look at the example. Which of the answers for the example below is correct and why?

> *For questions **1–6**, complete the second sentence so that it has a similar meaning to the first sentence, using the word given. **Do not change the word given**. You must use between **three** and **six** words, including the word given. Here is an example (**0**).*
>
> *Example:*
>
> (0) Attendance at the meeting wasn't compulsory, so she didn't bother to go.
> NEED
> She _____ the meeting, so she stayed at home.
>
> 1 needn't have gone to
> 2 wasn't needed at
> 3 didn't need to go to
> 4 thought she didn't need to go to

b Read the strategy on page 168, then do the task. Write only the missing words in CAPITAL LETTERS. Use the Help notes for support with certain items. Note that contractions (e.g. *haven't*) count as two words.

1 I know that it was wrong of me to upset Sam.
   SHOULD
   I know that I _____ Sam upset.
2 There's no way that my brother wrote this letter.
   POSSIBLY
   This letter _____ by my brother.
3 Because of the snow we couldn't get to the gig.
   PREVENTED
   The _____ the gig.
4 I've been too busy to watch the movie you sent, but I'll do it soon.
   ROUND
   I _____ the movie you sent, but I'll do it soon.
5 Sarah's card never arrived so it's possible she forgot to post it.
   NOT
   Sarah _____ the card, because it never arrived.
6 They didn't fix the computer problem, even though they said they would.
   SUPPOSED
   They _____ the computer working again but they didn't.

> ➤ **HELP**
>
> 2 A modal is needed here. Is it in the affirmative or the negative?
>
> 3 What type of word immediately follows *prevented* in this context, a preposition or a pronoun?
>
> 4 You will need a phrasal verb meaning *do something you have intended to do for a long time*. Do you need the affirmative or the negative?

2 Write a sentence using the modals in Questions 1, 2 and 5 in Exercise 1b. Ask another student to transform them without using the modal.

Task analysis

3 Answer these questions.
   1 What sort of changes (e.g. grammar and vocabulary) were necessary for each answer?
   2 Think of another example using the phrasal verb tested in Question 4.

Writing 2 Essay (Paper 2 Part 1)

Lead-in **1** Discuss these questions.

1 What are the main health and social benefits of leisure time? Why? How do you spend yours?

2 In what contexts do people write essays? What is their purpose? What types of essays can you think of?

Understand the task **2** Read the task and answer these questions.

1 How many of the 'profitable ways' in the notes must you choose? What must you decide?

2 How many 'opinions' from the notes must you include? How will you express them? What will you do if you don't include them?

3 Use the strategy in Module 2 (page 36) to analyse the question.

4 What will make the tutor think it is a well-written essay?

You have attended a talk on how people could spend their leisure time more profitably. You have made the notes below:

> Profitable ways of spending leisure time
> • helping others
> • learning
> • physical activities
>
> Some opinions expressed in the talk:
> 'At work we lose touch with friends, family and the community.'
> 'Passive entertainment makes us intellectually lazy.'
> 'We spend so long in front of screens, we are physically unfit.'

*Write an essay for your tutor discussing **two** of the profitable ways in your notes. You should **explain which way is more important**, **giving reasons** in support of your answer.*
You may, if you wish, make use of the opinions expressed in the talk, but you should use your own words as far as possible.

Plan your essay **3a** Brainstorm some notes which answer the question. Think of examples where appropriate (e.g. *helping in the community*).

b Look at an example of a 'spidergram' on page 48. Decide which of the points in your notes you will include and make a spidergram to show how your essay will be structured. How many boxes will you need? Where will you put the reasons to support your opinions? Where will you put the examples?
Which of these will you put in the central box?

helping others   losing touch   opinion   profitable use of leisure time

c Check that the points in the spidergram are all relevant to the answer and you have included everything necessary.

d Your essay will need an introduction and a conclusion. Make a paragraph plan. For example:

Paragraph 1: Introduction
Paragraph 2: _____
Paragraph 3: _____
Paragraph 4: Conclusion

Language and content

A | It is generally accepted that the pace of modern life has increased and more people work longer hours.

B | So for all the reasons I've said, we'd better look to do something more creative in our spare time.

C | In short, it is clearly desirable that we not only relax but that we do something worthwhile in our leisure time.

D | Here are two of the most profitable ways of spending leisure time.

EXPERT STRATEGY

Make sure:
- you select the key points and express them in your own words
- that every key point is backed up and possibly exemplified
- you avoid irrelevance, repetition and deviation.

Remember the main aim is to present an argument coherently. See page 169 for a full list of strategies.

Write your essay

Check your essay

4a Which of the sentences A–D could be used in the introduction and which in the conclusion?

b How could you rewrite these ideas for an essay?

1 Fun maybe, but these things don't do much for you long-term. (*Such activities …*)

2 As a society I don't think we're as together as we used to be. (*There is less …*)

3 I actually feel more chilled when I'm doing something useful. (*Doing something …*)

c Work with a partner and find at least one example in these sentence openings which:
- indicates the structure of the essay
- gives the writer's opinion
- adds extra information.

As (the pace of modern life increases) … so (it is more important) …
We simply cannot … or …
It is important to recognise that …
It has been claimed that …
However, although (leisure time can make us …), if we don't …

Main body
For a while (watching TV) … can be fun but …
This is due to …/This can lead to …
It goes without saying that (sports) …
The greatest benefit/biggest drawback is that …
The first point to bear in mind is that (many people) …
In my view, the best (use of leisure time) … is to …
It is often argued that …
It is my firm belief that …/There can be no doubt that …/
    It cannot be denied that …
It would be wrong to argue that (playing computer games) …/
    I would dispute the claim that …
These are (activities) which …
Another, often unacknowledged, (consequence of modern life is) …
Another way, then, of (using one's spare time) is to …/In addition, …
A further point is that …/Not only is … but …
And so therefore, if …

Conclusion
On the whole then, …
To conclude/sum up, whilst (having a daily workout) …,
    it is nevertheless (far more satisfying)
Clearly, if (leisure time is to become precious to us) …
On balance, while (it is clearly desirable that) …
All things considered, …/All in all, …

d Choose some of the sentence openings in Exercise 4c and complete them for your essay.

5 Now read the strategy and write your essay in 220–260 words, using some of the ideas and language above.

6 Edit your work using the Writing checklist on page 190.

Review

1 Choose the correct word to complete the sentences.

1 The taxi pulled __ at the entrance to the theatre and we jumped in.
   A off   B through   C up   D on
2 He only just managed to scrape __ his music theory exam.
   A through   B over   C by   D round
3 After thinking for a long time, I finally came __ with an idea for a book.
   A across   B round   C down   D up
4 The film company is hoping to __ the scandal concerning one of their big stars.
   A keep in   B cover up   C shut up
   D chill out
5 My school used to put __ an outdoor play every summer.
   A through   B forward   C on   D out
6 At the end of the film, the monster __ into a prince.
   A turned   B became   C appeared   D set
7 Have you ever __ part in a drama production?
   A played   B had   C formed   D taken
8 Technology has __ on considerably since the days of music CDs.
   A passed   B moved   C continued
   D progressed

2 Complete these sentences with a word from the box.

capture   convey   culminate   enhance
guarantee   insert   rectify   resemble

1 The stage manager is trying to ____ the problem with the props.
2 We will have to ____ the scene we forgot to record later on tomorrow.
3 The actor manages to ____ his emotions in an understated way.
4 The dancer doesn't in any way ____ her famous mother.
5 I ____ he'll be word perfect on the night. He always is.
6 Most of those films usually ____ in a car chase.
7 That brand has done everything it can to ____ the market for cool trainers.
8 His brilliant performance will only serve to ____ the reputation he's already got.

3 Rewrite each sentence so that it has the same meaning, using the modal verb in brackets.

1 It's possible I left the tickets in the car. (might)
2 It's obvious he hasn't been practising the piano every day. (can't)
3 I'm assuming they'll be doing their usual gig at the O2 stadium in June. (should)
4 I'm pretty sure he's already left by now, so it's not worth phoning. (will)
5 I was so happy, I nearly burst into tears of joy. (could)
6 There's no way she caught the train, given how late she left the house. (won't)
7 I'm sure they're enjoying themselves if they're staying an extra week. (must)
8 In the end, it wasn't necessary for them to have gone to all the trouble to get the visa as nobody asked to see it. (needn't)

4 Circle the correct words to complete the blog.

Browsing blogs

There is excitement in the house because my son **(1)** *is about to / is to* go to his first music festival. Everyone is telling him that it's **(2)** *due / bound* to rain because it always seems to at these events. Apparently, wallowing in mud is all part of the experience.

I've always fancied going to one too but I've been told it's no use applying because the tickets **(3)** *will have / are being* sold out by now.

Apparently, he'll **(4)** *share / be sharing* a small tent with a few friends, so at least they'll be warm! I was **(5)** *going to drive / on the verge of driving* him there, but he's now told me he prefers to go by coach with all the other festival-goers.

I expect he's **(6)** *living / going to live* on junk food for the three days he's there. There aren't **(7)** *sure / expected* to be any showers available either, so I imagine he **(8)** *'ll come / comes* home absolutely starving and looking pretty grubby.

4 The global village

Overview

4A
- **Reading and Use of English:** Multiple matching (Part 8); Word formation (Part 3)
- **Vocabulary:** Sleep; Similar words; Idioms: word pairs; Phrasal nouns
- **Listening:** Developing skills: Listening for attitude and opinion; Multiple choice: short extracts (Part 1)
- **Language development:** Word families: Adding suffixes; Making spelling changes; Adding prefixes; Word families
- **Writing:** Attitude phrases

4B
- **Listening:** Multiple choice: short extracts (Part 1)
- **Speaking:** Vocabulary: issues and opinions; Useful language: expressing probability and certainty; Long turn (Part 2)
- **Language development:** Noun clauses
- **Reading and Use of English:** Open cloze (Part 2)
- **Writing:** Proposal (Part 2)

Lead-in

1a What are the main characteristics of people in your country? On a scale of 0–5 (0 = completely untrue; 5 = very true), which of these are generally true?

Quiz

1. We are very punctual.
2. We use a lot of facial expressions and gestures.
3. We stand close to each other when we speak.
4. At work, relations between employers and employees are formal.
5. We show our feelings openly.
6. We are very family-oriented.
7. We have a good sense of humour.
8. Local communities are important even in big cities.
9. We are interested in what happens in other countries.
10. People in a community do a lot to help each other.
11. There's great respect for differences between people.
12. We are warm and friendly to strangers.

b Which of your country's characteristics are you most/least proud of?

2 What do foreigners think about your country? Which of their views are true? Which would you like to change and why?

55

4A A small world?

Reading (Paper 1 Part 8)

Before you read

1 Discuss these questions.

1 How 'normal' are your sleep patterns, compared to other people you know? Does a regular sleeping pattern matter? Why?

2 Are sleep patterns around the world generally the same or different? Give reasons.

Multiple matching

> EXPERT STRATEGIES page 169

2 Read the strategy on page 169, then do the task. Use the Help notes for support with certain items. Remember to read the questions carefully before you try to find the information.

*You are going to read an article about sleep. For questions **1–10**, choose from the sections (**A–E**). The sections may be chosen more than once.*

In which section of the article are the following mentioned?

a pragmatic advantage of having shared sleeping arrangements	1
beliefs about the potential risks of too deep a sleep	2
a widespread assumption that sleeping routines are universal	3
an awareness that scientific research methods may be flawed	4
a re-evaluation of ideas about what represents typical sleeping environments	5
the ability to fall asleep as a method of self-protection	6
investigations currently being carried out into the science of sleep	7
the link between darkness and periods of sleep	8
a lack of research into sleeping customs across cultures	9
different cultural attitudes to irregular sleep patterns	10

> **HELP**

2 How else can you say *a deep sleep*? Look for ways in which sleeping lightly is an advantage in some cultures.

4 Where does scientific research into sleep often take place? Why would this be a problem when investigating the way some cultures sleep?

5 Which part contrasts the beds used by Westerners and non-Westerners?

Task analysis

3 Discuss these questions.

1 Mark the key phrases in the options and compare them.

2 Find phrases in the text that mean the same as the phrases you marked in the options.

Discussion

4 How do you think other daily rituals might be different in your country from other countries? Think of some of the following and add any others you can think of.

- bringing up children
- shopping
- food/mealtimes
- welcoming guests
- transport
- family life

EXPERT WORD CHECK

allot   bear a resemblance   initiate   invaluable   nuisance
relegated   ritual   slump (*v*)   stifle   twist (*n*)

HOW THE WORLD SLEEPS

Is there something we can learn from how people in different cultures sleep?

A

It's a familiar ritual in many parts of the world. You climb into bed, stifling a yawn. Maybe a little reading or television to loosen you up for slumber. After a while, you nod off and sleep until an alarm clock starts ringing. The twist, however, is that this ritual doesn't apply to people currently living outside the modern Western world or even to inhabitants of Western Europe 200 years ago. Yet, as anthropologist Carol Worthman discovered, sleep scarcely figures in the literature of either cross-cultural differences or human evolution. It is generally relegated to the sidelines, treated as a biological given with little potential for variation from one part of the world to another.

B

Worthman contacted researchers who had intimate knowledge of one or more traditional societies, and uncovered a wide variety of customs, none of which bore any resemblance to what many modern Western people take for granted. She says that this finding raises profound questions for the research that is being done into our biological clock. Over the past 50 years, scientists have identified periods of rapid eye movement (REM) sleep, during which intense dreams often occur. Current efforts are examining genes involved in wakefulness and sleeping and have taken strides towards treating sleep disturbances. Although investigators assume that people sleep alone or with a partner for a solid chunk of the night, most studies take place in laboratories where individuals have naps while being hooked up to brain and body monitors. However, the distinctive sleep styles of non-Western, more traditional groups may shape the biology of sleep in ways undreamed of in sleep labs, which is why Worthman was keen to initiate relevant research.

C

Worthman assembled a preliminary picture of sleep practices in 10 non-Western populations. Having observed how sleepers in traditional societies recline on skins, mats, wooden platforms, the ground, or just about anything except a springy mattress, she says it brought it home to her just how odd the Western concept is of layers of bedding piled on a 'giant sleep machine'. Furthermore, unlike most Western bedrooms, sleep typically takes place in spaces that feature constant background noise emanating from other sleepers and various domestic animals. Communal space equates to safe space, invaluable in the event of a threat or emergency.

D

Virtually no-one in traditional societies, including children, keeps a regular bedtime. In these worlds without artificial light, activity is limited and affects the time allotted to sleep; individuals tend to slip in and out of slumber several times during the night, rather than sleeping in a solid block of time. In traditional settings, variable sleep cycles among individuals and age groups are useful so that someone can be awake or easily roused at all times. Whereas, as Worthman points out, the natural tendency of teenagers in the Western world to go to sleep late and wake up late is seen as a nuisance or as a sign of rebellion. Equally, extreme early birds get diagnosed as sleep disordered.

E

Some cultures, such as the Gebusi rainforest dwellers, are of the opinion that a person's spirit may wander off too far and fail to return if they sleep too heavily; dreaming makes this more likely. Whether or not one believes this, a quick nap may be preferable and has crucial effects on the body and mind. As an example, Balinese infants are carried about and held continuously by caregivers so that they learn to fall asleep even in hectic and noisy situations. This trains them to exhibit what the Balinese call 'fear sleep' later in life. Adults and children enter fear sleep by suddenly slumping over in a deep slumber when they or family members confront intense anxiety or an unexpected fright. They are literally scared into sleep. Conversely, it is possible that infants who sleep alone in the Western world may find it difficult to relax, fall asleep, wake up or concentrate because of the contrast between the sensory overload of the waking world and the dark quiet bedroom. Only cross-cultural studies of children's sleep and behaviour may be able to clarify such issues.

Vocabulary

Sleep

1a What have all these words got in common? Which of them is formal?

doze   kip   nap   slumber   snooze

b The following expressions all mean *the process of going to sleep*. Which is/are followed by *off* and which by *out*?

crash   doze   drift   drop   nod

c Ask each other these questions.
1 Are you a *light or a heavy sleeper*?
2 Do you ever *sleep through* your alarm?
3 What do you *lose sleep over*?
4 What time of day do you *feel drowsy*?
5 Do you ever *sleep in* at the weekends?
6 What times of day are you usually *wide awake* and *fast asleep*?
7 Do you ever *oversleep*?
8 Did you *have sleepovers* when you were a child?

Similar words

2 Circle the correct word to complete the sentences. Which ones do you agree with? Give reasons.
1 If I take part in a *heated / increased / large* discussion, it takes me ages to fall asleep.
2 I slept like a *stone / log / rock* last night.
3 Some people believe that young children and their parents shouldn't sleep *excluded / apart / separated*.
4 Without *artificial / imitation / pretend* light, our sleeping habits would change.
5 Some businesses are *doing / making / giving* the case for giving workers power naps.
6 I hope that different cultures manage to *keep / seize / hang* on to their traditions in the age of the internet.

Idioms: word pairs

3a Replace the definitions in *italics* with one of the word pairs below.

as and when   by and large   off and on
part and parcel   through thick and thin
touch and go

1 In this country, the unpredictable climate is *a necessary feature* of living here.
2 He supports the government *despite its difficulties and problems*.
3 Julia sleeps *at whatever time she can*.
4 I've been running *for short periods but not regularly* for six years.
5 *In general*, I think that's an excellent idea.
6 Whether we get a pay rise or not is *in the balance*.

b Ask and answer the questions.
1 Are you allowed to arrive at school/college/work *as and when* you feel like it?
2 Who would you support *through thick and thin*?
3 Which activity do you do *off and on*?
4 Have you ever been in a situation where the outcome was *touch and go*?
5 Which strange things are *part and parcel* of living in your country?

Phrasal nouns

4a Look at the words in *italics*. Which ones can also be used as a phrasal verb? How would you rephrase these sentences to include a phrasal verb?
1 There was a sharp *intake* of breath when Simon made the announcement.
2 The *onset* of winter gets earlier every year.
3 I always get *back-up* from Tania at meetings.
4 There were *setbacks* for a while in her training because of the bad weather.

b Complete the second sentence so that it means the same as the first sentence, using a phrasal verb.
1 I was a bit disappointed with the band, actually. It was a bit of a letdown.
I felt as if the band had ____ us ____ .
2 Last week there was a break-in at our local bank.
Last week, somebody ____ ____ our local bank.
3 There is an outbreak of measles at my school.
An epidemic of measles has ____ ____ at my school.
4 There is always a build-up of traffic there at this time.
Traffic always ____ ____ there at this time.
5 I think there may be a downpour later on.
I think it's going to ____ ____ later on.
6 Kick-off was delayed for ten minutes while the disturbance was sorted out.
The game didn't ____ ____ until the disturbance was sorted out.

Use of English 1 (Paper 1 Part 3)

Lead-in

1 Discuss these questions.

1 What are the most common ways of commuting to work/university in your country?

2 What are the disadvantages of commuting? Are there any advantages?

Word formation

2a Read the text quickly for the general meaning without changing the words in capitals.

➤ EXPERT STRATEGIES page 167

b Read the strategy on page 167, then do the task. Use the Help notes for support with certain items.

➤ **HELP**

1 This is an adjective meaning *large in size* (not *made longer/bigger*).

4 You need a common prefix which makes a verb from an adjective.

8 What is the prefix which adds the meaning *too many*?

*For questions **1–8**, read the text below. Use the word given in capitals at the end of some of the lines to form a word that fits in the gap **in the same line**. There is an example at the beginning (**0**).*

The daily commute

At 7.30 on a weekday morning, Tokyo's rush hour is at its peak. (**0**) *Countless* commuters pour into the world's largest city, via an (**1**)_____ network of bullet and overground trains, all of which operate with impeccable (**2**)_____ . As the trains pull into the station and the doors slide open, more and more workers force themselves on board. To do this, they need the (**3**)_____ of the white-gloved 'pushers' who are employed to (**4**)_____ that people get to work on time. This morning ritual is the downside of the rapid (**5**)_____ in Tokyo's population. Seats have been removed from trains in an attempt to find a (**6**)_____ to the problem, but this has not been a popular move with some people, who complain about even more people being crammed into the same limited space. A new subway system, which takes a (**7**)_____ route around the city, has helped a little but, until more is done to ease (**8**)_____ , it seems that commuters will just have to grin and bear it.

COUNT
EXTEND

RELY

ASSIST

SURE
GROW

SOLVE

CIRCLE
CROWD

Task analysis

3 Answer these questions.

1 How many other words do you know which take the same prefixes as in numbers 4 and 8? Check your ideas in a dictionary.

2 Which of the words change their stress pattern when they become a different part of speech?

Discussion

4 In what ways could commuting be made more pleasant?

Listening 1 Developing skills

Before you listen

1 What do you think the typical characteristics are of the British? How do they compare with other nationalities?

Listening for attitude and opinion

2a 🎧 26 Listen to Extract One, in which two Americans are having a discussion, and answer these questions.

   1 What do the speakers agree on? What do they disagree on?
   2 How does the woman sometimes feel when she's listening to British people?

b Give examples of language used to indicate that the speakers agree and disagree.

c Give examples of language used to express attitude and opinion.

Multiple choice: short extracts (Paper 3 Part 1)

3a You will hear two extracts about cultural differences. (In the exam you will have three extracts and they will all be on different topics.) Read the context sentence and the questions for Extract One first (the same extract you heard in Exercise 2a) and predict what the answers will be. Don't look at the options yet.

b 🎧 27 For questions 1–2, listen once and discuss what the answers might be. Then listen again and choose the answer (A, B or C) which fits best according to what you hear.

Extract One

You hear two Americans discussing how people in Britain and the USA communicate differently.

1 The man mentions the conversation with his neighbour as an example of British people's tendency
  A to undervalue their achievements.
  B to understate personal successes.
  C to underestimate cultural differences.
2 How does the woman feel about the way British people speak?
  A She gets frustrated by their inability to be direct.
  B She wishes they would be less polite.
  C She's amused by their humour.

c 🎧 28 Follow the same procedure as in Exercises 3a and 3b for Extract Two.

Extract Two

You hear two people talking about places where they have lived.

3 What did the man dislike about living in the place where he grew up?
  A being made to conform
  B being unable to get on with people
  C being judged on his appearance
4 They both appreciate the place they live now because
  A it gives off a sense of energy.
  B it benefits from ethnic diversity.
  C it's possible to be your own person there.

Discussion

4 Discuss these questions.

   1 Have you ever lived in another city/country, etc.? What was it like?
   2 Under what conditions would you move abroad? (e.g. for work) What would you miss most?
   3 What would people find difficult about living in your country? What would they enjoy about it?

EXPERT WORD CHECK

apologetic   baffle   immaculate   norms
outfits   play (something) down   put out (*adj*)
straightforward   tattoo   toe the line

Language development 1

Word families

> **EXPERT STRATEGY**
>
> In Paper 1 Part 3, you have to form a
> word from a given stem to fill in gaps in
> a text. You may have to make up to four
> changes. These may involve:
> - adding a suffix, e.g. *popular* (adj) →
>   *popularise* (v); *fortunate* (adj) →
>   *fortunately* (adv)
> - adding a prefix, e.g. *tolerant* →
>   *intolerant*; *large* (adj) → *enlarge* (v)
> - making a spelling change, e.g. *deep* (adj)
>   → *depth* (noun); *thief* (concrete noun) →
>   *theft* (abstract noun)
> - making a word plural, e.g.
>   *responsible* (adj) → *responsibility* (n) →
>   *responsibilities*
>
> In the exam, your spelling must be
> accurate.

Adding suffixes

1a For each section below, form a
different word by adding suffixes,
underlining the word stress. Use
your dictionary as support. There
may be more than one answer.

    1 Adjectives from verbs
    amuse amusing/amused
    depend differ hesitate influence
    produce
    Adjectives from nouns
    affection aggression fun history
    hope will

    2 Nouns from verbs
    amuse confront decide defend
    discover participate persist
    please save
    Nouns from adjectives
    accurate cruel confident diverse
    happy jealous popular tolerant

    3 Verbs from nouns and adjectives
    beauty deep general legal
    strong width

b Make a note of the prefixes/suffixes used
to form adjectives, nouns and verbs.

Making spelling changes

2 Change these adjectives and verbs
into nouns by making a spelling change.

    broad choose die fly long prove
    strong succeed

Adding prefixes

3 Look at the table of prefixes and their general meaning. Add
more examples using the words in the box. Some words
can be used more than once, with a different meaning.

appear	arrange	conformist	danger	date	develop
exist	populated	print	reversible	rich	school	secure
willing	worker				

Prefix	General meaning	Examples
un-, im-, in-, is-, irr-, non-	not; the opposite of	*unbelievable, non-fiction*
mis-	wrongly	*misunderstanding*
co-	together; with	*co-production*
en-	cause to be; make into	*enlarge*
re-	again, in a different way	*replace*
under-	not sufficient	*underpaid*
over-	too much	*overtired*
pre-	before	*pre-book*

Word families

4a A good way of increasing your vocabulary is to make a record
of other forms of a word you know, or other forms of a new
word you come across. Use your dictionary as support to help
you complete these word families. Mark the stressed syllables.

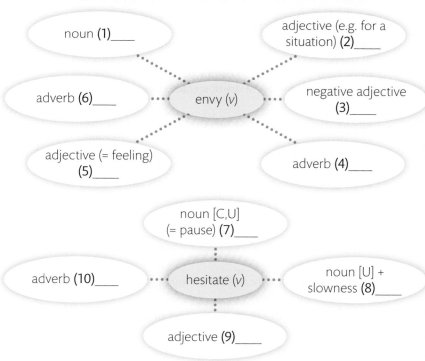

b Choose some other words from Modules 1–4 and make
word families, following the model in Exercise 4a.

Writing 1 Attitude phrases

EXPERT STRATEGY

In some types of writing, you are required to give or report facts and opinions and give recommendations or persuade. Using 'attitude phrases' to indicate your opinion on the information or comment on its truth will make your writing sound natural and fluent.

1a Compare two different versions of a report. In extract B:

1 Which expression introduces a statement that is true in most cases?
2 Which structure is used to emphasise the importance of a point?

> **A** Many of the people we spoke to said that they would welcome the idea of the town hosting an international festival, but very few of them had a firm idea about what kind of focus they thought it should have.

> **B** Generally speaking, the people we spoke to said that they would welcome the idea of the town hosting an international festival. What was noticeable, though, was that very few of them had a firm idea about the kind of focus they thought it should have.

b Read these two further extracts and add the expressions in *italics* to the categories below.

> **C** *Understandably*, perhaps, the general level of interest was higher among older people than teenagers or young adults. What became clear, moreover, was that, *on the whole*, young people were far more interested in music and dance than anything else. *Indeed*, this came near the top of the list for many older people, too, although food and drink attracted most interest.

> **D** Apparently, a lot of people feel that we do not organise enough cross-cultural events in the town. Surprisingly, though, most of them had had very little contact with the international college and had been to no events here. Presumably, this is partly our fault for not publicising it sufficiently well.

> **Generalising:** generally speaking, by and large, as a rule, in the main, ____
> **Giving your opinion/reaction:** annoyingly, naturally, strangely, to be honest, ____ , ____
> **Commenting on the truth/likelihood of something:** possibly, doubtless, in all probability, ____
> **Emphasising what you have said:** in fact, ____
> **Reporting/commenting on an opinion:** seemingly, one assumes, ____

2a Circle the correct words to complete the text.

We also interviewed several people about our idea for offering foreign language courses at the college in the evenings. (1) *In the main / Frankly*, the people we interviewed, both young and old, were very positive about it. (2) *Presumably / Indeed*, some languages will have more takers than others, but I feel it's well worth progressing to the next stage and investigating which ones we could offer. Most people felt it would be a hugely popular initiative. (3) *To be honest / Apparently*, it was a great success when the school used to run evening classes years ago, according to many people. (4) *Quite rightly / Naturally*, we will need to do further research but we really should follow up our ideas as soon as we possibly can. As well as making money, I feel absolutely sure that the lessons would be an excellent way of integrating our college into the life of the town. And (5) *personally / doubtlessly*, I'd be absolutely delighted if our students could benefit from more contact with people from the town. It would be wonderful if this could be the start of a new ongoing relationship.

b Work in pairs and find different ways in which the writer tries to persuade the reader to accept his/her suggestions.

3 You are at a college in the USA. The students are putting on an international festival; it will include a variety of entertainment and food and drink will be provided. You have been asked to suggest ideas which represent your country.

1 Make a note of some ideas for food, drink, entertainment, costumes, etc. which would best represent your country.
2 Discuss your proposals with other people. If there are others from your country, choose the best ideas.
3 Write an email, trying to persuade the committee to include your suggestions. Use some of the expressions of attitude and persuasive expressions from Exercises 1 and 2.
4 Exchange emails. Decide which proposals are the most original and which are the most persuasive.

Listening 2 (Paper 3 Part 1)

1 Discuss these questions.
1 Where you live, what local issues do people feel most strongly about (e.g. public transport)?
2 What action can people take? Is it effective? Give reasons.

2 Read questions 1–6 opposite and the options. Can you guess answers to the following?
1 What rights is Hector trying to get?
2 What is *guerrilla gardening*?
3 What is the aim of *craftivism*?

Multiple choice: short extracts

3a Read the task opposite. Mark the key words in the question or sentence stem and think about who you are listening to and what information you are listening for.

b 🎧 29 Read the strategy on page 170, then do the task. Use the Help notes for support with certain items.

Task analysis

4 Look at all the options again. Why are the other two options for each question not correct?

Discussion

5 Discuss these questions.
1 What do the three forms of activism have in common? What are your views of them? Which would be most effective in your country?
2 Can you think of other unusual kinds of activism?

---

*You will hear three different extracts. For questions **1–6**, choose the answer (**A**, **B** or **C**) which fits best according to what you hear. There are two questions for each extract.*

Extract One

You hear part of a radio interview with a man called Hector Ramírez, who campaigns for the rights of cyclists.

1 What has been the main aim of Hector's campaign?
   A to get the government interested in his ideas
   B to provide a facility which is both attractive and useful
   C to make it easier for people to move around his city
2 What aspect of the scheme is Hector particularly pleased with?
   A the way it has grown
   B the attitude of influential people
   C the flexibility shown by motorists

Extract Two

You hear two friends talking about an activity called guerrilla gardening.

3 The woman thinks it's special because
   A it's risky and exciting.
   B it brings local people together.
   C it saves local residents money.
4 How does the man feel about it?
   A He suspects it's being funded by big business.
   B He thinks that it should be made illegal.
   C He distrusts the motives of the people involved in it.

Extract Three

You hear two students talking about a form of protest called craftivism, which the woman is involved in.

5 The woman's movement has been successful because
   A she's had a lot of experience of public protests.
   B her supporters keep in touch with each other on the internet.
   C the messages that she sends make people laugh.
6 What do they agree about?
   A People should think of others as well as themselves.
   B All forms of protest have an effect.
   C The support of international bodies is welcome.

> HELP

1 One of these is only partly true, the other isn't stated as an aim. Only one answer can be deduced as a main aim.

4 Listen for the phrase *getting arrested*. The answer comes after that.

6 The man does not completely agree with two of the options.

EXPERT WORD CHECK

cash in (*v*)   chuck (around)   cross-stitched (*adj*)   cycle rack
discounted (*adj*)   empower   enforce   infrastructure
jump on the bandwagon   terminology

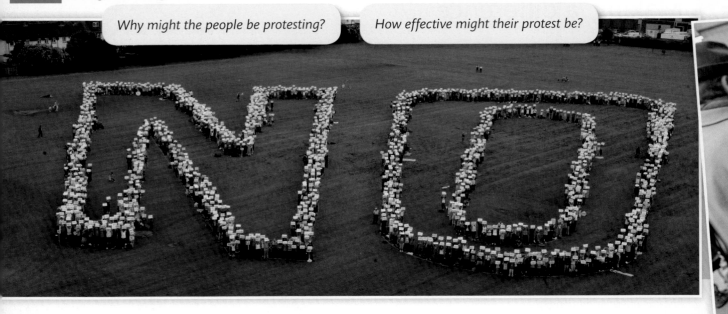

Why might the people be protesting?   *How effective might their protest be?*

Speaking (Paper 4 Part 2)

Vocabulary:
issues and opinions

1a Match the verbs and nouns to make a form of protest. There might be more than one possibility.

distribute	draw	go on	hold	organise	sign	take part in

write to

demos	graffiti	leaflets	marches	meetings	newspapers

petitions   sit-ins   strike

b Which forms of protest can you see in the pictures?

c In what situations do people use the other forms of protest?

d Circle the correct word.
  1 to be totally *against / opposed* something
  2 to demonstrate *for / in favour of* something
  3 to (make someone) *back down / back under*
  4 to put pressure *at / on*
  5 to have an influence *on / in*
  6 to generate publicity *for / to*
  7 to have major doubts *of / about*
  8 to have your say *on / in*
  9 to force people to come *at / to* a compromise
  10 to change people's minds *in / about*

e Answer these questions. Use the expressions from 1a and 1d.
  1 What do you think the people in the pictures hope to achieve?
  2 What effect might their protest have?

2 Complete these extracts from news articles, using words and phrases from Exercise 1 in the correct form.

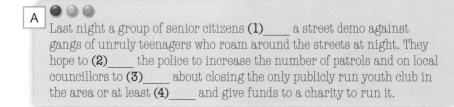

A

Last night a group of senior citizens **(1)**____ a street demo against gangs of unruly teenagers who roam around the streets at night. They hope to **(2)**____ the police to increase the number of patrols and on local councillors to **(3)**____ about closing the only publicly run youth club in the area or at least **(4)**____ and give funds to a charity to run it.

B ● ● ●
Most people are **(5)____** car parking charges, saying that the measure will hurt local traders. Twenty-five thousand people had **(6)____** , which was handed in at the meeting. When local activists had **(7)____** on the issue the meeting finally broke up and the protesters dispersed peacefully.

C ● ● ●
Campaigners have **(8)____** about the number of tourists coming to the city and are **(9)____** to local residents on the difficulties it causes for the city's infrastructure. However, they are not very hopeful of **(10)____** of the city councillors about their current open-door policy.

> EXPERT STRATEGIES page 172

3 a 🎧 30 Look at the pictures again. Listen to the interlocutor's instructions. What do the candidates have to do?

b 🎧 31 Listen to Thérèse doing the task. How successful is she? Did she follow the advice in the strategy on page 172? How could her answer have been improved?

c 🎧 32 Now listen to Francesca. How successfully does she carry out the task?

Useful language: expressing probability and certainty

4 🎧 33 Listen again to the second candidate's answer and complete the text.

The people **(1)____** because they are unhappy. If you live in a small village where there is no public transport, it **(2)____** difficult for some older people to travel to the next town to go to the post office. And if something is built on the playing field, young people **(3)____** nowhere to go to play sports. **(4)____** how effective the protests might be – it **(5)____** how well organised they are. If it gets reported in the newspapers and on TV, people **(6)____** and take notice. The petition **(7)____** have a big effect too.

Long turn **5** Work in pairs. Do the task in Exercise 3, using a different set of photos.
Student 1: Talk about photos A, C and E (page 204).
Student 2: Talk about photos B, D and F (page 204).

Task analysis **6** Which aspects of the Speaking assessment criteria on page 171 did you meet/not meet? Did you provide evidence of a range of vocabulary and structures? How could your performance be improved?

Language development 2

Noun clauses

1a Read the following paragraph. What does it take to be a good volunteer at the Olympic Games?

◉ **Browsing blogs**

No Olympic Games can be successful unless there is an army of well-briefed volunteers to help out. Experience of past Games suggests **(1)** that it's not just a question of getting them to smile. The aim should be **(2)** to make sure that they provide a real service. **(3)** What needs to be done is **(4)** to see to it that they have enough information to answer the difficult questions, and it is encouraging **(5)** that the organisers of recent Games have taken the challenge seriously. The first aspect of the challenge is **(6)** how to select the volunteers and that depends on **(7)** who applies in the first place. At the London Games, the organisers interviewed all the credible candidates. It was then of the utmost importance **(8)** to host a series of 3-hour-long mass meetings as well as location-specific sessions for the selected 70,000 to energise and inform them. **(9)** Whether or not that was enough is debatable but, even as it was, **(10)** organising it was quite a challenge.

b The underlined clauses function like a noun in the sentence. Match them to the three types of noun clauses listed in the grammar reference on pages 179–180.

c Match the underlined noun clauses (1–10) in Exercise 1a to the following.

   A This is the subject of the sentence.   ___
   B This is the object of the sentence.   ___
   C This follows an adjective, noun or preposition.   ___
   D This follows the verb *be*.   ___

2a Circle the correct word in each pair. In some cases both are possible.

   1 I was looking forward to finding out *which / what* event I had been allocated to.
   2 It was soon clear *how / that* it was going to be incredibly hard work.
   3 We had already been told *that / when* we would get fares and food paid for.
   4 *Why / How* they couldn't put us up in hostels was a mystery to me.
   5 *It was highly likely / There was a strong likelihood* that I would have to look for a room a long way from the city.
   6 Many people asked *how far / whether* we were doing it because we wanted to be part of a major event.
   7 *To do / Doing* voluntary work of any kind takes a lot of commitment.
   8 *That / How* we felt about the uniforms was thought to be very important.

b Complete the text with a suitable word in each gap.

● ○ ○
Making sure **(1)**____ volunteering is a positive experience is critical. The idea **(2)**____ people only do it for selfless reasons is wrong. **(3)**____ inspires many people to get involved is the possibility of giving themselves a new lease of life.

Kerry started as a volunteer and now manages a community centre. 'It's critical **(4)**____ our volunteers live in the community and they know **(5)**____ the local people think. If you can't help someone you also need to know **(6)**____ to send them and **(7)**____ they need to see.'

It is easy to see **(8)**____ Kerry's centre is a success, and **(9)**____ it has helped regenerate the neighbourhood. It's because she listens. Her main worry now is **(10)**____ the Government is listening and **(11)**____ effects their cuts will have. Everyone knows **(12)**____ no community can survive without its volunteers and just **(13)**____ dependent we are on them is becoming increasingly clear.

3 Complete the second sentence so that it has a similar meaning to the first sentence. Use between three and six words, including the word given.

   1 The conflicting information we receive can be confusing.
   EASY
   It _____ by all the conflicting information we receive.
   2 It's highly likely that they will close the school.
   STRONG
   There's a _____ being closed.
   3 There was a debate about how the community could raise funds to keep the service open.
   SUBJECT
   How the community could raise funds to keep the service open _____ debate.
   4 I suddenly thought how well he was looking.
   STRUCK
   It _____ was looking well.
   5 You can completely understand people looking for ways of overcoming loneliness.
   QUITE
   It _____ for ways of overcoming loneliness.
   6 Tania didn't know to what extent illness had affected Mark's work.
   UNCLEAR
   How far Mark's work had _____ to Tania.

4 Use noun clauses to complete these sentences in a way that is true for you. Then compare your answers with a partner.

   1 It is easy/hard/impossible for me ____ .
   2 My main worry is how/when/whether ____ .
   3 I love/hate things that ____ .
   4 I can never remember how/where ____ .
   5 I think ____ is a useful/clever way ____ .
   6 Whether or not I ____ depends on ____ .

Use of English 2 (Paper 1 Part 2)

Lead-in **1** Read this quote from Ivor Gormley, director of *The Good Gym*, and answer the questions.

> 'Gyms are a ridiculous invention. People have got too much energy and go to these weird places where they use machines to get rid of all their energy. I thought we could channel people's excess energy into something more productive.'

1 Do you agree with what Ivor says about gyms? Why?/Why not?
2 What do you think his idea was?

Open cloze **2a** Read the title and the text below quickly and answer these questions. (Ignore the gaps at this stage.)

1 What is the answer to question 1.2 above?
2 How does it benefit everyone?
3 How are the elderly protected?

➤ EXPERT STRATEGIES page 167

b Read the instructions and do the task.

*For questions 1–8, read the text below and think of the word which best fits each gap. Use only **one** word in each gap. There is an example at the beginning (0).*

THE GOOD GYM

The Good Gym, based in East London, encourages members to make good (0)*use* of their energy by combining street-running exercise with helping others. What the gym (1)____ is work with charities and local community groups to assign runners to elderly people and encourage them to drop in for a chat while they're out on their run. (2)____ came up with the idea must have realised that visits like this would make (3)____ the difference to some old people's lives. Having a break in the running can work well from a training (4)____ of view too. Runners can do a speed run to the house, rest there, have a chat, then do a more gentle, warm-down jog on the way back.

So far, the initiative has been a great success (5)____ the fact that elderly people living on their own are usually reluctant to let strangers into their homes. (6)____ a safety measure, every runner, (7)____ exception, has to have a criminal record check.

The idea has taken off locally, but (8)____ it will catch on nationally or even further afield is yet to be seen.

Task analysis **3a** Which of these were tested in the task? Give an example.

adjectives   concrete nouns   fixed phrases   noun clauses
reduced relative clauses   subject-verb agreement

b Which would not usually be tested in this task?

Discussion **4** What do you think of *The Good Gym*? Could the idea work in your country? Give reasons.

Writing 2 Proposal (Paper 2 Part 2)

Lead-in **1** Discuss these questions.

1 In what ways could college students help the local community? Think of some worthwhile projects involving voluntary work. (e.g. environmental protection; archaeology digs; helping the physically/ mentally disabled, the homeless, orphans, the elderly)
2 Choose one project. You are going to write a proposal to get one of the projects started. Who would you send the proposal to? What kind of arguments would you put forward?

Understand the task **2** Read the task below and answer the questions.

1 Use the strategy in Module 2 (page 36) to analyse the question.
2 In what ways is a proposal similar to and different from a report? (Think of: structure and layout, style, time referred to, verb forms.)
3 What will make yours a good proposal?

> *You see this notice on the noticeboard of the college where you are studying English.*
>
> The college is planning to provide funding for a new local community project and is looking for suggestions. The principal invites you to send a proposal outlining an idea, explain why it is worthwhile **and** how it would work. A decision can then be made about how the money should be spent.
>
> *Write your proposal in 220–260 words.*

Plan your proposal **3a** Brainstorm some areas for a community project where students help in a local shelter for the homeless.

b Make notes under these headings.

1 What is the general idea?
2 How would the project be set up?
3 Why would the project be worthwhile?

c Your proposal will have an introduction and a conclusion, and a middle section of recommendations. What will be the key recommendations? (Use an imperative *Get students involved …* or a modal *The commitment should be ongoing …*) What is the reason for each recommendation?

Recommendation 1: _____
Reason: _____
Recommendation 2: _____
Reason: _____
Recommendation 3: _____
Reason: _____

d Where could you add an example?

Language and content

4a Which of these sentences could be used in the introduction and which in the conclusion?

A This proposal is for a way of getting students involved in helping the homeless.

B So for all the reasons I've said, I think you ought to get this thing going.

C The project is clearly worthwhile, as it would be of considerable benefit to the homeless.

D Here are some ways of making sure students do their bit for the local community.

b How could you rewrite these suggestions for a proposal?

1 The homeless usually have loads of other probs too.

2 What you do – it always works best – is to get students to teach something they're good at.

3 OK, my idea is that you get one student and you say, all right you look after that person.

4 Right, anyone who wants to take part would come up to us and say what they're good at.

c Match these headings with the groups of sentence openings below.

Explaining the practicalities   Justifying a recommendation
Making a recommendation

1____
It's obvious that people work best when …
The project could be counterproductive if/unless …
This would enable/mean that …
It is clear that, in this way …

2____
To set the scheme up …
One/Another/A good idea would be to …
If (we want to be able to …)
Make sure students …

3____
The way it would work is like this. … would …
How we would organise it would depend on …
This would mean that … would have to …

d Choose and complete some sentences for your answer.

e Complete these sentences with one of the formal connecting words in the box.

furthermore   hence   moreover   therefore   thus

1 There is often a lack of life skills among the homeless. ____ , illiteracy and mental illness can often contribute to an already difficult situation.

2 The hostel staff are overwhelmed with problems, ____ voluntary help is desperately needed.

3 Students would not receive special training. They need, ____ , to concentrate on the things they are good at.

4 Students would see the problems for themselves, ____ helping them understand the difficulties that many people face.

EXPERT STRATEGY

Make sure that every key point is backed up and possibly exemplified and that you avoid irrelevance, repetition and deviation. Remember the main aim is to persuade the reader to take a course of action.
For a full list of strategies see page 170.

Write the proposal

5 Read the strategy, then write your proposal in 220–260 words, using some of the ideas and language above.

Check your proposal

6 Edit your work using the checklist on page 190.

Review

1 Complete the sentences with one word in each gap.

1 I am usually ____ asleep by 10 p.m., whereas my wife is still ____ awake until after midnight.
2 Alex very rarely loses sleep ____ anything.
3 If I'm watching TV at night, I tend to drift ____ after about ten minutes.
4 At the weekend, I sleep ____ whenever I can to make up for the early weekdays.
5 My son always wants to stay up late so we have had to come ____ a compromise.
6 I wake up on and ____ all night at the moment.
7 ____ and large, I have no problems sleeping.
8 I'm such a heavy sleeper that I frequently sleep ____ the alarm.

2 Complete the phrasal nouns with the particles below.

back down in in off on out up

1 The end of the film was a complete let____ . I was so disappointed.
2 After the break-____ , I had new locks fitted.
3 When I announced the new sales figures, there was an audible ____take of breath.
4 I often get depressed at the ____set of winter.
5 There has been an ____break of cholera, so our trip is cancelled.
6 As a result of the cut in funding, my research is suffering a set____ .
7 The referee delayed kick-____ because of fighting in the stands.
8 The police appealed for back-____ to control the crowds.

3 Circle the correct words to complete the sentences.

1 There's a good chance *how far / that* a new supermarket will affect local business.
2 *What / Why* I enjoy campaigning so much is the range of people I get to meet.
3 I must give some thought to *who / which* of these local causes most deserves a donation.
4 It remains to be seen *how / whether* committed the newly elected council is to local issues.
5 *Who / That* she decided to give the lecture at all was very unexpected.
6 We were asked *whether / why* or not we would vote for the green party.
7 *Using / To use* graffiti as a method of protest is common everywhere.
8 It is difficult *seeing / to see* what the protesters hope to achieve.

4 Read the text. Use the words in capitals at the end of some of the lines to form a word that fits in the gap in the same line.

◎ Browsing blogs

The main problem at the moment in my small town is the **(1)**____ building which is taking place. The normally **(2)**____ residents are now beginning to lose patience as a dramatic **(3)**____ in housing starts to put a strain on the infrastructure, especially roads and schools.	EXTEND TOLERATE GROW
At first, it seemed highly **(4)**____ that any form of protest would go beyond **(5)**____ discussions around the dinner table and letters in local newspapers. However, petitions, letters and even demonstrations mean that open **(6)**____ cannot be ruled out, even in this sleepy town. Opinions will doubtlessly **(7)**____ as a couple of local celebrities and other **(8)**____ people have now thrown their weight behind the protest.	LIKE HOT CONFRONT STRONG INFLUENCE

5 Controversy

Lead-in

1   Which difficult topics are in the news in your country at the moment?

2a These are some controversial statements. Tick the ones you agree with and rewrite those you disagree with to reflect your own opinion. Can you think of any others?

'Global warming is vastly exaggerated.'

'Security has become an obsession in the modern world.'

'A woman's place is in the home.'

'Celebrities should not expect to have their privacy respected.'

'Children who are out of control are the result of poor parenting.'

'Nuclear power is the only viable energy source for the future.'

'All health care should be free.'

'People who are obese should not receive free medical help.'

'People who want to sell their blood or one of their kidneys should be allowed to do so.'

'Murderers should face capital punishment.'

'Free university education should be available to everybody.'

 b Select some of the issues and compare your opinions, giving reasons.

Reading (Paper 1 Part 5)

Before you read 1 Which animals do people keep as pets in your country? Why? What are the advantages and disadvantages?

Skimming 2 Read the book review quickly, focusing on the first and last paragraphs. What do the authors identify as the main problem with owning pets?

Multiple choice 3a Highlight the key phrases in the questions or stems 1–6. Which part of the text answers each question?

b Read the strategy on page 168, then do the task. Use the Help notes for support with certain items.

*You are going to read a review of a book about the environmental impact of keeping pets. For questions **1–6**, choose the answer (**A**, **B**, **C** or **D**) which you think fits best according to the text.*

1 What do we learn about UK pet owners in the first paragraph?
 A They are prepared to spend more than any other nation on pet food.
 B They tend to spend less on feeding their pets during a financial downturn.
 C They are now showing an interest in the contents of the food they buy for their pets.
 D They want the pet food industry to become more accountable for the quality of its products.

2 *New Scientist* magazine finds it particularly disturbing that
 A dogs can make more demands on the natural world than some people do.
 B feeding a dog and running a large car use the equivalent amount of resources.
 C keeping a cat has a worse impact on the environment than running a small car.
 D wealthier people tend to own more pets than people who have less money.

3 In order to lessen the ecological impact of pets, the authors of the book propose that owners
 A train household pets to take responsibility for finding their own food.
 B consider using pet animals as an additional means of nutrition for humans.
 C find small non-domesticated animals to use as the main supply of food for pets.
 D make a point of buying pet food which is made only from sustainable ingredients.

4 On what basis does the pet food industry defend the environmental impact of its food production?
 A It only recycles food which is unsuitable to sell to humans.
 B It is an eco-friendly way to process excessive amounts of food.
 C It is responding to public demand for a convenient source of pet food.
 D It is acceptable practice if humans are to benefit from pet ownership.

5 How does one report recommend reducing the risk to UK wildlife?
 A by restricting cats to certain areas of the country
 B by convincing cat owners not to let them out overnight
 C by limiting the number of cats that one is allowed to own at one time
 D by making it illegal to breed from cats for profit

6 The authors of the book urge people to
 A be more economical when spending money on pets.
 B refrain from owning a pet for the good of the planet.
 C assess whether their ecological footprint justifies having a pet.
 D take an active part in determining the role of pets in modern society.

> **HELP**

3 Look for the sentence beginning *In other words* to answer this question.
4 The justification is given in the sentence beginning *If we didn't recycle animal by-products.*

How green is your pet?

Robert and Brenda Vale – the authors of a provocative new book
Time to eat the dog? The real guide to sustainable living – have bad
news for animal lovers.

At Europe's largest pet show, *Pet Index*, onlookers gather around as Henrietta Morrison places a spoonful of dog food in her mouth. She has a point to prove; her company sells the most expensive pet food on the UK market, with the promise that the contents are 'proper food'. The UK pet food industry has been the recipient of unkind remarks and rumours as to the true origin of its ingredients for decades but the market continues to be dominated by products containing delights such as 'animal derivatives'. However, despite the economic recession, there is now a significant move towards using only 'premium' products.

Now the industry faces another source of criticism as a new book triggers a debate about the environmental impact of owning a well-fed pet. The *New Scientist* magazine, in a recent editorial, largely agreed with the book's findings that some pets, due to the food they eat, have a surprisingly high 'ecological footprint', which is a way of quantifying human demand on the planet's ecosystems using a measure called 'global hectares'. According to the authors of the book, 'it takes 0.84 hectares of land to keep a medium-sized dog fed, which is twice that needed to run a large car. An even more shocking comparison is that in 2004, the average citizen of Vietnam had an ecological footprint of 0.76 hectares. Dogs are not the only environmental sinners: the eco-footprint of a cat equates to about 0.15 hectares, almost the equivalent of a small car. In a world where scarce resources are already hogged by the rich, can people really justify keeping pets that require more than some people?'

The authors of the book say they were 'genuinely surprised' when calculating the environmental impact of pets. And some of the ideas they put forward to alleviate this are likely to shock some pet owners. For example, the book suggests catching pests such as rats and processing them into a 'natural' cat food, getting a pet which serves a dual purpose such as keeping chickens and eating the eggs or keeping a pair of rabbits and eating their offspring. When feeding a pet, however, the advice is to 'think feathers and long ears'. In other words, favour pet foods made from rabbit and chicken meat, which is less damaging to the environment than red meat and fish.

As you might expect, the Pet Food Manufacturers' Association puts up a spirited defence, arguing that the vast majority of meat and fish used in pet foods is of adequate quality for human consumption but surplus to requirements. 'If we didn't recycle animal by-products to sell, they might otherwise be disposed of via landfill, which is not very green,' says the chief executive. In addition, he points out that pets should not be viewed just on their 'carbon pawprint'. 'Our environment is greatly enriched by the part they play in our lives. Pets in the home instil responsibility, encourage social awareness and have positive health benefits.'

That people greatly benefit from pets isn't really disputed. But of course, it's not just the food they eat that's the problem. Conservationists have long been saying that cats, as opportunistic predators, are having a detrimental effect on small mammals. One UK university report points out that in the US, animal welfare groups recommend keeping only 'indoor cats', while some Australian states are contemplating 'feline-free zones' as well as compulsory neutering to cut down on the cat population. It concludes that, realistically, education rather than legislation is the answer for the UK, urging people to take measures such as putting bells on cats' collars and keeping them in during their natural hunting time, which is between dusk and dawn.

The authors of the book do not – as some of their critics seem to assume – advocate a mass killing of all the world's pets. 'All we are arguing in the book is that we should be making sensible informed choices. So it's not going to be that much of a problem if you have a big dog but take the bus everywhere, don't fly, live in a small home and have a small family. We can't go blind into this debate. If we are to examine the way we live,' the authors argue, 'nothing should be off limits, no matter how uncomfortable it is to discuss. We have to recognise that we live in a world of finite resources where pets are an extravagance rather than a right.'

Task analysis **4** Discuss the different strategies that you used to complete the task, and then compare with the strategy on page 168.

Discussion **5** Do you think it is right to spend money on keeping pets when so many people in the world live in poverty? Give reasons for your answer.

EXPERT WORD CHECK

derivatives   dual   feline   hog (*v*)   instil   offspring
premium (*adj*)   recipient   sinner   spirited (*adj*)

Vocabulary: global issues

Similar words

1a Circle the correct words to complete the sentences.

1 Big cars over 1.6 litres tend to *spend / consume* a lot of fuel.
2 Pet food is claimed to be made from food which is *surplus / excess to* our needs.
3 In many parts of the world, resources are *rare / scarce*.
4 The Vales' book has *triggered / activated* a fierce debate.
5 If you keep a pet, you should *cancel out / compensate for* this by cutting your carbon footprint in other areas.
6 If leftover food were not used for pet food, it would have to be *disposed of / given up*.

b Match the more formal expressions in Exercise 1a with the less formal/neutral ones a–f.

a sparked off
b thin on the ground
c use up
d more than enough for
e thrown away
f make up for

c Discuss these questions.

1 What could everyone consume less of in order to help the planet?
2 Should there be stricter legislation on the disposal of household rubbish?
3 Which global issues have sparked off debates in your country recently?
4 Should people with a big carbon footprint (e.g. who fly a lot) compensate in other ways? How?

Collocation

2a Match the verbs 1–5 with the words and phrases they collocate with a–e. There may be more than one possibility.

1 pollute
2 emit
3 give rise to
4 wipe out
5 spray

a crops with pesticides/chemicals
b natural disasters (famine/drought/flooding)
c natural habitats
d water supplies/the atmosphere
e toxic fumes/carbon dioxide

b Match the nouns/adjectives 1–6 with the words/expressions they collocate with a–f.

1 a build-up
2 global
3 rising
4 exhaust
5 soil
6 organic

a produce
b sea levels
c of greenhouse gases
d erosion
e warming
f fumes

3a Read what three people say about global problems and match them to one of these three issues: climate change; food resources; pollution.

b Complete the paragraphs using one suitable word in each gap. Use the vocabulary from Exercise 2 in the correct form.

Laura

The most serious problem is that cars (1)____ poisonous gases because of the (2)____ which come out of their exhaust pipes. This (3)____ the atmosphere and helps to destroy the ozone layer.

Will

The (4)____ of greenhouse gases has led to (5)____ warming, which in turn often (6)____ disasters such as famine and (7)____ . There are also more and more floods, due to (8)____ sea levels.

Nicola

I worry about what I'm eating. I don't like the idea of eating food which has been sprayed with (9)____ , so I try to eat (10)____ produce where possible. I haven't made up my mind yet about the idea of genetically modified (11)____ .

c Which global issue worries you most? Think about the issues mentioned in Exercises 1–3 and also other issues such as:

- the loss of rare species
- asylum seekers
- homelessness
- economic migrants
- the gap between rich and poor
- inequalities in the international labour market.

Word formation

4a Complete these sentences with the correct form of the word in capitals.

1 Pollution from the ____ of exhaust fumes leads to an increase in allergies. **EMIT**
2 Over-____ of fast food is contributing to an increase in rubbish. **CONSUME**
3 The ____ of natural habitats in many parts of the world reduces biodiversity. **DESTROY**
4 Local councils should be much more proactive in the ____ of waste products. **DISPOSE**
5 I believe that chemicals sprayed on our food could be ____ in large quantities. **POISON**
6 Some people are ____ concerned about the dangers of global warming. **EXCESS**

b List the opinions in Exercise 4a in the order you agree with them (1 = most, 6 = least).

Use of English 1 (Paper 1 Part 1)

Lead-in 1 Tell each other any stories you have heard about animals which have predicted natural disasters. Discuss how it is possible for them to do this.

Multiple-choice cloze 2a Read through the text once quickly. In what way could whales help prevent a disaster?

b Read the strategy on page 167, then do the task. Use the Help notes for support with certain items.

*For questions 1–8, read the text below and decide which answer (**A**, **B**, **C** or **D**) best fits each gap. There is an example at the beginning (0).*

Can whales predict disasters?

As photographer Andrew Sutton was filming whales just off the coast of Sri Lanka, warnings were given on land that a tsunami was **(0)** C in the area. However, Andrew and his crew were totally **(1)**__ to what was about to happen, and so watched in amazement as every species of cetacean, **(2)**__ from massive blue whales to tiny spinner dolphins, disappeared within the **(3)**__ of around five minutes. **(4)**__ the humans on the boat felt nothing, the animals had obviously sensed the shocks from beneath the sea and **(5)**__ the area seconds after the earthquake had begun and minutes before the tsunami actually took place.

In a similar incident, a recent scientific report from Mexico appears to prove that a fin whale accelerated quickly away from the **(6)**__ of an underwater earthquake.

The **(7)**__ of all this are very interesting to scientists, because it suggests that sea mammals might be able to give crucial warnings a few seconds **(8)**__ to a potentially dangerous seismic activity in the same way that some animals are alleged to be able to do on land.

0	**A** forthcoming	**B** expectant	**C** imminent	**D** gathering
1	**A** unaware	**B** unconscious	**C** oblivious	**D** ignorant
2	**A** ranging	**B** reaching	**C** ranking	**D** running
3	**A** duration	**B** space	**C** time	**D** length
4	**A** Whilst	**B** Yet	**C** However	**D** Despite
5	**A** vanished	**B** fled	**C** disappeared	**D** escaped
6	**A** point	**B** setting	**C** place	**D** site
7	**A** expectations	**B** propositions	**C** assumptions	**D** implications
8	**A** approaching	**B** prior	**C** previous	**D** leading

➤ **HELP**

1 Only one of these adjectives collocates with *to*.

5 Which one of these verbs can be followed by a direct object?

Task analysis 3 Look at numbers 1 and 5 and say how the sentence would have to change grammatically in order for the incorrect options to fit.

Discussion 4 Discuss these questions.

1 In what other ways have animals helped humans in the present and past? Think about transport, food, farming and medical research.

2 Which animals do you think are the most intelligent? Why?

Listening 1 (Paper 3 Part 2)

Before you listen

1 Discuss these questions.

1 What do bees feed on? What might threaten their source of food?
2 In what ways do bees help the planet?

Sentence completion

2 Read the extract and try to predict what type of word(s) might fit in each space. Remember it will be a single word or a short phrase (usually up to 3 words).

3 🎧 34 Read the strategy on page 171, then do the task. Use the Help notes for support with certain items.

*You will hear a man called Simon Dickson, who is a member of a wildlife organisation, talking about the decline of the bee population. For questions **1–8**, complete the sentences with a word or short phrase.*

The decline of the bee population

Simon mentions (1)_____ as the year when there began to be widespread anxiety about the disappearance of bees.

Simon points out that bee-pollinated plants produce (2)_____ which benefit humans.

Simon makes a comparison with (3)_____ to underline the seriousness of declining bee numbers.

Simon thinks that innovations in (4)_____ provide the main explanation for the decline of bees.

Simon says the problem of (5)_____ in bees could be reduced if a wider range of food was available to them.

Simon gives the example of (6)_____ as places where bees now stand a good chance of survival.

Simon explains that chemicals may be causing loss of (7)_____ in bee populations.

Simon is convinced that it is (8)_____ which is making it difficult for bees to locate vital scents.

➤ **HELP**

1 Several dates are mentioned. Which date tells us when the rest of the world started becoming anxious about the decreasing bee population?

3 Simon mentions several global problems, but which does he think is the most serious?

Task analysis

4 Were your predictions in Exercise 2 correct? What helped you to guess that you were listening for a date in number 1? In number 2, what clue did you have that you were listening for a plural noun?

Discussion

5 What information in Simon's talk was new to you? What, if anything, did you find particularly interesting?

EXPERT WORD CHECK

deteriorate   disoriented (*adj*)   diversity   further afield
immune system   pests   phenomenon   prone to   thrive
wipe out

Language development 1

➤ EXPERT GRAMMAR page 180

Modifying gradable and ungradable adjectives

1 Look at this extract from the listening text on page 76 and answer the questions below. Then check with the grammar reference on page 180.

*It is **extremely important** that human beings change the way they manage the planet.*

1 What is the function of the adverb?
2 Give examples of other adverb(s) that would fit here.
3 Why is *absolutely* not possible?

2a Make pairs of words using an adverb from A and an adjective from B. There are many different possibilities.

A	absolutely	bitterly	completely	extremely
	incredibly	rather	really	totally	very
	virtually			

B	different	disappointed	excited	empty
	expensive	perfect	quiet	relieved	unspoilt

b Complete the text below, using the collocations from Exercise 2a.

The night before we went on holiday, I could hardly sleep because I was (1)____ about returning to the resort where we always went on holiday as children. I could still remember the place vividly; it was very simple and uncommercialised and because there were very few tourists, it was still (2)____ . The roads used to be (3)____ because there was hardly any traffic, and the beaches were often (4)____ even during the summer, despite the fact that they were (5)____ in every way – clean and sandy, with crystal-clear water.

So I was (6)____ when I returned for the first time in 20 years to find that the resort was (7)____ from how it was before. No doubt some people appreciate the fashionable, (8)____ hotels and restaurants, but I didn't! In fact, I was (9)____ to go home again.

c Compare your answers with other students. Which different combinations are possible?

d Describe a place which you used to go to on holiday and your feelings about it.

Adverb and adjective collocations

3a Some adverbs are only used in combination with certain adjectives. Complete the text by choosing the adverb that collocates with the adjective in bold.

Until recently, progress on the tiny African states of São Tomé and Príncipe has been (1)____ **slow**. For many years, the islands have been (2)____ **dependent** on foreign aid. With the discovery of oil, however, life for the 140,000 inhabitants is about to become (3)____ **different**.

Not all the changes are likely to be (4)____ **beneficial**. The islanders are (5)____ **attached** to their unspoiled beaches and rainforest, and some people worry that the islands' (6)____ **balanced** environment will become (7)____ **polluted**. The government has drawn up (8)____ **publicised** plans on how the new income will be spent on improving education and health, for which funds are currently (9)____ **inadequate**. However, a few residents remain (10)____ **opposed** to the development.

	A	B	C
1	A completely	B painfully	C absolutely
2	A heavily	B bitterly	C usually
3	A highly	B seriously	C totally
4	A heavily	B entirely	C perfectly
5	A completely	B fully	C deeply
6	A perfectly	B totally	C painfully
7	A highly	B immensely	C heavily
8	A entirely	B widely	C deeply
9	A greatly	B totally	C heavily
10	A bitterly	B painfully	C widely

b Discuss the advantages and disadvantages of global tourism.

Writing 1 Supporting sentences

1a Your class recently had to write an essay
entitled: Why is tourism a threat to some parts of
the world? What can be done about it?

1 Discuss your views with other people.
2 Read these sentences from some students' essays.
Which ones introduce a point (topic sentences)
and which are sentences to support the argument
(supporting sentences)?

> However, it is clearly crucial to keep tourists
> away from the areas where wild birds nest.

> The main impact of this would be to have only the
> very rich visiting, which would be unfair.

> It would be a pity if tourist numbers
> were restricted even further.

> This would be the responsibility of
> the guides escorting the groups.

> An example of this would be oil spills from tourist boats.

> Equally, there must be close monitoring
> of potential dangers to marine life.

b Complete the supporting sentences for these
topic sentences. Then work in pairs to
compare answers.

1 It seems that we have to accept mass tourism as a
reality. All the evidence suggests …
2 First of all, it's reasonable that tourists should be
well informed about the local culture. The reason
for this is …
3 Local people should be encouraged to get
involved in the tourist industry. One way of doing
this is …
4 Tourists should pay a fee for visiting the sites. In
some places, …

EXPERT STRATEGY

For an essay based on notes, select the main points
to put at the beginning of a paragraph and then
write supporting sentences, which include more
ideas, information or examples.

2a Look at these possible main points for the essay
on tourism in Exercise 1a and add any other
points you can think of.

1 Local culture
2 Regulation
3 Revenue
4 Local population
5 Threats to habitat

b These are some notes you made of your own
opinions. Match them to the main topics in
Exercise 2a. Add any others you can think of.

a *Profits often go to outside tourist agencies.*
b *Tourist controls needed – tighter monitoring.*
c *Indigenous people there for thousands of years.*
d *Wildlife being destroyed at alarming rate.*
e *The site has great historical significance for the
population.*

c Select your two most important points. Write
a topic sentence and a supporting sentence for
each. You may want to use adverbs of attitude
(e.g. *clearly, obviously*) and, where appropriate,
expressions to report people's opinions such as:

It is generally believed that …
Supporters of … maintain that …
According to many people …
It is sometimes claimed that …
It could be argued that …

d Work in pairs. Make a paragraph plan for your
essay. Include an introduction, two main points
and a conclusion.

e Compare your sentences and paragraph plan
with other people's. Then work with your partner
to improve the plan you made in Exercise 2d.

Listening 2 (Paper 3 Part 3)

Before you listen

1 Discuss these questions.

1 What is computer hacking and why do people do it? What can the consequences be?

2 When, if ever, is it morally justified?

2 Read the multiple-choice questions 1–6 opposite and underline the key words.

Multiple choice

3 🎧 35 Read the strategy on page 171, then listen and do the task opposite. Use the Help notes for support with certain items.

Task analysis

4 Compare and justify your answers. Were any of the other answers tempting? Why?

Discussion

5 Discuss these questions.

1 In what way does the discussion confirm or change your opinion about hacking? How would you have reacted in Grace's situation?

2 Is the anonymous posting of secret official documents on the internet a good or bad thing? Why?

---

*You will hear an IT consultant called Jack Warne and a journalist called Grace Martin taking part in an interview on the subject of online crime. For questions **1–6**, choose the answer (**A, B, C** or **D**) which fits best according to what you hear.*

1 How does Jack feel about the current threat to personal information?
   A confident that the latest technology will ensure security
   B convinced that the problem is not a new one
   C concerned that too much data is being stolen in paper form
   D worried that people underestimate the dangers

2 Grace thinks the most disturbing aspect of technology is
   A the range of people who carry out computer crime.
   B the number of large organisations which have lost data.
   C the amount of information which can get stolen.
   D the ease with which an individual's reputation can be destroyed.

3 What did Grace mind most about someone hacking into her email account?
   A the feeling that she had lost contact with her friends
   B the idea that the criminal might be watching her
   C the fear that people she knew might be deceived into giving money
   D the knowledge that someone was pretending to be her

4 Jack thinks that identity theft is
   A almost inevitable when criminals can operate remotely.
   B nearly impossible to protect oneself against.
   C often the fault of the victim.
   D sometimes the result of an unexpected meeting.

5 Why does Grace feel that hackers are worse than street muggers?
   A They know the name of the person they attack.
   B They might get in touch with their victim again.
   C They ask for such large sums of money.
   D They don't think of themselves as criminals at all.

6 Unlike Grace, Jack believes that hacking
   A can be justified in certain circumstances.
   B is wrong when governments are its victims.
   C should always be punishable with a prison sentence.
   D has to be the responsibility of companies offering internet access.

➤ HELP

2 Grace finds one aspect more disturbing than the other.

4 Listen to Jack talking about identity theft. His answer comes towards the end of his turn.

6 Listen to both Jack and Grace after the interviewer assumes they both agree. There is one thing they completely disagree on.

EXPERT WORD CHECK

dire   discard   ferret (*v*)   hush up   hardened (*adj*)   outsmart
scam   sharp-witted   stalk (*v*)   unsettle

Speaking (Paper 4 Part 3)

Vocabulary: security

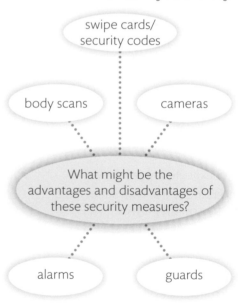

1a Look at the spidergram and say in which situations each measure might help to protect security and why.

b 🎧 36 Underline the syllables which are stressed in these words/ word pairs. Then listen and check.

alarm system	biometric	body scans	CCTV cameras
code number	high fencing	phone tap	pilotless planes
security guards	spy satellites	swipe card	

c Complete these extracts from a magazine article, using words from Exercise 1b.

A The company's headquarters are an intimidating fortress. To deter intruders the buildings are surrounded by very (1)_____ with a sophisticated (2)_____ on the wall and (3)_____ recording everything. At the main entrance there are private (4)_____ checking on people coming and going. Once inside you can't get into any of the individual buildings without passing a (5)_____ through an electronic device or keying in a (6)_____ . In the more sensitive areas there are (7)_____ checks using iris or finger scans.

B The US military uses a whole battery of security systems, including (8)_____ with telescopes pointing back down towards earth to check on what countries are doing or (9)_____ , sometimes called drones, to patrol the skies. Many governments cite security as a reason for listening to other people's conversations, by putting a (10)_____ on a suspect's mobile and hacking into their emails. At airports too increasing use is being made of whole (11)_____ instead of physical body searches.

d Which of the approaches to security in Exercise 1b do you think sometimes cause people to worry? Give reasons.

2a Read the strategy on page 172 and the Speaking assessment criteria on page 171 before you start.

b 🎧 37 Look at the spidergram and listen to the interlocutor's instructions. What are the candidates required to do?

c 🎧 38 Listen to two people doing the task. Which points of view do you agree/disagree with?

d 🎧 39 Now listen to the interlocutor's instructions for the second part of the task and the candidates' discussion. Do you agree with their conclusion? Why?/Why not?

e How successfully did they carry out the task? Did they follow the advice in the task strategy?

Useful language: intensifying expressions

3a 🎧 40 Listen to the sample answer again and complete these sentences.

1 Body scans at airports are not ____ as a physical body search.
2 In body scans, there isn't ____ protection of our basic human rights.
3 Security cameras might be by ____ of preventing crime.
4 ____ security cameras we have ____ we seem to need.
5 We are being snooped on ____ each year.
6 Alarms are ____ at catching criminals as some other measures..
7 The number of thefts is getting ____ each year.
8 A security guard is probably the ____ deterrent ____ .
9 Having security guards everywhere would be ____ – people couldn't afford it.

b Which words are most stressed in the intensifying expressions in the answers?

c Which statements above do you agree/disagree with?

Collaborative task

4a Work in pairs. Look at the spidergram and do the task in Exercise 2. Time yourselves and follow the task strategy.

b Tell the class which security measure you have chosen and why.

Task analysis

5a Which aspects of the Speaking assessment criteria did you meet/not meet?

1 Did you initiate and respond appropriately?
2 Did you avoid dominating the exchange?
3 Did you maintain the interaction appropriately?
4 Did you use a good range of language?

b How could your performance be improved?

Developing the discussion

6 Work in pairs. Take it in turns to ask and answer these questions.

1 In which public places do you feel most secure and insecure?
2 Why do you think that there has been an increase in personal security devices in recent years (e.g. personal defence sprays)?
3 Are there enough police on the streets in your country? Is it a safe place for tourists?
4 What could we all do to improve our personal security?
5 Some people say that we are too obsessed with security these days. What's your opinion?

EXPERT STRATEGY

- Participate in developing the discussion. Don't just give one-word answers.
- Develop your ideas and give your opinions in an interesting way. Respond to and develop the points made by your partner.
- You can disagree with your partner but don't interrupt or dominate the discussion.

Language development 2

Review of conditionals

1a Read this headline, then match sentences 1–4 with the four types of conditionals in grammar reference 2A on page 181.

> **JOURNALIST ARRESTED FOR HACKING INTO CELEBRITY'S PHONE**

1 It might be easier if we used a scanner to track their phone calls.
2 If we hadn't been caught, we would have hacked into the president's phone by now.
3 We all intercept phone calls if we want a good story.
4 If the police come round, I'll deny everything.

b Choose the correct form to complete the sentences.

1 If they *carry on / 'd carry on* like this, there *can / could* be a great scandal.
2 If a celebrity *reports / would have reported* them to the police, they *started / might start* to get worried.
3 If he *knew / 'd known* his calls were being listened to at the time, he *wouldn't say / wouldn't have said* all the things he did.
4 If there *is / was* any danger of being overheard, I *won't / should* use my phone.
5 If they *managed / 'd managed* to hack into his phone, they *'d got / could have got* to the truth.
6 If I *knew / know* who tapped your phone, I *'d tell / will tell* you!

Mixed conditionals

2a What two different conditional patterns are combined in these sentences? What time does each refer to?

1 If this country <u>had</u> a privacy law, we <u>wouldn't have been able</u> to expose their behaviour.
2 If I <u>had thought</u> the information wasn't in the public interest, I <u>wouldn't be telling</u> you about it now.
3 I <u>would have taken</u> pictures of her sunbathing if I <u>were</u> less moral!
4 The public <u>would still be</u> in the dark if we <u>hadn't run</u> that story.

b Complete these sentences with the correct form of the verbs in brackets. Use a modal if necessary.

1 If our politicians at that time ____ (be) more honest, they ____ (still, govern) the country today.
2 Journalists don't always check their facts. If they ____ (do), our newspapers ____ (not sue) for such huge amounts last year.
3 We ____ (not get) so many good scoops in the last few years if people in the public eye ____ (always be) as innocent as they say they are.
4 If they ____ (not write) such terrible things about her private life, she ____ (live) today.

c Complete the sentences with as many results as you can think of in the present and past.

1 If newspapers ____ (not invent), ____ .
2 If there ____ (be) no internet, ____ ,

Alternatives to *if*

3 Rewrite these sentences using the words given in brackets. Make any changes necessary.

1 If we don't give our stories emotional colouring, nobody will read them. **(unless)**
2 People only read our stories if they can identify with the people in them. **(unless ... not)**
3 Many journalists will continue to embellish the facts even if they are sometimes proved wrong. **(whether ... or not)**
4 I would have taken more time over the story if I hadn't been under pressure from my editor to liven it up. **(But for)**
5 I'll give you an interview, but only if I can check the story before you print it. **(on condition that)**
6 A good story needs good pictures because if it hasn't, it won't have much impact. **(otherwise)**
7 The press industry can recover its good reputation, but only if it cleans up its act. **(provided/providing that)**
8 Newspapers can compete with other media, but not if they can't be trusted. **(as long as)**

Omission of *if*

4a Compare these opening clauses. What is the difference in grammatical form and level of formality?

If anyone objects,
If anyone should object,   → *tell them to put their*
Should anyone object,   *complaint in writing.*

b How could you say these sentence openings using *if*?

1 Were anyone to object ...
2 Had I realised ...
3 Were it not for his help ...

c Rewrite these sentence openings beginning with *had, should* or *were*. Then complete the sentences in any way you like. Mark the words which are stressed.

1 If I had known my ____ was going to be so ____ , ____ .
2 If it weren't for the fact that my/our ____ was present, ____ .
3 If you need any ____ , ____ .
4 If he/she was my (son/sister/friend) ____ , ____ .

Reading and Use of English (Paper 1 Part 6)

Cross-text multiple
matching

1 a Read the title and introduction to the text. What is the film about?

b Look at question 1 and underline the key information. Then look carefully at Extract C and underline the opinion you are looking for.

c Underline the main points in questions 2–4 and find the opinions in the extracts which will help you to answer the questions.

d Read the strategy on page 168, then complete the task.

You are going to read four reviews of a film about a social network. For questions 1–4, choose from the reviews A–D. The reviews may be chosen more than once.

The social network

Four reviewers comment on a film (written by Aaron Sorkin and directed by David Fincher), which is based on Mark Zuckerberg's creation of the social network Facebook.

A

From the very outset, the rapid-fire dialogue in *The Social Network* identifies itself unmistakably as the work of the writer Aaron Sorkin. And while the superb script has a tendency to fall into 'geek-speak' at times, this is skimmed over where necessary to get to the heart of the movie, which focuses on a gloomy contradiction: teenager Zuckerberg creates a half-billion network of 'friends' by betraying his only real friend. Rebels and outsiders have always been a fixation for the director, David Fincher, and this movie is no exception: his 'hero' does all he can to shift power from the rich and well-connected and overturn the social order in favour of the 'computer nerd'. He depicts his lead actor as complex and ambiguous: Zuckerberg's self-confidence is impressive, amusing, yet extraordinarily hostile. And after each of his many immature outbursts, one can just detect a tiny hint of regret.

B

On the face of it, the topic of this film – the founding of a relationship site by Zuckerberg, a computer whizz who is unable to connect with human beings and steps over anyone who stands in his way – comes across as rather dreary. But, surprisingly, the human drama at its core results in a fascinating story. Sorkin is well known for his intelligent, witty scripts. No surprises here, then, and this is his best to date. The unexpected element is Fincher, the director: there is none of the physical menace associated with his previous work, the real-world situations in this film are treated sensitively, and he allows time for us to absorb the impact of a word or a gesture. In the writer and director's view of him, Zuckerberg demonstrates a selfishness and total

inability to understand people's feelings, a serious weakness in any context other than the world of computer science. It is an impressive performance.

C

Director David Fincher has created a gripping story in which the self-centred and uncommunicative protagonist comes over not quite as a hero but not exactly a mediocre character either. The director, being even-handed, requires us to make up our own minds about the other characters too. Fincher has modified his usually distinctive style, so that the sharp engaging dialogue takes centre stage: this may disappoint his fans but it keeps the audience glued to the screen. The film has as its focal point the bitter legal dispute as to who gets the credit for Facebook's start-up. It successfully manages to convey the passion of a very recent social network revolution along with the thrill of big money moving fast to create the world's youngest billionaire. It is an entertaining and hyperactive account of its time, cleverly highlighting the unpleasant atmosphere and lack of trust which surrounded the origins of the now much more 'friendly' Facebook.

D

The opening scene, a dialogue between Zuckerberg and the girlfriend who wants to break up with him, sums up our hero's flaws: arrogance, obsessionalism and a lack of empathy. Coldly analysed in terms of what actually happens, the film is just scenes of people sitting in front of screens or in lawyers' offices, bars or diners. Frantic and information-crammed to a fault, Sorkin's fast-paced chatter is relentless, making it a struggle at times for those with no interest in technology to follow. However, this is a movie which succeeds in entertaining almost despite its subject matter – the fact that it's about Facebook is almost irrelevant. The relationship of Zuckerberg with his business partner is the main point: the genius and the tragedy of Zuckerberg is seeing the world in strictly practical terms, at the expense of real-world relationships.

Which reviewer

shares reviewer C's opinion regarding the portrayal of Facebook's creator?

1

expresses a different view from the others concerning the impact of the dialogue?

2

agrees with reviewer B that the film is a new departure for the director?

3

has a different opinion from the others about what constitutes the main theme of the film?

4

Writing 2 Essay (Paper 2 Part 1)

Lead-in

1 Discuss these questions.

1 Criminals get hold of our personal details through computer hacking. What other methods do they use? Has it happened to you?
2 What suggestions can you make for how to deal with the problem?

Understand the task

2 Read the task and answer these questions.

1 What type of essay is it? (e.g. advantages/disadvantages, problem/solution, persuasive)
2 What must you include? What will you have to invent?
3 What will make the tutor think it is a well-written essay?

> *You have attended a talk on ways in which people should be encouraged to protect themselves against identity theft. You have made the notes below:*
>
> Methods of protecting against identity theft:
> • protecting credit and debit cards
> • deleting suspicious emails
> • destroying documents
>
> Some quotes from the speaker:
> 'Fraudsters rely on young people in particular being too trusting.'
> 'Never give personal data or send money on request.'
> 'Everyone should use a shredder.'
>
> *Write an essay for your tutor discussing **two** of the methods in your notes. You should **explain which is more important**, **giving reasons** in support of your answer.*
> *You may, if you wish, make use of the opinions expressed in the talk, but you should use your own words as far as possible.*

Plan your essay **3a** Work together. Brainstorm some notes which answer the question. Make sure you think of reasons for any opinions and examples where appropriate.

b Organise your notes to show how your essay will be structured. For example, you could make a spidergram (see page 80 for an example).

c Check that the points you have chosen are all relevant to the answer and you have included everything necessary.

d Make a paragraph plan of between four and five paragraphs to include an introduction and conclusion, method 1 and method 2. Which of the ideas in the box will you include? If so, where? Where will you include a reason and/or an example?

the most important method of protecting yourself
the threat + what could be done about it
explaining identity theft
one way of protecting yourself
another way of protecting yourself

e Make notes of what you will include in each paragraph.

Language and content **4a** Read this introduction and match the sentences 1–4 with a–d below.

(1) *A growing phenomenon over recent years has been the way in which our personal identity has been threatened by criminals.* (2) *It can be done through the internet, by stealing our credit card, or by getting information from documents we throw away or leave lying around.* (3) *It is clear that to defeat this crime we must remain vigilant and be extra cautious about what we do with personal information.* (4) *This essay will focus on two ways in which we may help keep our identity safe.*

a telling the reader the aim of the essay
b adding a sentence to support the first
c focusing on the question in your own words
d writing a general sentence about the topic

b Rewrite the introduction in your own words and/or use some of the phrases in the box.

carried out by   for many of us it is hard   has become big business
increasing at an alarming rate   many people believe that
more than ever before   stay one step ahead   the aim of this essay is to

c Reread your introduction. What is the function of each sentence?

d How could you complete these sentences for the middle section of the essay?
1 Young people/Some people are particularly _____ .
2 (In such cases) they should be told/made aware _____ .
3 One area in which (we) need to be _____ .
4 Another way in which (we) make life easy _____ .

e What will be the aim of the conclusion? Look again at the question. How could you complete these sentences for your conclusion? You may want to use phrases from Exercise 4b.
1 Overall, in my view, _____ .
2 People need to remember that _____ .

Write your essay **5** Now write your essay, using the ideas and some of the language above. Write your answer in 220–260 words.

Review

1 Circle the correct words to complete the sentences.

1 Most people are *totally / really* oblivious to the extent of the threat pesticides pose to bees.
2 In this country, any changes to the law tend to be *absolutely / painfully* slow.
3 Some of the governors were *bitterly / heavily* opposed to any new health and safety restrictions.
4 The earth's ecosystem is *perfectly / extremely* balanced.
5 It's *deeply / incredibly* important that we find ways to protect children's safety online.
6 The advantages of renewable energy are being *completely / widely* discussed.
7 Some people are more *heavily / deeply* attached to their pets than others.
8 I'm *absolutely / extremely* disappointed by the lack of response to my advert for volunteers.

2 Complete the sentences with the correct form of the word in capitals.

1 Local residents will be offered _____ if permission is granted for a third runway. **COMPENSATE**
2 The local council is responsible for the _____ of household waste. **DISPOSE**
3 Toxic vehicle _____ need to be reduced by half. **EMIT**
4 The debate about national _____ is becoming ever more urgent. **SECURE**
5 The level of _____ caused by the recent floods has been underestimated. **DESTROY**
6 An increasing number of people are now realising the _____ of the economic downturn. **IMPLICATE**
7 Farmers should try to avoid _____ use of chemicals. **EXCESS**
8 Border guards can be a useful _____ to illegal immigrants. **DETER**

3 Choose the correct words to complete the sentences.

1 __ we had CCTV cameras installed when I suggested it, this robbery may have been avoided.
   A Whether   B Had   C Should   D But for
2 Your online bank account should be safe __ you change your password frequently.
   A as long as   B unless   C supposing
   D imagine
3 I'm going to resign __ you like it or not.
   A supposing   B whether   C unless   D were
4 I have decided to buy only local produce from now on, __ it gets too expensive.
   A whether   B supposing   C unless
   D but for

5 __ you need more information, don't hesitate to contact us.
   A Should   B Providing   C Imagine   D Were
6 The privacy of celebrities would be more likely to be respected __ we to stop buying the tabloids which publish such sensationalist stories.
   A had   B if   C were   D should
7 Racism in football will decline __ there is a zero tolerance approach towards it.
   A otherwise   B but for   C were   D providing
8 You should complain if you have a bad meal __ nothing will ever change.
   A had   B otherwise   C but for   D whether

4 Complete the text with the words below.

been	fled	globally	given	have	imminent
prior	ranging	sites	scarce	space	triggered

Tew technology has always (1)_____ health panics. Microwave ovens, computer screens and telephones have all (2)_____ rise to anxiety at one time or another. The latest of these scares appears to be wind farms, which have been blamed for a variety of illnesses (3)_____ from weight gain and grey hair to cancer! Every type of psychiatric problem seems to have either already happened or is (4)_____ because of this technology. Apparently, chickens won't lay eggs either, and other animals have (5)_____, never to return.

Wind farms first appeared 20 years ago in the USA and since their appearance the number has risen to just under 200,000 (6)_____. Some people claim that acute symptoms can appear in the (7)_____ of 20 minutes if people are exposed to wind turbines. But if the claims are true, why wouldn't people (8)_____ reported more diseases much earlier? The first complaints came a decade after the first wind farm. What was happening (9)_____ to this time that made it safer for people?

Perhaps it is more to do with a recent rise in the number of anti-wind activists, possibly those with connections to the fossil fuel industry. After all, many windfarm (10)_____ have been operating for years without any complaints. If windfarms affect some people, why haven't others (11)_____ suffering too? And why do they appear to affect certain communities, whereas in other areas complaints are (12)_____ or non-existent?

Overview

6A
> **Reading and Use of English:** Gapped text (Part 7); Word formation (Part 3)
> **Vocabulary:** Communication; Phrasal verbs; Expressions with *speak*, *talk* and *say*; Informal expressions of speaking and understanding
> **Listening:** Multiple matching (Part 4)
> **Language development:** Spelling; Easily confused words; Hyphens
> **Writing:** Cohesion

6B
> **Listening:** Sentence completion (Part 2)
> **Speaking:** Vocabulary: Emotional reactions; Long turn (Part 2)
> **Language development:** Verb + *-ing* or infinitive with *to*?; Verb + object + infinitive/*-ing*; Verb + *-ing* form/infinitive with a change of meaning
> **Reading and Use of English:** Key word transformations (Part 4)
> **Writing:** Essay (Part 1)

Lead-in

1   **Look at the photographs and answer the questions.**

  1   In what way are the people in the photographs communicating a message about themselves?
  2   In what other ways do people communicate without using words?
  3   How do animals communicate

  a   with each other?
  b   with people?

2   **What makes somebody a good communicator? Is it mainly facility with language?**

3   **How aware are you of your senses?**

  1   Which smells, sights and sounds are important to you?
  2   Do your senses ever cross over? For example, do you ever see music as colours or colours as smell?

Reading (Paper 1 Part 7)

Before you read   **1**   How is the language you use different from the way your parents or grandparents express themselves? (e.g. different grammar, more colloquial vocabulary, etc.)

Skimming   **2**   Read the main text. Ignore the gaps at this stage. What aspect of language change is the text about?

You've been verbed

Mothers and fathers used to *bring up* children: now they *parent*. Critics used to *review* plays: now they *critique* them. Executives *flipchart* and almost everybody *googles*. The English language is in a constant state of flux. New words are formed all the time, while old ones fall into disuse.

1	

Further evidence of this linguistic phenomenon is found in all areas of life, though some are more productive than others. Financiers have a wealth of imaginative ideas. As do politicians, who have come up with the verb *to doughnut*. Apparently, this means to sit in a ring around a colleague who is making a parliamentary announcement, so that it is not clear to television viewers that the room is practically deserted.

2	

Yet another productive field is technology, partly because it's constantly seeking names for things which did not previously exist: we *text* from our mobiles, *bookmark* websites, *inbox* our email contacts and *friend* our acquaintances on Facebook – only, in some cases, to *unfriend* them later. *Blog* had scarcely arrived as a noun before it was adopted as a verb. Conversely, verbs such as *twitter* and *tweet* have been transformed into nouns, although the process of verbing – or denominalisation, as it is known to grammarians – is much more common.

3	

There is a difference today, though, in that potential changes in our language are picked up and repeated faster than they would have been five or six hundred years ago when print was the only mass communication medium, and fewer people were literate. They can now be tried out around the world and given the green light (or *greenlighted*!) straightaway.

4	

So while in French the noun *action* has to become the verb *actionner*, English can use the same form for both verb and noun. In German, (apart from *essen*, meaning *food* or *to eat*) such words are virtually unknown; the same is true of Chinese – although the noun meaning *thunder* can also be used as the verb *to shock*. In Arabic, such formations are not found at all.

5	

Which is fine, but sometimes the results are ridiculous – notably when verbs come from nouns which were formed from verbs in the first place. To say 'Let's conference,' instead of 'Let's confer,' or 'I'll signature it' instead of 'I'll sign it' makes the speaker come across as either ignorant or pretentious.

6	

Certain verbs seem to upset people more than others. Verbs connected to place are particularly clumsy: 'I'd like to showcase/workshop this.' And *actioning*, *progressing* and *impacting* seem to wind people up too. Of course, not every newly invented word or phrase passes into general use and hopefully some will gently fade away. But as for trying to end verbing altogether, no chance! There is no turning back the clock.

EXPERT WORD CHECK

deserted (*adj*)   flux   literate   obtrusive   pretentious
revel (in something)   vibrant   virtually   (a) wealth of (something)
wind someone up

Gapped text   **3**   Read the strategy on page 168, then do the task. Use the Help notes for support with certain items.

*You are going to read a magazine article about language change. Six paragraphs have been removed from the article. Choose from the paragraphs **A–G** the one which fits each gap (1–6). There is one extra paragraph which you do not need to use.*

A What is the driving force behind *wanting* to do it, though? 'Looking for short cuts, especially if you have to say something over and over again, is a common motivator,' says the editor of a popular dictionary.

B Sport is another ready source: *Rollerblade*, *skateboard* and *snowboard* have all graduated from names of equipment to actual activities. Football referees used to book players or send them off, now they *card* them.

C On the other hand, it has been welcomed by linguists as evidence of a vibrant linguistic culture. Many people applaud its entertainment value, especially when it is applied to someone's name.

D What makes these innovations so easy is that English, unlike other Indo-European languages, uses few inflections. It rarely changes the form of its words to show different meanings.

E Using a complicated verb when there is a far simpler alternative, such as *dialogue* for *talk*, has the same effect, which is why some lovers of the language dislike the whole business of verbing so much.

F No trend has been more obtrusive in recent years, though, than the changing of nouns into verbs. 'Trend' itself (which used to be a noun and is now also used as a verb meaning *change or develop in a general direction*) is an example of the way the language is adapting.

G The practice goes back a long way too. Steven Pinker, in his book *The Language Instinct*, points out that 'easy conversion of nouns to verbs has been part of English grammar for centuries; it is one of the processes that makes English English'. Sixteenth-century writers such as Shakespeare revelled in it and there are many examples of nouns used as verbs in his plays.

➤ **HELP**

1 Two extracts from the base text, on either side of the first gap, *The English language is in a constant state of flux* and *Further evidence of this linguistic phenomenon* will help you to find the link in the options.

2 As well as finance, politics and new technology, what other area of language has provided a lot of new verbs?

3 You are looking for information about 500 years ago, to contrast with *There is a difference today, though.*

Task analysis   **4**   Discuss these questions.
1 What words or phrases do *another ready source* (B) link back to?
2 Find other examples of linguistic links.

Discussion   **5**   Do you think people should resist language change? Is it generally better or worse to change?
Think about things which have affected your language, e.g.
• words and expressions from other languages
• slang and 'teen speak'
• text language.

Doughnut is used as a verb in political circles

Vocabulary: communication

Phrasal verbs

1a Rephrase the sentences by saying the phrasal verbs in *italics* in another way.

1 I dropped hints that she should go, but I obviously hadn't *got* my message *over*.
2 It's quite hard to *get through to* my uncle at times.
3 There are some subjects I try not to *bring up* very often.
4 When I'm chatting to my friends, the same topics *crop up* again and again.
5 I finally managed to *talk* my son *out of* playing rugby.
6 I encourage my children to *talk over* potential issues before they become a problem.

b Work with a partner and use some of the phrasal verbs to talk about your own life.

Expressions with *speak*, *talk* and *say*

2a Match 1–8 with a–h to make sentences.

1 Unless you *speak up*,
2 It's *easier said than done*
3 If you're going to *talk business* all night,
4 I'm not going to *say a word*
5 Andrew always *speaks his mind*
6 She doesn't always know what she's *talking about*
7 I can't *say for certain* that it's Jane's husband
8 She's here to *speak on behalf*

a so try not to get offended by him.
b we won't be able to hear a word.
c because you know my opinion already.
d but he looks just like him.
e but I'm going to give up sugar.
f of her client.
g but she likes the sound of her own voice.
h I'm not coming with you!

b Complete the sentences with *talk, speak* or *say* in the correct form.

1 She's half an hour late again, needless to ____ .
2 I'm afraid I'm still not on ____ terms with Clarissa after our row.
3 Sorry I'm late. I've been trying to ____ some sense into my son.
4 He hasn't done his homework and is ____ nonsense again.
5 Bad? You can ____ that again! It was terrible!
6 Tim was ____ very highly of you yesterday.
7 I'm useless at making small ____ to people I'll never see again.
8 It goes without ____ that I'll do anything I can to help.

c Ask each other if you have recently

• spoken your mind about something
• spoken highly of anyone
• talked business
• spoken on behalf of anyone
• stopped being on speaking terms with someone
• had to make small talk.

Informal expressions: speaking and understanding

3a Match the expressions in *italics* to the definitions (a–h).

1 I could hardly get a *word in edgeways* when he was speaking.
2 Carol *missed the point of* what we were saying.
3 I can't make *head or tail* of this homework.
4 I'd better explain the arrangements to Carol before she *gets the wrong end of the stick*.
5 They were *having a go at* each other all the time.
6 Sadie was *going on* about work all evening again.
7 I *dropped hints* about what I might like for my birthday but I don't think he noticed.
8 You *took the words right out of my mouth!*

a talking endlessly in an annoying way
b any sense
c got the wrong idea about
d criticising/arguing with
e chance to say anything
f suggested (something) indirectly
g misunderstands
h said exactly what I was going to say

b Ask and answer the following questions.

1 In what situations have you not been able to get a word in edgeways?
2 Have you ever missed the point of something, or got hold of the wrong end of the stick?
3 What have you dropped hints about?
4 Do you know anyone who goes on about something all the time?
5 Is there something you haven't been able to make head or tail of?

4 Make a note of useful expressions from this section. Remember to include any dependent prepositions.

Use of English 1 (Paper 1 Part 3)

Before you read

1 What are the advantages of mobile phones? What are the disadvantages? (e.g. health, the environment)

Word formation

2 Read the text. What advantages and disadvantages are mentioned?

3 Decide which part of speech fits into each gap, and whether the word should be plural, negative, etc.

4 Read the strategy on page 167, then do the task.

*For questions **1–8**, read the text below. Use the word given in capitals at the end of some of the lines to form a word that fits the gap **in the same line**. There is an example at the beginning (0).*

Mobile phones: a benefit or social nuisance?

Few people under 30 will be able to imagine a time before the **(0)** _existence_ of mobile phones. | EXIST
Neither will they be aware of the **(1)**_____ effect | HARM
that many people predicted text language would have on young people's language skills. Interestingly, linguists nowadays believe that expressing oneself clearly in texts is evidence of a good **(2)**_____ in grammar and sentence structure. | GROUND
Mobile phones are credited with encouraging people to communicate more. They can also provide **(3)**_____ to people who are alone in | REASSURE
dangerous situations. Some people use mobile phones as a kind of barrier to unwelcome social contact; texting can signal your **(4)**_____ to other | AVAILABLE
people in the same way that wearing sunglasses and headphones does.
Some issues with mobile phones are still **(5)**_____. | CONTROVERSY
Talking loudly on the phone while on public transport is thought to be rude and **(6)**_____ by | CONSIDER
many people in the UK. However, a significant **(7)**_____ of people still do it, despite the sighing | MINOR
and other obvious signs of **(8)**_____ from their | APPROVE
fellow passengers.

Task analysis

5 Answer these questions.

1 Why was more than one change required for some items?
2 Make a note of the words in capitals and the words you formed from them. Underline the stressed syllables and notice where the stress changes according to the part of speech.

Discussion

6 Discuss these questions.

1 Do you think that texting encourages creative use of language? Why?/Why not?
2 How many textspeak abbreviations can you think of? (e.g. cu l8r) Do you know any international ones?
3 What 'rules' would you like to introduce for the use of mobile phones in public?

Listening 1 (Paper 3 Part 4)

Before you listen **1** Discuss these questions.

1 Which foreign language do you think is the most useful to learn? Which is the easiest/most difficult/most attractive?
2 Which would you most like to learn, apart from English, and why? What would people find hard/interesting about learning your own language?

Multiple matching **2a** You will hear five short extracts in which various people are talking about learning a foreign language. Read the options in Task One and Task Two.

b 🎧 41 Read the strategy on page 171, then do the task.

TASK ONE
For questions 1–5, choose from the list (A–H) why each speaker decided to start learning a language.

TASK TWO
For questions 6–10, choose from the list (A–H) how learning a foreign language affected each speaker's life.

While you listen you must complete both tasks.

A to improve job prospects	
B to obtain a qualification	Speaker 1 □ 1
C to go travelling	Speaker 2 □ 2
D to meet people	
E to keep busy	Speaker 3 □ 3
F to support a family member	Speaker 4 □ 4
G to impress people	
H to deepen knowledge of a culture	Speaker 5 □ 5

A It enabled my business to expand.	
B It helped me to find a partner.	
C It inspired me to change my course.	Speaker 1 □ 6
D It led to me changing my career.	Speaker 2 □ 7
E It helped me to find my dream job.	Speaker 3 □ 8
F It challenged me intellectually.	Speaker 4 □ 9
G It helped me to fulfil my potential.	Speaker 5 □ 10
H It made me re-evaluate my life.	

Task analysis **3** Read the first part of the first extract. Why does the speaker decide to learn French? Which words or phrases might tempt you with other options, and why are they not correct?

Speaker 1: My French evening class was a means to an end really – my son was having problems at school and I wanted to be able to help. Actually, he gave it up in the end, whereas I got more and more interested in the French way of life. I then met someone who owns a flat in France and we often get cheap flights out there for weekends.

Discussion **4** Discuss these questions.

1 How important are foreign languages in life?
2 Do you think everyone is capable of learning another language successfully? Why?/Why not?
3 What is your motivation for learning a language? Which person in the extracts, if any, do you identify with?
4 What tips would you give to somebody who wants to learn a foreign language?

EXPERT WORD CHECK

a means to an end   from scratch   inadequate   incentive
narrow (something) down   payoff (*n*)   stuck in a rut   switch (*v*)
time on my hands   tough going

Language development 1

Spelling rules

1 Discuss which of these techniques you use to help you to remember spellings. Add any others you use.

- rules, e.g. *-y* changes to *-ie* when adding *-s* or *-d* (*cry – cries – cried*)
- grouping words with similar patterns (e.g. *pay – paid, say – said, lay – laid*)
- mnemonics (e.g. rhymes or songs which help you to remember)
- breaking the words into parts (e.g. *in-de-pend-ent*)
- associating words with pictures
- writing out a word many times
- using a dictionary to check words
- keeping a record of words you find a problem

2 Choose the correct alternative for these words with double consonants.

1 I would *recommend / reccommend* living in the country if you want to learn a language *successfully / sucessfully*.
2 It is hard to *exagerate / exaggerate* the *diference / difference* learning a second language can make to your life.
3 *Acording / According* to Tom, you're *disappointed / disapointed* with your progress.
4 In *adition / addition* to German, I am also a *beginner / beginer* in Turkish.
5 I've been given the *oportunity / opportunity* to set up a *business / businness*.
6 Is it *neccessary / necessary* to find our own *accommodation / accomodation*?
7 She *was embarassed / embarrassed* by her lack of *professionalism / proffessionalism*.
8 She was able to find an *appartment / apartment* almost *imediately / immediately*.
9 It *occurred / ocurred* to her that she *preffered / preferred* to be at home.
10 Because of the decisions she made, she went on to have a wonderful *carreer / career*.

3 Make the following words plural. What are the rules? Check with Expert writing on page 200.

box	chief	enquiry	fly	hero	journey	leaf
life	potato	radio	thief			

4 Correct a commonly misspelt word in each sentence.

1 It is impossible to finish the job without assistence.
2 Could we have seperate bills, please?
3 I have a neice and a nephew.
4 Medecine is much safer than it used to be.
5 I need your advise about what to wear.
6 She panicked when she heard they were arriveing shortly.
7 You need to practice your swimming.
8 She's a lot prettyer than her sister.
9 Our familys often go on holiday together.
10 Did you recieve an invitation to the party?

Words that are easily confused

5a Choose the correct word for each pair.

1 *lose/loose*
   a She wears her hair ____ when she's not at work.
   b Try not to ____ your temper with the kid.
2 *stationary/stationery*
   a The traffic on the motorway has been ____ for hours.
   b You can buy paper, pens, etc. in the ____ department.
3 *insure/ensure*
   a Can you ____ you check all the details before signing below.
   b I can't decide whether or not to ____ the washing machine.
4 *affect/effect*
   a How will the tax changes ____ you?
   b All this uncertainty is having a bad ____ on us.

b Make sentences to show the difference between these pairs. Use your dictionary to help.

1 their/there	4 heal/heel
2 past/passed	5 your/you're
3 hear/here	6 principal/principle

Hyphens

6 Add hyphens where necessary in these sentences.

EXAMPLE:
We went for a ten kilometre walk.
We went for a ten-kilometre walk.

1 The band split up in 2001, but reformed after a break.
2 We very rarely get break ins in this area.
3 Do you ever see your ex husband these days?
4 Day to day life can be quite stressful at times.
5 Her costar in the film was a very down to earth character.

Writing 1 Cohesion

1a Read the sentences and decide what the reference links in bold refer to. Check your ideas with a partner.

1 There are several ways of improving your brain. **One method** is to perform tasks like completing crosswords. **Another** is to learn a language.

2 Rebecca joined a class in Mandarin at the local college last month. She's been going **there** every day since **then**. **That's why** I never see **her** these days.

3 Are you one of **those people** who find it difficult to learn a language? If **so**, you are probably one of the many **millions** with a memory problem.

4 Get a big dictionary – **one** with lots of examples. **The ones** which just have definitions are less useful.

5 Sara doesn't want to join the class, and **neither** do I.

b Complete the text using expressions from the box.

---
firstly   in the process   instead of   on the contrary
secondly   since   such as   such claims   the reason
their   what's more   whatever   which is why

It used to be thought that children exposed to two languages from birth become confused and fall behind in (1)____ development but there is absolutely no evidence for (2)____ . (3)____ , recent research has shown that (4)____ holding you back, bilingualism has several advantages, (5)____ regularly speaking two languages can have a profound effect on the brain. (6)____ , bilinguals, (7)____ their age, are generally more effective at multitasking, (8)____ they often perform better in creative thinking tasks (9)____ problem solving. (10)____ , they do a better job at prioritising information in potentially confusing situations. (11)____ , in old age they are shielded to a certain extent from dementia. (12)____ for this seems to be that having to keep two languages separate in the brain and ignore distractions means that the brain's control system is constantly being exercised and, (13)____ , gets a lot stronger.

2a Read these extracts from a leaflet advertising a university language support programme. Underline examples of repetition.

INTRODUCTION

language support programme

Studying for a degree in a second language can be a challenge. It doesn't matter what the academic goals may be. There is another thing. Studying in a second language is something that very few people are capable of. Students should remind themselves what an amazing achievement studying in a second language represents. Students are bound to feel frustrated at times. Because most international students feel frustrated at times, we believe that most students will benefit from English language training to ensure that the students can fulfil the students' academic potential.

OUR COURSES

language support programme

Do you have language difficulties in your seminars? Do you suffer from lack of confidence? Having language difficulties and lacking confidence can affect your academic performance. If you have language difficulties, then our Language Support programme aims to help students with difficulties. Our programme is free. Our programme is open to all students for whom English is not their first language. The programme offers individual tutorials for students who wish to discuss their academic writing. The programme also offers language training in groups. We think our programme offers the best available support and, we are pleased to say, our students also think it offers the best available support.

---

b Now rewrite the extracts to make them more cohesive and avoid repetition. Use some of the expressions from Exercises 1a and 1b.

3 Work with a partner.

1 Plan and write an information sheet about a place to study English or another language.

2 Compare in groups. Who has the place you would most like to go to?

Listening 2 (Paper 3 Part 2)

Before you listen   **1**   Discuss these questions.

1 Would you use your instincts in these situations, or would you make a decision based on reason? Why?

applying for a job   buying a car   deciding whether to marry

2 In general, are you a rational person or do you base important decisions on your emotions? Or both? What are the advantages of your approach?

Sentence completion   **2**   🎧 42   Read the task below. What kind of information is missing? Try and predict the kind of words you will hear before you start. Read the strategy on page 171.

You will hear a student called Derek Charles giving a presentation about his research into the subject of intuition. For questions 1–8, complete the sentences with a word or short phrase.

> ### INTUITION
>
> Derek originally assumed he would take up a career in the world of (1)_____ .
>
> Derek uses the word (2)_____ to describe how he felt when he first decided to study psychology.
>
> Derek wanted people who thought of themselves as (3)_____ as volunteers for his research.
>
> Derek found using the (4)_____ the most successful way to attract volunteers.
>
> The researchers asked the volunteers to write a (5)_____ as a matter of routine.
>
> The researchers tracked the volunteers' (6)_____ during the memory test.
>
> The volunteers lost concentration by listening to (7)_____ during the memory test.
>
> The computer detected a different (8)_____ when the volunteers recognised images they had seen unconsciously.

Task analysis   **3**   Compare and justify your answers and then answer these questions.

1 If you had wrong answers, what made them incorrect?
2 What advice would you give a candidate doing this task?

Discussion   **4**   Do you think men or women are generally more intuitive? Give reasons.

> **EXPERT WORD CHECK**
>
> dawn on   detail (*v*)   dream up   electrode   eminently
> flash (*v*)   freak (*n*)   kaleidoscopic   mull over   snap judgment

What might the person's first reaction be in this situation?

A

B

Speaking (Paper 4 Part 2)

Vocabulary: emotional reactions

1a Look at the photos and discuss these questions.

1 What do the photos have in common?
2 How is one photo different from the other two?
3 Judging from the expressions and body language, how do you think the people are feeling? Do they look *frustrated*, *seething with anger* or *absolutely delighted*?

b 🎧 43 Listen and underline the words in these sentences which are most stressed.

1 I was absolutely livid because I was stuck.
2 I immediately burst into tears.
3 I was in two minds and had to weigh up what to do next.
4 It's thoroughly depressing when you're stranded and can't move.
5 I welled up – I was so moved.
6 When people do things like that, it winds me up.
7 My patience soon wore thin – the situation was driving me mad.
8 I was really down and a bit grouchy beforehand – but I cheered up straightaway.

c Match the sentences to people in the photos.

d Compare with a partner how you would react in these situations. Who would be calmer/ more agitated?

2a Circle the correct words to complete the text. Use a dictionary if necessary.

◉ **Browsing blogs**

We'd had a great meal and all of us were **(1)** *in high spirits / out of sorts* but when the waiter presented the bill, I **(2)** *lost my cool / mulled it over* and **(3)** *did my head in / flew into a rage* – it was far higher than it should have been. **(4)** *On reflection / In the heat of the moment* I **(5)** *brooded over / snapped at* him and told him he'd made a mistake, which made my wife get extremely **(6)** *ratty / beside herself* – she hates it when I **(7)** *make a scene / pull myself together* and ruin an otherwise **(8)** *delightful / delighted* evening. I don't know why but things like this **(9)** *get to me / get over it* more than they should. Of course, after I'd **(10)** *calmed down / kept my head* I realised it was me that had made the mistake – I'd forgotten the bill included two bottles of champagne!

b Find an expression which means the person was

1 angry. 2 happy. 3 behaving normally again.

c Make questions with any words/expressions which are new to you. Then ask your partner.

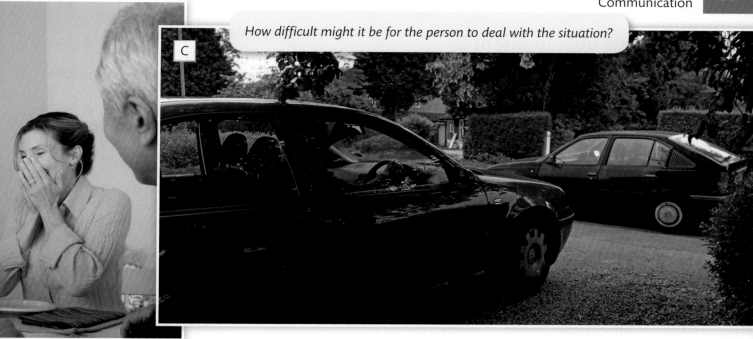

How difficult might it be for the person to deal with the situation?

C

3a 🎧 44 Look at the photos in Exercise 1 again. What do you think the interlocutor's instructions will be? Listen and check.

b 🎧 45 Listen to Axel doing the task. Which two photos does he talk about? How far do you agree with his interpretations?

c 🎧 46 Listen again. How successfully did Axel follow the strategy on page 172 and the Assessment criteria on page 171 for this task? Did he deal with both parts of the task? Did he include anything irrelevant to the task?

Useful language

4a What expression(s) does the speaker use for

1 making a contrast
2 expressing probability
3 expressing certainty

b Change these sentences to what the speaker actually says.

1 It is difficult. (**possibility**)
   *It m*_____ .
2 A lot of people don't these days.
   (**adding new information/contradicting**)
   *A*_____ .
3 A lot of people don't these days. (**emphasis**)
   *I d*_____ .
4 I've never done it. (**emphasis**)
   _____ *done it m*_____ .
5 She's shocked.
   (**possibility/emphasising something surprising**)
   *P*_____ .
6 It won't be long before she's entered into the spirit of the occasion.
   (**Speculating**)
   My _____ .

Long turn

5 Work in pairs.

TASK 1
STUDENT A: Do the task in Exercise 3. (about one minute)
STUDENT B: Look at the photos and listen to your partner, then answer this question: 'Do you think that most people react in the same way in unexpected situations?' (about 30 seconds)

TASK 2
STUDENT B: Look at the photographs on page 205 and do the task. (about one minute)
STUDENT A: Look at the photos on page 205 and listen to your partner, then answer this question. 'Which decision do you think would be the hardest to make?' (about 30 seconds)

Task analysis

6 Assess how well you carried out the tasks.

- I paraphrased when I couldn't remember a word.
- My timing was good.
- I was mainly fluent.
- I used some complex structures and a wide range of vocabulary.
- I made few mistakes.

Where do you need to improve?

Discussion

7 Discuss these questions.

1 How important is it to learn to control our emotions? When is it most important?
2 To what extent are we more impatient and less considerate these days? Do you think it is the same with young and old people?
3 Why do some people not like surprises, even 'nice' surprises?

Language development 2

Verb + -*ing* or infinitive with *to*?

1a Some verbs can only be followed by an -*ing* form or an infinitive with *to*. Divide these verbs into two groups. One verb fits both patterns.

agree	attempt	choose	consider	contemplate
deny	deserve	fancy	guarantee	hesitate
hope	imagine	involve	long	neglect	put off
practise	resent	struggle	volunteer	

b Check your answers in the grammar reference on page 182.

c Use a verb from Exercise 1a in the correct form to complete the sentences. There may be more than one possibility.

1 Could you ever ____ losing one of your five senses?
2 Derek's eyesight was damaged and he ____ to see anything very clearly.
3 Fortunately, many people ____ to help him.
4 Derek had always ____ to be able to play the piano one day.
5 I couldn't ____ to teach him myself because he lived so far away.
6 But I felt he shouldn't ____ having lessons, so I ____ to pay the cost.

d Complete the questions using a verb in the correct form. Then take turns asking and answering with a partner.

1 Have you ever struggled … ?
2 Would you ever consider … ?
3 Have you ever attempted … ?
4 Could you imagine … ?
5 Have you ever neglected … ?
6 Do you think you deserve … ?

Verb + object + infinitive/-*ing*

2 Rewrite the sentences using the phrases in italics and an infinitive or -*ing* form.

1 They enjoyed the holiday a lot.
(*I didn't expect* …)
2 We went to a very exotic market.
(*Friends had encouraged* …)
3 Don't try the very sour milk, you two!
(*I warned* …)
4 Leah loved the mysterious atmosphere.
(*I can imagine Leah* …)
5 The excursion was cut short by a sandstorm.
(*A sandstorm caused* …)
6 A taxi took her back to her hotel.
(*Their guide arranged for* …)

Verb + -*ing* form/infinitive with a change of meaning

3a Complete the text with the -*ing* form or infinitive to complete the sentences.

I'll never forget (1)____ (walk) into a friend's kitchen a few years ago and (2)____ (feel) intoxicated by the scent of wild strawberries. I had meant (3)____ (stay) only a couple of hours, but that's not how it turned out. I remember (4)____ (him/tell) me where he'd got the strawberries and then (5)____ (go) out straightaway to look for some for myself. 'Don't forget (6)____ (hurry) back if the weather breaks,' he warned. Of course, when I came across this delicious fruit I stopped (7)____ (collect) some and went on (8)____ (pick) what I could, despite rumbles of thunder. I even went on (9)____ (explore) another clearing nearby, but very soon the rain started. This meant me (10)____ (have) to find shelter and I regretted (11)____ (not/take) my friend's advice. I tried (12)____ (find) a hut, but there was nothing. As a last resort, I even tried (13)____ (shelter) under an oak tree but, by that time, I was soaked to the skin.

b Explain the difference in meaning.

1 go on *to* … / go on -*ing*
2 forget *to* … / forget -*ing*
3 remember *to* … / remember -*ing*
4 try *to* … / try -*ing*
5 stop *to* … / stop -*ing*

4 Match the halves to complete the sentences and discuss the difference in meaning in each pair.

1 a I can't bear to listen
  b I can't bear listening
  i to music when I'm working.
  ii to any music today.

2 a I watched him painting
  b I watched him paint
  i a portrait, which only took 30 minutes.
  ii a portrait, which he'd begun the previous day.

3 a I prefer tasting
  b I'd prefer to taste
  i wine before I buy it.
  ii this wine before I buy it.

4 a I don't want you to wear
  b I don't want you wearing
  i my coat tonight.
  ii my coat every night.

5 a I saw Molly use
  b I saw Molly using
  i Joe's phone once when he wasn't looking.
  ii Joe's phone all evening.

6 a I left Jake waiting
  b I left Jake to wait
  i for the shop to open while I bought us some coffee.
  ii for the shop to open and went home.

Use of English 2 (Paper 1 Part 4)

Key word transformations

1 Read the strategy on page 168. Complete the second sentence so that it has a similar meaning to the first sentence, using the word given. **Do not change the word given.** You must use between **three** and **six** words, including the word given. Here is an example (0).

0 He'll never be able to read the small print, I'm sure.
   IMAGINE
   I could _never imagine him being able_ to read the small print.

1 Lara doesn't like it when people speak to her as though she were a young girl.
   BEING
   Lara resents _____ she were a young girl.

2 'Certainly, no machine will last forever,' said Theo.
   GUARANTEED
   Theo said that no machine could _____ forever.

3 What made you accept the job?
   PERSUADED
   What was _____ accept the job?

4 Everything was fine before Emily arrived and then things started to go wrong.
   ONLY
   It _____ that things started to go wrong.

5 'When we used to fight, I never hurt him,' said Amy.
   EVER
   Amy denied _____ when they used to fight.

6 Sam didn't feel like getting into an argument with his brother.
   MOOD
   Sam _____ into an argument with his brother.

Task analysis

2 Some students 'over-transform' their answers. (e.g. by adding extra words, by making unnecessary changes) Were any of your answers 'over-transformed'? How?

3 Why would these be wrong answers in Exercise 1?
   Q1 *resents being thought of as if*
   Q2 *have a guarantee to last*
   Q3 *the reason that you were persuaded to*
   Q5 *ever being in the silly situation of hurting him*

4 Write a sentence using a verb + infinitive and a sentence using a verb + *-ing* form. Ask another student to transform the sentences without using the same structure.

Writing 2 Essay (Paper 2 Part 1)

Lead-in **1** Discuss these questions.

1 What do the pictures suggest about young people today?
2 Do you think young people are more or less caring towards other people than they used to be? Give examples.

Understand the task **2** Read the task and answer these questions.

1 What type of essay is it?
2 What must you include? What will you have to invent?
3 What style will you use?

You have attended a panel discussion entitled: 'Today's youth is the same mixture of good and bad characteristics as always.' You have made the notes below:

Characteristics of today's youth
· caring
· confident
· self-centred
· need constant
  stimulation

Some opinions expressed in the discussion:
'They do more voluntary work than ever.'
'They are more self-reliant.'
'The "Me"-generation have no empathy.'
'They are obsessed with material possessions.'

*Choose **two** of the characteristics in your notes and write an essay **explaining whether today's youth is different from previous generations**, **giving reasons** in support of your answer.*
You may, if you wish, make use of the opinions expressed in the discussion, but you should use your own words as far as possible.

Plan your essay **3a** Work with a partner. What are the main positive and negative characteristics of today's youth? Read the question carefully and decide on your answer. How many characteristics are you asked to write about? Think of reasons and examples where appropriate.

b Make a paragraph plan for your essay. How many paragraphs will you have? Where will you give your point of view?

c Choose from your notes in Exercise 3a what you will include in each paragraph.

Language and content

4a Compare these introductions. Which do you prefer and why? Which is more appropriate for the opening sentence of an essay?

A In my view, young people are probably much the same as they have always been.

B In recent years, there has been concern that youth attitudes have changed as living standards have risen and that young people have become less empathetic. But is this true?

C Young people now spend time on their own in front of computers and in many countries only mix with people like themselves.

b How could you continue these sentences to make a topic sentence to begin a paragraph for your essay?

1 (To begin with,) it is certainly true that (many young people in the West) …

2 On the other hand, in some countries …

c Choose the correct alternative in these opinion phrases and decide whether the phrase is used to introduce (I) a new opinion or support (S) an opinion already stated.

1 It is also my firm *view / belief / argument* that …   ___

2 Nowadays, many older people *concern / bother / worry* that …   ___

3 Despite their *claims / views / attitudes* that …   ___

4 This is because they *criticise / hold the view / allow* that …   ___

5 Conversely, it could be *argued / expressed / uttered* that …   ___

6 While it has to be *thought / conceded / believed* that …   ___

7 Another commonly held *point of view / claim / way of thinking* is that …   ___

d Complete some of the phrases in Exercise 4c for your essay.

e Match the headings in the box with the expressions. Then choose and complete expressions for your essay.

Beginning a conclusion   Conceding   Disputing   Emphasising
Expressing general views   Giving reasons

A ____
It is often said/felt/thought that …
It's widely agreed that …
B ____
It is certainly true that … It is true to some extent that …
It's difficult to accept the idea that … (but …)
It cannot be denied that … (but ….)
There can be no doubt that … (but …)
Though it is true that … (one should bear in mind that …)
C ____
It seems to me that … On balance I feel that …
Taking all the arguments into account …
D ____
What is (particularly noticeable) is that …
If there is one thing that is really … , it is that …
E ____
It is simply not the case that … I would dispute the claim that …
F ____
This factor could account for …

Write your essay

5 Now write your essay, using some of the ideas and the language above. Write your answer in 220–260 words.

Check your answer

6 Edit your essay using the checklist on page 190.

Review

1 Choose the correct word to complete the sentences.

1 Her comment may be annoying, but you mustn't let it __ you.
   A get at   B get by   C get to   D get up

2 I wish he wouldn't __ what a good linguist he is.
   A go on about   B go through with
   C go on with   D go in for

3 Megan's __ up all the options before deciding which phone to get.
   A snapping   B bringing   C taking   D weighing

4 Sam's __ livid with you for parking outside her house.
   A completely   B absolutely   C thoroughly
   D incredibly

5 The victims were __ with indignation when the newspaper published the article.
   A angry   B enraged   C seething   D infuriated

6 You look a bit __ sorts. I hope you cheer up soon.
   A out of   B under   C beyond   D without

7 She's been __ hints that we are ignoring her.
   A dropping   B making   C giving   D saying

8 Tom's a poor speaker – he takes ages to get his point __ .
   A out   B through   C away   D across

2 Complete the expressions in each sentence.

1 Tania's never afraid to speak her _____ when she disagrees.

2 You can't get a _____ in edgeways once he starts talking!

3 Sssh! Please don't _____ a scene in front of all these people.

4 Mark's still _____ over whether to study Portuguese or not. He needs to make a decision soon.

5 No, you've got the wrong _____ of the stick.

6 Needless to _____ , minor languages are disappearing fast.

7 I'm upset because my daughter had a go _____ me on the phone.

8 It was a lovely day and we set off in high _____ .

3 Correct the spelling, vocabulary and punctuation mistakes. There are two mistakes in each sentence.

1 His ex girlfriend gave him some good advise.

2 The principle reason for there communication failure was old-fashioned technology.

3 He effected an upper-class accent to try and insure success at the interview.

4 Make some enquirys about how to get independant assistance.

5 Aditional passengers will recieve separate information.

6 On a day to day level the immigrants made absolutely no difference to the lifes of villagers.

7 Unbelievibly, I think they might loose the election.

8 My niece's leg wound has heeled very succesfuly.

4 Circle the correct words to complete the email.

To:	Darren Bates
From:	Sean O'Donnell
Subject:	Elephants

Hi Darren!

Do you remember me **(1)** *to say / saying* that elephants can communicate with each other over several miles and that they use low sounds which we can't hear? Well, I forgot **(2)** *to tell / telling* you about our experience with that very noisy sound they make! Our guide on safari had arranged for us **(3)** *driving / to drive* out to a river where elephants like **(4)** *bathe / to bathe*. Of course, we could hardly wait **(5)** *to see / seeing* these huge creatures **(6)** *to splash / splashing* about in the water. The minute we got there, we stopped **(7)** *taking / to take* pictures. Our presence must have caused one of the old females **(8)** *to panic / panicking* because she started **(9)** *trumpet / trumpeting* loudly and was obviously furious. Our guide warned us **(10)** *being / to be* as still as possible. He also told us to stop **(11)** *taking / to take* pictures and **(12)** *to try / trying* not **(13)** *provoke / to provoke* them. We hadn't expected the elephants **(14)** *reacting / to react* this way and it was quite frightening.

Luckily, after a few minutes, the herd quietened down, but not long after we chose **(15)** *to leave / leaving* them in peace and went back to our hotel.
I'll tell you more when I see you.

Sean

7 Values

Lead-in

1a Look at the photographs and discuss the questions. Under what circumstances will people do these things? What will affect their decision?

   1 live away from their parents while studying
   2 buy or rent a flat/house and start a family
   3 live apart from their family after they finish their education
   4 spend their college holidays travelling
   5 take a year off to travel abroad before finding a job

  b What are the advantages and disadvantages of each situation?

2 What are your personal experiences of the situations in Exercise 1a? Do you believe that young people in your country are encouraged to have too much independence from their parents? Why?

Before you read 1 How does a child's relationship with their parents affect their character? In what ways does the relationship change when the person grows up and moves away from the parental home?

Skimming 2 Read the article quickly for the general meaning. Why can going back home be 'dangerous'?

Multiple choice 3 Try to answer the questions first before looking at the options. Then read each part again carefully and do the task.

*For questions 1–6, choose the answer (**A**, **B**, **C** or **D**) which you think fits best according to the text.*

1 How did Julia react to her boyfriend's comments, following the visit to her parents' home?
A She blamed her parents for her unusually negative attitude that day.
B She found it difficult to accept that criticism of her attitude was justified.
C She was surprised to realise that she had repeated old patterns of behaviour.
D She was annoyed at having the issue of the relationship with her family brought up.

2 In the second paragraph, the writer suggests that it's difficult for people to visit their old family home because
A it can remind them of negative events that happened in the past.
B it can make them feel as if they are being treated like children again.
C it is necessary for them to re-establish a good relationship with the family.
D it can cause them to have unexpectedly strong reactions to the experience.

3 In the third paragraph, the writer says that unless people are aware of what can trigger negative emotions,
A it can be harmful for important relationships with loved ones.
B it can complicate relationships between parents and children.
C it can impede their transition into becoming mature adults.
D it can give rise to a rebellious attitude towards authority figures.

4 In the fourth paragraph, the writer suggests that when parents become angry,
A the stress they are under is passed on to their children.
B their children fail to understand what they have done to upset them.
C their children lose sight of the good points of their relationship.
D the words they use may make a lasting impression on their children.

5 In the fifth paragraph, the writer suggests that a common way for a child to react to parental anger is to
A try and defend themselves physically.
B want to get revenge in some way.
C experience a strong sense of insecurity.
D attempt to escape from what is going on.

6 The writer's main message is that readers should
A accept that past ways of behaving will negatively affect the present.
B try to avoid transferring childhood reactions to adult relationships.
C acquire a greater understanding of how bad parenting can affect lives.
D put out of their minds any negative incidents that happened in the past.

Why going back home can be dangerous

An American psychologist discusses the downsides of a family visit after a person has left home to live independently.

A friend of mine, Julia, recently took her boyfriend along on a visit to her parents' house. It was the first time he'd met her parents, who he found to be kind, laid-back people, and certainly not critical in any way. Yet several times during the visit, he noticed Julia's voice take on an uncharacteristically high-pitched tone as she defensively reacted to seemingly innocent comments from her parents. When he mentioned this observation on the drive home, Julia was taken aback by how his description of what she had said sounded like her teenage self arguing with her parents over their strict, controlling style.

It is not uncommon for people returning to visit their parents to react in this way. Although there are obviously real joys in reconnecting with one's loved ones, the downside is that it can stir up implicit memories. These are memories that exist deep down and can surface without conscious awareness, automatically triggering feelings we had in the past. Dr Daniel Siegel, author of *The Mindful Brain*, says that, 'When we retrieve an element of implicit memory into awareness we just have the emotional response without knowing that these are activations related to something we've experienced before. This is distinct from an explicit memory – a concrete experience that exists in our minds, such as learning to ride a bike.' It is implicit memories which make it possible to experience even a seemingly pleasant visit home while at the same time unconsciously taking on the identities and attitudes we had as children and reacting as we would have done then.

If Julia's boyfriend hadn't made her aware of her childlike reaction, she would in all likelihood have carried on being defensive or defiant in less appropriate situations. This regression to the past would not seem so significant if it was restricted to interactions with parents but the closer someone gets to another person or the more we let them mean to us,

the more likely it is that the strong feelings we have will spark off sub-conscious memories from early relationships. When this happens, negative feelings are re-experienced that are irrelevant to the present. The impact is particularly obvious in romantic relationships, but can be observed in many areas of people's personal and professional lives. When someone has an emotional reaction to something, for example, something a boss said, it's helpful for them to evaluate how they feel. When a feeling is particularly intense, it indicates a connection to childhood occurrences. The more people fail to recognise the way they have grown up and differentiated themselves from their parents, the more likely they are to act out old behavioural patterns in their current life.

Of course, not all parental influences are negative. Yet it's an unfortunate fact that children are more likely to be affected by a single destructive outburst from a parent than by a series of positive experiences with them. This is simply because humans are programmed to remember what scares them. Even the most aware of parents have lapses in which they lose their temper or fail to respond sensitively to their children. Sadly, it's in these moments that children tend to identify with their parents or internalise the message being communicated to them. For example, if a parent accused a child of being lazy whenever the parent was feeling overwhelmed with work, the child would be more likely to identify themselves as lazy and still hear this accusation in their heads as adults.

Why should this be? If a parent suddenly responds with harsh anger, the size difference alone between an adult and a child causes a difference in the way we perceive things. While the child experiences the adult's angry outburst or severe annoyance as intensely threatening, to the adult the interaction is just something that irritated them at the time. When children feel frightened by the very person they depend on for survival, they don't know which way to turn; they want to both run towards and away from the parent. Their only solution is to unconsciously identify with the parent's point of view, finding it too emotionally threatening, not to mention physically impossible, to fight back.

By remaining aware of what triggers reactions from the past, people are less likely to recreate past scenarios and relive the emotions they produced. The more people make sense out of implicit memories and construct a cohesive narrative of their lives, the more they can live free from the limitations created by the past.

Task analysis   **4**   How would you explain to someone how to do this task effectively?

Discussion   **5**   Discuss these questions.
1 How can criticism by parents influence your view of yourself?
2 Give examples of how people see themselves as different from their parents.

EXPERT WORD CHECK

defiant   harsh   high-pitched   laid-back   lapse (*n*)   outburst
overwhelmed   perceive   retrieve   stir up

Vocabulary

Words that are easily confused

1 Complete the sentence in each pair with the correct expression. What is the difference in meaning?

intense/intensive
  1 The heat was so ____ that we had to stay indoors.
  2 I've just finished an ____ course in Spanish.

childish/childlike
  3 It's very ____ to argue like this.
  4 Laura looked at me with ____ delight.

occurrence/incident
  5 Traffic jams have become a daily ____ in this city.
  6 Apparently there was a serious ____ in the town last night.

limited/restricted
  7 You can't park here. It's a ____ area.
  8 The offer is only available for a ____ period.

differ/differentiate
  9 You must learn to ____ between fact and fiction.
  10 Their ideas ____ in many very basic ways.

Idiomatic expressions: home and family

2a Look at the expressions in *italics* to do with *home* and say the sentences in another way.
  1 Where do you feel most *at home*?
  2 Some of the things my boss said to me really *hit home*.
  3 My son is always hungry; he *is eating me out of house and home*.
  4 You can complain *until the cows come home* but I'm not changing my mind.
  5 It took a few weeks before *it came home to me* that she wasn't coming back.
  6 Where is *your home town*?
  7 She immediately *homed in* on what I'd said about Daisy and asked me more about it.
  8 I only go and see my football team if they're playing *at home*.

  b Choose some expressions and use them in sentences which relate to your own experience.

Word formation

3 Complete the sentences with the correct form of the word in capitals.
  1 She was ____ quiet today. I hope she's not ill! **CHARACTERISTIC**
  2 Tom was quite ____ when I asked him where he'd been. **DEFEND**
  3 James has a lot of very ____ friends. **INFLUENCE**
  4 My daughter, who is 16, can be ____ at times. **REBEL**
  5 Laura's boyfriend has a rather ____ personality. **DESTROY**
  6 Don't make wild ____ like that if you can't back them up. **ACCUSE**
  7 Jane tends to ____ her feelings. **INTERNAL**
  8 Adam has very little ____ of what is going on. **AWARE**

My ideal home

4a Make notes on your ideal home under the following headings. (Imagine money is no object!) Use the notes in *italics* to give you ideas.
  1 The location
  (rural or urban, sea view, close to shops, etc.)

  _____

  2 The type of building
  (detached house, newly built modern flat, historic property, tiled roof, big windows, etc.)

  _____

  3 Outside
  (mature/fenced/walled garden; hedges, trees, landscaping, terrace, etc.)

  _____

  4 The rooms
  (open-plan kitchen, bright, airy bedrooms with lots of light, utility room, en suite bedrooms, basement, cellar, attic, loft conversion, large landing, porch, etc.)

  _____

  5 Decoration and furnishings
  (wooden floors/tiles/carpets/rugs/curtains/blinds; painted walls or wallpaper; built-in or free-standing/ modern or traditional furniture; a place to develop/ extend/convert, etc.)

  _____

  b Share your ideas.

Use of English 1 (Paper 1 Part 1)

Before you read 1 Where do you feel most at home: in the family house where you grew up, where your loved ones are, or wherever you are at the moment?

Skimming 2 Read the text. In what ways has the idea of 'home' changed in recent years?

Multiple-choice cloze 3 Read the strategy on page 167, then do the task below.

*For questions **1–8**, read the text below and decide which answer (**A, B, C** or **D**) best fits each gap. There is an example at the beginning (**0**).*

What is a home?

Is it a house, a family, or just a sense of belonging?

Many stories, such as the *Odyssey* or *The Wizard of Oz*, (**0**) A journeys home. Perhaps this is why so many people closely (**1**)__ with them. Interestingly, many people still (**2**)__ their parents' home as home, even when they have their own house and family.

Feeling at home is also about one's surroundings. Having a flat or house (**3**)__ people with the opportunity to stamp their own personality on a place. As traditional communities have fragmented, our homes have become places where people are (**4**)__ to find privacy and relaxation.

Yet, as the workforce has become more (**5**)__ and people have started to move house much more often, perhaps 'home' is no longer home in the same (**6**)__ that it used to be. It is now more a feeling of belonging that moves with people wherever they go. The concept will continue to change as more people work from home. (**7**)__ , for many people home is now an integral part of their working lives, as (**8**)__ to somewhere to go at the end of the day.

0	A feature	B refer	C deal	D focus
1	A involve	B identify	C respond	D relate
2	A regard	B think	C believe	D look
3	A allows	B enables	C provides	D offers
4	A dedicated	B convinced	C committed	D determined
5	A mobile	B shifting	C portable	D changeable
6	A meaning	B concept	C sense	D significance
7	A Nevertheless	B Otherwise	C However	D Indeed
8	A opposed	B instead	C apart	D different

Task analysis 4 Look at items 1–3. What make the 'wrong' options wrong?

Listening 1 (Paper 3 Part 1)

Before you listen

1 What would you miss most about your home town if you had to move away?

Multiple choice: short extracts

2 🎧 47 Read the rubric and questions for each extract to familiarise yourself with the context and the people you are going to listen to. Read the strategy on page 170, then do the task.

*You will hear three different extracts. For questions **1–6**, choose the answer (**A**, **B** or **C**) which fits best according to what you hear. There are two questions for each extract.*

Extract One
You hear two colleagues talking about living in the north and south of their country.

1 What do they both miss about life in the north?
  A the friendliness of the locals
  B the way people speak
  C the physical surroundings

2 When she visits the north, the woman feels
  A embarrassed by all the fuss that's made of her.
  B detached from the people she used to be close to.
  C relieved that she decided to move south.

Extract Two
You hear an interview with a man who went to live in a tent with his family.

3 He moved into a tent
  A for financial reasons.
  B for ecological reasons.
  C for research reasons.

4 What has he appreciated most about living in the tent?
  A having more time with his wife and child
  B learning some practical skills
  C being close to nature

Extract Three
You hear two students talking about living in a university hall of residence.

5 What do they disagree about?
  A how convenient it is
  B how costly it is
  C how comfortable it is

6 What disappointed the woman about the students she lived with?
  A their reluctance to spend time with one another
  B their inability to get on good terms with each other
  C their lack of interest in sharing meals together

Discussion

3 Which of the extracts did you find most interesting? Why?

EXPERT WORD CHECK

cramped   drift in   fair enough   hassle (*n*)   hoot (*v*)
pitch a tent   (a) stone's throw   sustainable   uproot

Language development 1

Cleft sentences: emphasis with *what, the thing, the reason, the place, all …*

> EXPERT GRAMMAR page 183

1a Match 1–4 with a–d to make sentences from the listening extracts.

1 The thing that's given us most pleasure
2 What our listeners want to know
3 The place where my sister lives
4 All we wanted to do

a was live a more sustainable life.
b is why anyone would be mad enough to live in a tent.
c is hearing the owls hooting.
d is only a stone's throw away from my parents' house.

b Answer the questions.

1 Which verb connects the two parts of the sentence?
2 Where is the emphasis – at the beginning or end of the sentence?
3 Which auxiliary can be added to give extra emphasis to a verb? (Look at 4a.)
4 How would you say sentences 1–4 in a 'non-emphatic' way?

c Practise saying the sentences in Exercise 1a. Which words are stressed?

Emphasis with *it + be*

2a Look at the examples of another type of structure used to emphasise parts of the sentence.

I missed the unexpected things most. →
It **was** the unexpected things **that** I missed most.

That article really inspired us. →
It **was** that article **that** really inspired us.

b Rephrase these sentences, giving more emphasis by using *It + be*.

1 We were initially attracted to the garden, rather than the house itself. (*It was …*)
2 The mature trees, in particular, were difficult to resist. (*It was …*)
3 The beautifully proportioned living room was the main attraction inside. (*It was …*)
4 The last time I saw somewhere I wanted to buy was five years ago. (*It was …*)
5 I didn't realise how much I wanted it until we got home. (*It wasn't until …*)
6 We will only be able to afford it if I go back to work. (*It's only by …*)

3 Rewrite the sentences so that the emphasis is on the words in *italics*.

1 I prefer *the climate* in the south.
  What _____ .
2 Most people don't realise *how beautiful the countryside in the north is*.
  What _____ .
3 I left the north because *I went to university*.
  The reason why _____ .
4 I missed *my friends* more than anything.
  The thing that _____ .
5 I only intended to *stay for a couple of years*.
  All _____ .
6 I'd love to live in *Spain* for a while.
  The place _____ .

4a Complete these sentences so that they are true for you.

1 *All I've ever wanted to do* _____ .
2 *The reason why I* _____ .
3 *The place that I like best* _____ .
4 *The thing that I like most about my hometown*
  _____ .
5 *What I miss/would miss most about living away from home* _____ .
6 *It was my mother/father who* _____ .
7 *It wasn't until* _____ .
8 *It's my family* _____ .

b Discuss your answers with a partner.

Writing 1 Punctuation

1a Read this extract and add these punctuation devices where appropriate: apostrophe ('), comma(,), full stop(.), capital letter (T), exclamation mark (!), hyphen(-), speech marks ('…').

The place where I spend lots of my time is my bedroom its got all my things there and ive painted it in my favourite colours which are purple black and red and ive put posters on the walls theres a three seater sofa too so I can watch tv there with my friends my mother calls it a hamsters nest because there are lots of cosy throws on the bed there are also piles of clothes all over the floor unfortunately Im not the worlds tidiest person

b Compare your answers. Which punctuation device do you have problems with?

Punctuation devices

2a Find examples of the following in the sentences below: apostrophe ('), comma (,), full stop (.), capital letter (A), colon (:), semi-colon (;), dash (–), speech marks ('…'), exclamation mark (!). What are the functions of each?

1 I love all fruits: pineapple, oranges, mango – fruit's my favourite food!
2 I'd like to go to Prague; it's famous for its architecture.
3 My sister's room is on the left and my brothers' room is on the right.
4 If you allow yourself time to do nothing, inspiration often strikes.
5 Unfortunately, it is difficult for some people to accept criticism.
6 Picasso was a painter, sculptor, print-maker, stage-designer and ceramicist.
7 Michael Morpurgo, whose book *War Horse* was made into a film, writes mainly for children.
8 'You can't wait for inspiration – you have to go after it with a club.' (Jack London)

b Check the Writing reference on page 199.

3a Add commas and apostrophes to these sentences where necessary.

1 If youre planning to start learning the piano youll need a good teacher a lot of time and a lot of patience.
2 Nureyev was the best dancer there has ever been in my view.
3 The DVDs that I watch the most are Wallace and Gromit.
4 *The Artist* which won most of the Oscars was a very imaginative movie.
5 Madame Tussauds is one of Londons oldest attractions.
6 My parents dog was looked after by my friends mother.

b Add speech marks and appropriate punctuation to the following quotes.

1 *ideas are like rabbits you get a couple and learn how to handle them and pretty soon you have a dozen* (John Steinbeck)
2 *you write your first draft with your heart and you rewrite with your head the first key to writing is to write not to think* (Sean Connery)

c Punctuate these sentences using a semi-colon, a colon, a dash and an exclamation mark once each.

1 To be successful you need three things talent, determination and good luck.
2 I'd like to see the show again in fact, I'm going to book tickets tomorrow
3 Katie is a great actress she has sensitivity and a good voice.

4 Use the punctuation devices in Exercise 2 to correct this extract. The devices can be used more than once and there may be more than one possibility.

Because Im a singer I spend lots of time on the tour bus we get on board after one of our gigs at about 12 pm once weve unwound we get into our bunks to sleep while the driver takes us on to the next venue

I sleep really well on the bus in fact when I go home to my flat in manchester i find it too empty very quiet and its difficult to get to sleep on our current bus we have engineers and managers to go with us it accommodates 12 14 people

when we started out we travelled around in a mates old van we now have a double decker and my mum said yesterday you could be in a nightclub when youre on your bus its decorated in red and black and has all the necessities a tv fridge and a microwave

Listening 2 (Paper 3 Part 4)

Before you listen   **1**   Read the instructions for the tasks below and look at the list A–H in Task One.

1 In what circumstances could people learn these things when travelling?
2 Which are the most important lessons, in your view?

Multiple matching   **2**   🎧 48   Read the strategy on page 171, then do the task.

You will hear five short extracts in which people are talking about going travelling.

TASK ONE

*For questions **1–5**, choose from the list (**A–H**) what each speaker learnt when they were travelling.*

TASK TWO

*For questions **6–10**, choose from the list (**A–H**) how each person's life has changed as a result of travelling.*

While you listen you must complete both tasks.

TASK ONE		TASK TWO	
A to keep possessions to a minimum		A I enjoy routine domestic tasks.	
B to be more polite with strangers	Speaker 1 1	B I throw away things I no longer care about.	Speaker 1 6
C to rise to a challenge	Speaker 2 2	C I make my job less of a priority.	Speaker 2 7
D to have a more relaxed lifestyle	Speaker 3 3	D I make an effort to meet new people.	Speaker 3 8
E to save money	Speaker 4 4	E I live for the moment.	Speaker 4 9
F to plan carefully	Speaker 5 5	F I visit towns I've never been to before.	Speaker 5 10
G to be more aware of the natural world		G I like entertaining people I know.	
H to be prepared to change an arrangement		H I am more emotional.	

Task analysis   **3**   Compare and discuss your answers. What clues in the recording helped you to identify the information you needed? Did anything mislead you?

Discussion   **4**   Work in pairs.

Student A: Think of a difficult travel adventure. (e.g. *motorcycling through Africa, sailing solo around the world*) Explain what you think the difficulties would be and ask for advice.

Student B: Give your partner advice on how to deal with such an experience. Use expressions like these: *Have you thought of ...? If you ..., you might ... I think you should/it'd be a good idea if you ... You could always ...*

EXPERT WORD CHECK

backwash effect   be blown away by   on the spur of the moment
reserve (*n*)   savour   select (*adj*)   substitute (*n*)   tag along

Speaking (Paper 4 Part 3)

going on an adventure with other travellers

finding oneself alone in a dangerous situation

What might travellers learn from these experiences?

travel plans going wrong

watching a religious festival

living among different cultures

A

B

C

D   COACH

E

Vocabulary: travel

1a Work with a partner. Think of specific contexts for each of the situations in the spidergram.

b Match the situations in the spidergram to the contexts in the pictures.

2a Match 1–6 with their endings a–f to make sentences.

1 I needed to *get away* and *have some time to myself,*
2 I've never been very *self-reliant,*
3 It was foggy when we got to the airport,
4 We *soaked up the atmosphere*
5 It was a *tricky situation* when the bus broke down
6 Cycling on these roads is *fraught with danger*

a so we were stranded and had to *sleep rough.*
b and tried to *pack in* as much as we could.
c because we were *marooned in the middle of nowhere.*
d and you *run the risk of* serious injury.
e so I *took* three months *off* work.
f but you soon learn to *fend for yourself.*

b Which expressions in *italics* can you match with the situations in the spidergram?

c Take it in turns to pick a situation and describe it to your partner.

d Imagine yourself in the different situations and take it in turns to tell a partner what happened in each. Use some of the expressions in *italics* above and any others you may know.

Collaborative task: sample answer

3a 🎧 49 Now look at the question in the spidergram. What does the task involve? Listen to the interlocutor's instructions and check.

b 🎧 50 Listen to two people doing the task. Which of their opinions do you agree/disagree with?

c 🎧 51 Listen again and say whether these statements are *True* (T) or *False* (F).

1 They cover all the points.
2 They invite each other's opinions.
3 They talk about their own experience.
4 They fail to justify their opinions.
5 They exchange ideas and keep the conversation flowing.
6 They fail to speculate.
7 They have a poor range of vocabulary.
8 They use grammar accurately and appropriately.

d Compare and justify your answers in Exercise 3c.

e 🎧 52 Now listen to the interlocutor's instructions for the second part of the task and the candidates' discussion. Do you agree with their conclusion? Why?/Why not?

f How successfully did they carry out the task?

Useful language

4a What expressions do the students use for agreeing and disagreeing with each other?

b Complete these extracts from the sample answer.

1 All right, I'll ____ . (**Beginning the task**)
2 Yes, I ____ agree. (**Imprecise language**)
3 ____ it's more of a test of your character if there's no-one to help you? (**Asking for agreement**)
4 ____ in some places is to make sure you avoid the tap water. (**Emphasising**)
5 ____ being invited to stay in someone's home? (**Asking for clarification**)
6 It seems to ____ staying in someone's home or putting yourself in an unsafe situation. (**Deciding**)
7 Which one shall we ____ ? (**Asking for opinion. Expressing a choice**)
8 Not ____ . (**Disagreeing**)
9 ____ , and the same goes for the adventure. (**Agreeing**)
10 I'll go ____ with that! (**Agreeing**)

c 🎧 53 Listen again and check.

d Match these expressions to the categories in brackets in Exercise 4b above and add any others you know.

absolutely right   but that's not always the case   I'm not so sure about that
settle for   Sorry, I don't really see what you're getting at
Sorry, I don't quite follow you   start the ball rolling   stuff like
The thing that   Wouldn't you say that

e Practise the expressions in Exercises 4b and 4d. Make sure you stress the most important word(s) and you use the correct intonation.

Collaborative task

5a Work in pairs. Do the task in Exercise 3. Time yourself. Remember to follow the strategy on page 172 and the Assessment criteria on page 171.

b Tell the class briefly which experience you have chosen and why.

Task analysis

6 Compare your answer with the sample answer. Did you express the same ideas? Did you use any of the same language?

Discussion

7 What memorable travel situations or holidays have had an impact on your life? Name your dream holiday and companion.

Language development 2

Past tenses for hypothetical meanings

1a Compare the form and meaning of these sentences. What verb form is used in each? What time does each sentence refer to? Why are past forms sometimes used? Check your answers in the grammar reference on page 183.

I'd rather go travelling around Peru.

I'd sooner we went to Mexico.

If only you could get more time off work.

I wish you hadn't told me the cost of the flight!

b Circle the option in the second sentence that best reflects the meaning of the first sentence.

1 She wishes she had more time.
   She *is / was* always busy.
2 If only it would stop raining.
   I'm *optimistic / not optimistic* that it will stop.
3 I'd rather we'd bought a mosquito net.
   We should *get / have got* a mosquito net.
4 He talks as though he lived there.
   He *might / doesn't* live there.
5 It's time we were leaving.
   We *should leave now / have already left*.
6 I'd sooner you didn't wear my sandals.
   You *wear / shouldn't wear* my sandals.
7 Supposing I said something to her, would it help?
   I *might / won't* say something.

wish / if only

2a Circle the options which are possible in each sentence. If more than one is possible, discuss any difference in meaning.

1 I *wish / hope / want* I can pass my exams.
2 I wish I *can / could / will* see Graham more often.
3 If only I *was / am / will be* going away with you tomorrow!
4 My brother *wishes / wished / had wished* he could drive.
5 I wish James *doesn't / didn't / hadn't* cut his hair so short.
6 I wish *you / he / I* wouldn't smoke in here.
7 If *you / you only / only you* knew how happy I was to get back home!

b Complete the following sentences so they are true for you. Discuss with a partner.

1 I sometimes wish I could …
2 If only I didn't have to …
3 I often wish I hadn't …
4 If only people wouldn't …

Other expressions

3a Circle the options which are possible in each sentence. If more than one is possible, discuss any difference in meaning.

1 It's time *I buy / to buy / I bought* a tablet computer.
2 Suppose I *get / got / had got* one for this trip. Do you think it would be useful?
3 I'd prefer it if you *didn't bring / wouldn't bring / won't bring* any technology at all.
4 Why do you talk to me as if I *am / was / were* stupid?
5 What if your smartphone *gets / got / will get* stolen?
6 You look as though you *see / have seen / saw / had seen* a ghost.

b Complete the second sentence so that it has a similar meaning to the first sentence. There may be more than one possibility.

1 I wish you hadn't suggested I order the seafood.
   I'd rather _____ .
2 Why don't you eat more protein and get your strength back?
   It's time _____ .
3 Instead of crossing the river at night, shall we do it at daybreak?
   Would you prefer it _____ ?
4 Do you think we should have stayed on in the village a bit longer?
   What if _____ ?
5 Something did happen, but you pretend it didn't.
   You talk as though _____ .
6 I'd like to have met her family, but imagine what would have happened.
   Suppose _____ ?

4 Complete the text with the correct form of the verbs in brackets.

My friend Rob says it's time we all **(1)**____ *(give up)* non-essential flying to protect the ozone layer. If only it **(2)**____ *(be)* that simple! I have been a travel writer all my life and it's not as though at my age I **(3)**____ *(can/find)* another job. I wish he **(4)**____ *(not keep)* having a go at me. I need to have things to write about and I'd rather he **(5)**____ *(give)* practical suggestions instead. Last month, I wrote about a cycle journey in my country, which my editor rejected and I wished I **(6)**____ *(not bother)*. I felt as if I **(7)**____ *(waste)* time and money!

5 Ask a partner about one of these imaginary situations.

1 having a year off to do what you want
2 being born in a different century

Use of English 2 (Paper 1 Part 2)

Lead-in

1 Discuss these questions.

1 What kind of souvenirs do you collect on your travels?
2 What's your favourite travel souvenir? Why?

Open cloze

2a Read the title and the text below quickly and answer these questions. (Ignore the gaps at this stage.)

1 Why do people collect travel souvenirs?
2 How did collecting become a serious passion for one person?

b Read the strategy on page 167, then do the task.

*For questions **1–8**, read the text below and think of the word which best fits each gap. Use only **one** word in each gap. There is an example at the beginning (0).*

MEMORIES ARE MADE OF THIS

We don't normally collect souvenirs for **(0)** _any_ great significance they might have in themselves. Nor **(1)**____ we collect them for practical reasons, **(2)**____ than to brighten up some empty shelf. When **(3)**____ comes to it, as the word suggests, the real reason we buy souvenirs is for the memories we associate with them. Some tourists buy cheap mass-produced goods and others will only buy handmade folk art. But **(4)**____ both sets of travellers have **(5)**____ common is that for them the object acquires sentimental value, even on those occasions they feel they **(6)**____ kick themselves for having paid too much. How often do we all wish we hadn't parted with our precious money so easily!

However, for some people collecting can become a serious passion. A few years ago, the writer Paul Theroux was in a market in Mumbai when he saw a nineteenth-century glass painting. 'All I did was stop and admire it,' he says. 'I don't know **(7)**____ it should be, but when I tried to move away, I realised that I had to buy it.' Now, wherever he travels, he goes looking for glass paintings, almost as **(8)**____ he were hunting for treasure.

Task analysis

3a Find an example of these in the tested items.

| conjunction | fixed phrase | modal verb | preposition | pronoun |
| question word | verb | | | |

b What other areas of grammar might be tested in Part 2?

Discussion

4 Discuss these questions.

1 What advice would you give a visitor to your country looking for travel souvenirs? (e.g. where to get them, what to be careful of)
2 Would you give the same advice to different people? (e.g. teenagers, men, women, rich people)

Writing 2 Letter of complaint (Paper 2 Part 2)

Lead-in **1** Discuss these questions.

1 In what contexts do people make written complaints?
2 Why might you want to write a complaint to an airline?

Understand the task **2a** Read the task and check who you are writing to and why.

> *You were booked in on a flight to Sri Lanka via Amsterdam, but when you got to your local airport you found that your connecting flight to Amsterdam was first delayed, then cancelled. You were unhappy with the way the situation was handled by the airline. Write a letter to the airline. Your letter should:*
> *• describe what happened*
> *• explain why you were unhappy*
> *• say what you want the airline to do.*
> *Write your **letter**.*

b What do you hope or expect to achieve by writing your letter? (e.g. to please, annoy or persuade the reader) Decide on the style and register you will use. (e.g. aggressive, friendly or diplomatic but firm)

Plan your letter

3a Work with a partner and brainstorm some ideas for your letter. Which points will you include? (e.g. *refund, staff attitudes, friend waiting, alternative flight, previous experience with airline, communication failures, airline's customer guarantee*)

b Make a paragraph plan for your letter and write notes for each paragraph.

Language and content

4a Circle the correct alternative in these phrases. Which phrases could you use in your letter?

1 (my) *recent / late* experience with
2 *get into / catch* a connecting flight
3 *incur / earn* a lot of expense
4 *meet / take charge of* (a person's) needs
5 *contribute / provide* assistance
6 take *good / full* responsibility for
7 (the plane will) arrive *shortly / sharply*
8 *break / split* a promise
9 dissatisfied *at / with* the service
10 a very offhand *manner / behaviour*
11 as the *planned / scheduled* flight time (grew nearer)
12 *decidedly / tremendously* unhelpful

b Which of these sentence openings would be better and why?

1 I'm writing to express my deep disappointment at …
2 I'm writing because I'm angry that …

c Divide these expressions into:

1 making the complaint and explaining what happened
2 providing evidence
3 future action.

I shall expect to hear from you …
I appreciate that …/the reasons why … but …
Upon checking …
I knew that if I missed …
As it turned out, …
May I remind you …
As you may remember, …
I enclose … herewith
I immediately contacted …
I believe your airline needs to …
If I hear nothing from you, I will have no/little choice but to …
I would be grateful if you could …
Not only was I unable …
I await your response to …
Please find attached …

d Decide which of the expressions above you could use in your letter and match them to the paragraphs in your plan in Exercise 3b. How can you complete them in an appropriate way?

Write your letter

5 Now write your letter in 220–260 words, using some of the language above.

Check your letter

6 Edit your work using the checklist on page 190.

Review

1   Circle the correct word or phrase to complete the sentences.

1 Some children are left at home to *keep / fend* for themselves when both parents work.
2 Don't go down that route! It's *fraught / loaded* with danger.
3 What would you do if you found yourself *marooned / deserted* in the middle of the ocean?
4 My parents' criticisms about our lifestyle really *homed in / hit home*.
5 Most teenagers have a *rioting / rebellious* streak – it's nothing to worry about.
6 We were waiting to move into our new house and had to sleep *rough / hard* for a few weeks.
7 Katie is on a *restricted / limited* diet – she can't eat any sugar.
8 There's no need to sound so *preventative / defensive* – I'm not getting at you.

2   Complete the sentences with the correct form of the word in capitals.

1 In our company, we do not _____ between men and women in terms of pay. **DIFFER**
2 Transport problems are a common _____ when you travel a lot. **OCCUR**
3 Every society should protect the weak and _____ . **DEFENCE**
4 We used decorative lighting to make the room more _____ . **ATMOSPHERE**
5 Ryan behaved _____ , which I find annoying. **CHILD**
6 I might be able to get you a cheaper flight but it'll be _____ . **TRICK**
7 I noticed that the _____ didn't really match the wallpaper. **FURNISH**
8 Our hostel is heavily _____ on charity. **RELY**

3   Complete the second sentence so that it has a similar meaning to the first sentence.

1 I'm closer to my sister Sarah than I am to anyone else.
 The person _____ my sister Sarah.
2 Imagine living in a big city – how would you cope?
 Supposing _____ cope?
3 William's trip across Asia didn't go well but he likes to pretend it did.
 William talks as _____ well.
4 My parents' lack of tact upset me most.
 What _____ tact.
5 Instead of moving to Spain, I'd like it much better if we moved to Norway.
 I'd really prefer it _____ Spain.
6 We'll only get on if we are completely open with each other.
 It's only by _____ get on.
7 I wish it were possible for us to go trekking in the Andes.
 If only we _____ in the Andes.
8 I'm more worried about living on my own.
 The thing that _____ on my own.

4   Complete the text with one word in each gap.

It wasn't **(1)**_____ his son Mark developed a rare muscle disease that Matt decided to try and raise money for a special children's home. '**(2)**_____ I decided to **(3)**_____ was run a series of fundraising marathons in Death Valley, California, the hottest desert in the world. The **(4)**_____ why I did them there **(5)**_____ to generate publicity. Obviously, I **(6)**_____ rather have done them somewhere cooler but **(7)**_____ I cared about was raising money as quickly as possible. Since I now realise how difficult life is for wheelchair users, I wish I **(8)**_____ acted sooner. Of course, I also wish other people **(9)**_____ get involved. Frankly, it's **(10)**_____ the government did something to raise awareness. If only there **(11)**_____ more volunteers helping the cause, we **(12)**_____ soon have our home!'

Lead-in

1a Decide whether these statements are *True* (T) or *False* (F). (See answers on page 205.)

1. Cattle were used as a medium of exchange before money was invented.
2. Gold bars were the earliest form of currency.
3. Before coins, silver, shells and other metals were used in trade.
4. Coins were first used because they were easier to carry.
5. Banks were invented before coins.
6. Coins were first introduced about 700BC.
7. The first paper currencies were used in China.
8. The euro was first introduced in 1980.
9. At the present time there are no currencies backed by gold.
10. The dollar is the oldest currency in the world.

b What do you know about the history of the currency of your country?

2 Discuss these quotes. What do you think they mean? Do you agree or disagree with them? Give reasons.

1. 'Money isn't everything, but it sure keeps you in touch with your children.' J. Paul Getty
2. 'The lack of money is the root of all evil.' Mark Twain
3. 'Making money is art and working is art and good business is the best art.' Andy Warhol
4. 'The thing that differentiates man from animals is money.' Gertrude Stein
5. '640,000 dollars ought to be enough for anyone.' Bill Gates
6. 'Money won't create success, the freedom to make it will.' Nelson Mandela
7. 'A business that makes nothing but money is a poor business.' Henry Ford
8. 'The easiest way for your children to learn about money is for you not to have any.' Katherine Whitehorn

Reading (Paper 1 Part 8)

Before you read

1 Imagine going into business with a close friend or member of your family. Would it be easy to work together? What would be the advantages and disadvantages?

Multiple matching

2 You are going to read a magazine article about four married couples who have started their own businesses. Read the strategy on page 169, then do the task.

For questions 1–10, choose from the couples (A–D). The couples may be chosen more than once.

Which couple

mentions how lack of experience may have helped them to get business?	1
says their instant success was not achieved without some setbacks?	2
mentions the advantages and disadvantages of working together?	3
believes in the importance of getting direct customer feedback?	4
tries to run their own business according to the principles it promotes?	5
feels disappointed about how their previous jobs turned out?	6
appreciates the positive effect of the business on their relationship?	7
was inspired to go into business by their own unsatisfactory experiences?	8
makes efficient use of their differing skills and abilities?	9
admits that there is little personal contact between them on a working day?	10

Task analysis

3 What advice would you give an exam candidate doing this task?

Discussion

4 Discuss these questions.
1 Which of the businesses in the text would you find most interesting to be involved in? Why?
2 What personal qualities are necessary if you want to set up a successful business?

EXPERT WORD CHECK

constraint   dodgy   hemp   launch (*v*)   lucrative   plain sailing
practise what you preach   reckless   take the plunge   venture (*n*)

TWO'S COMPANY

We speak to four married couples who have started their own businesses.

A   James and Tamara have a hotel-booking service

James and Tamara started their hotel guides as a hobby. 'It all began with me taking Tamara away for some pretty miserable weekends in some dodgy hotels, thanks to a guidebook that shall remain nameless,' explains James. 'We decided we should write our own.' The couple turned their spare bedroom into an office and worked on the venture in their free time. However, when the first guide was published, it took off immediately, encouraging them to expand into an equally lucrative hotel-booking service. 'It just took on a life of its own, although there were downs as well as ups while we were actually researching and writing the guide. It certainly wasn't all plain sailing,' Tamara says. She describes the tensions of writing to tight deadlines and having their first manuscript turned down. There is a natural split in their areas of expertise: as chief executive, James looks after the overall business and brand while Tamara deals with the technology side of the company, which is not James' strong point. Tamara says her husband is more entrepreneurial. 'James wants to crack on with an idea immediately, whereas I like to think things through.'

B   Kim and Jason co-own three furniture shops

When Kim started going out with Jason, they were both working for the same investment bank but when Jason suggested starting up their own business, selling eco-friendly wooden furniture, Kim saw it as an adventure. 'I'd got rather disillusioned with the world of finance. Helping rich people to get even richer didn't tie in with my values. I wanted to do something which would help the world.' Jason felt much the same, although he now admits it was reckless to give up their jobs at the bank before they had got the business up and running. 'But we had bags of energy and believed in what we were doing, so we just decided to take the plunge.' After they took over a furniture shop which was losing money, sales soon increased by 70 percent, enabling them to take on additional staff and eventually open a further two shops. At one stage, the couple tried having their office at home. 'It didn't go well. Jason is messy and I'm tidy; the plan to just get up and be in your office has quite a high failure rate,' says Kim. Both of them also regularly spend time serving in the shop. 'It's an essential way of getting feedback from the people who buy our products,' explains Kim.

C   Chris and Joanna have a coaching and consultancy company

While Chris and Jo were doing executive training, they were told that many companies were not very good at managing women who left to have children and later returned to work. So they launched Talking Talent, a company that helps organisations attract, retain and maximise the potential of women. 'Since setting it up, we've had three children ourselves. As a working mother, I understand the problems and constraints, and by making it possible for me to still be involved in the company, we like to think we're practising what we preach,' says Jo. But work–life balance can be a double-edged sword. 'We can do things during the working day that we might not otherwise be able to do, such as popping home to have lunch with the children. The challenge is that when there's a lot going on, it's not just one of us feeling stressed, it's both of us,' says Jo. They don't tread on each other's toes. Chris enjoys managing teams and delivering executive coaching, while Jo looks after client relationships and wins new business. Jo says people have the perception that the couple spend all their time together. 'But our business is very client-focused so we'll probably cross paths at work once a week, if that,' she says.

D   Henry and Glynis produce healthy cooking oils

Having worked together in the film industry for much of their married life, Henry and Glynis embarked on a project to bring them back to their farming roots. 'When we started out, we had absolutely no knowledge of the retail business. At first when we talked to potential customers about our products – oils made from hemp seed – nobody understood why we were doing it. We couldn't seem to get it right. But our innocence was probably to our advantage because people seemed to like the idea that here were two people who had stumbled across something and put years of effort into it. Eventually a big supermarket gave our product a try. It just went from there.'

Henry and Glynis don't mind that their office work spills over into their home life. 'Every business decision that's made has to be run past each other so that we both agree. One of the greatest things about us running the company is that there's this mutual goal, and every success seems to make us stronger as a couple,' says Glynis.

Vocabulary: business

Fixed expressions

1 Work in pairs. Discuss these questions.
Give reasons for your views.

1 Do you tend to *leap at* an idea or *think things through* before you make a decision?
2 When you have made a decision, do you like to *crack on* straightaway or are you *more measured*?
3 Do successful business people *stumble across* good ideas or do they have a *clear vision* of the future?
4 How would you avoid *treading on each other's toes* if you worked with your partner?
5 Is working together likely to *strengthen the bonds* between a couple or is it *a recipe for disaster*?
6 Would you be prepared to *take a gamble* in business or would you prefer to *play it safe*?

Collocations

2a Circle the verb in each phrase which does not collocate with the noun.

1 *do / make / go into* business with someone
2 *develop / grow / implement* a business plan
3 *set up / build up / open up* a company
4 *wind down / take up / buy out* a business
5 *take on / run / lay off* staff
6 *achieve / break / win* a contract
7 *raise / generate / make* funds
8 *embark upon / target / break into* a market
9 *do / carry out / see through* market research
10 *do / make / earn* a profit

b Complete the text with verbs from Exercise 2a in the correct form.

After Sarah resigned from her job as a family doctor, she was **(1)____** on by a company which produced expert medical reports. Her husband, Mark, quickly realised how much profit the company was **(2)____** and suggested that Sarah should **(3)____** up her own business. Mark then **(4)____** enough funds to help his wife and **(5)____** a business plan so that they could get a bank loan. He also gave up his job to help and **(6)____** out market research. Unfortunately, the recession meant that work slumped and they had to **(7)____** off staff and eventually **(8)____** down the business altogether.

Compounds

3a Match 1–8 with a–h to make a compound noun or verb connected to business. There may be more than one possibility.

1	take	a	line
2	share	b	load
3	net	c	up
4	work	d	turn
5	feed	e	holder
6	turn	f	work
7	dead	g	back
8	down	h	over

b Which part of the compound word is stressed in each case?

c Work with a partner to make a few sentences using the compound words from Exercise 3a.

Prepositions

4 Complete the sentences with *down, on, in* or *of*.

1 He's away ____ business at the moment.
2 OK, it's late. Let's get ____ to business.
3 To stay ____ business, you have to work very hard.
4 It's none ____ your business how old I am.
5 We embarked ____ a new project together.
6 We put our success ____ to hard work.

5a Work in groups to think of an idea for a business (e.g. a new drink, restaurant, shop). Use some of the vocabulary from Exercises 1–4. Decide:

• what the business will be
• how many staff you will need
• how you will raise funds to set it up
• what the target market will be
• what your own role will be
• whether you will work from home or have special premises
• how you will advertise it
• the name and logo.

b Present your idea to the class.

c Vote on who has the best idea.

Use of English 1 (Paper 1 Part 3)

Lead-in **1** How much do you know about Amazon.com?

    1 What does it sell?

    2 When was it set up?

Word formation **2a** Read the text and see if your answers were correct.

    b Read the strategy on page 167, then do the task.

*For questions **1–8**, read the text below. Use the word given in capitals at the end of some of the lines to form a word that fits in the gap **in the same line**. There is an example at the beginning **(0)**.*

Amazon.com: a success story of our time

Amazon.com was **(0)** *originally* founded by Jeff Bezos in 1994 as an online bookstore. One of Amazon's ideas was to give customers the **(1)____** of writing a review of any books they bought. These product reviews helped to build trust and **(2)____** amongst customers, who appreciated the opportunity to get honest opinions from other people, some of whom would write reviews every week. It was a simple yet **(3)____** popular idea. Amazon's business plan was unusual in that the company didn't anticipate being **(4)____** for several years. However, when a businessman invested $100,000 in the company, Bezos was able to upgrade his website and **(5)____** hosting opportunities, which was attractive to customers. Other items, such as movies and CDs, were soon added to the **(6)____** of goods available to buyers, although Amazon stayed close to its roots and continued to **(7)____** in books.	ORIGIN OPT LOYAL EXPECT PROFIT FACILITY SELECT SPECIAL
In 1999, Bezos was named the Person of the Year by *Time* magazine in **(8)____** of his success in promoting online shopping.	RECOGNISE

Task analysis **3** Look at the words in Exercise 2b.

Find two words in which the stress changes when it becomes a different part of speech.

Discussion **4** What are the pros and cons of online shopping?

- Which things are best bought online?
- Which things would you never buy online?
- Which is your favourite online retailer? Give reasons.

Listening 1 (Paper 3 Part 3)

Before you listen

1 Why do people do yoga? What kind of people do you associate with the activity?

2 Read questions 1–6 and guess what the answers might be. Read the strategy on page 171, then do the task.

Multiple choice

3 🎧 54 You will hear an interview with an ex-businessman called Jason Clarke, who works as a yoga instructor and consultant. For questions **1–6**, choose the answer (**A**, **B**, **C** or **D**) which fits best according to what you hear.

1 Jason was originally attracted to the idea of taking up yoga because he was
   A hopeful that it might help solve a physical problem he had.
   B keen to find a less strenuous leisure activity.
   C curious to investigate the reason for its popularity.
   D interested in whether it would relieve symptoms of stress.

2 Jason decided to start teaching yoga because he felt it would
   A be a financially profitable area to go into.
   B enable him to make a difference to people's lives.
   C give him the excuse to spend more time on it.
   D provide an opportunity for him to travel widely.

3 What inspired Jason to set up a yoga consultancy for businesses?
   A ideas he heard connected to eastern philosophies
   B his respect for the writings of high-profile practitioners
   C his experience of witnessing yoga in action in the workplace
   D advice from health care professionals in various parts of the world

4 What advantages do company managers get from introducing the workforce to yoga?
   A It encourages workers to maximise their potential.
   B It attracts prospective members of staff.
   C It reduces the amount of sick leave taken.
   D It requires employees to increase their working hours.

5 Jason says that some business people fail to benefit from yoga because
   A they're not prepared to spend enough time on classes.
   B they don't come to class in the right frame of mind.
   C they regard paying for classes as a waste of money.
   D they prefer to address issues on a conscious level.

6 Jason thinks the main reason for combining the principles of yoga with business is to
   A increase productivity by developing the techniques of relaxation.
   B highlight that kindness to others is equally as important as personal gain.
   C make people aware of the potential dangers of materialism.
   D find the balance between ancient beliefs and modern management techniques.

Task analysis

4 Which strategy has helped you most in doing this part of the listening paper?

Discussion

5 Which activities do you do when you want to unwind?

EXPERT WORD CHECK

associate (v)   burnt out   get hooked   hunched   low-key
mutually exclusive   oblivious   philanthropic   rolled out
sceptical

Language development 1

Emphasis using negative introductory expressions

➤ EXPERT GRAMMAR page 184

1a Compare the sentences. Which is the most emphatic in each pair? How has the emphasis been created?

1 a Friends swore that yoga had reduced their back pain and helped them cope with the pressure at work.
   b Friends swore that not only had yoga reduced their back pain, but it had also helped them cope with the pressure at work.

2 a I only seriously considered trying to do the same in the UK when I saw what was happening in the States.
   b Not until I saw what was happening the States did I seriously consider trying to do the same in the UK.

3 a It doesn't say anywhere in yoga teachings you can't have wealth.
   b Nowhere in yoga teachings does it say you can't have wealth.

b Look at Expert grammar on page 184 to find other ways of making sentences more emphatic. Then complete the second sentence so that it means the same as the first sentence, making any necessary changes.

1 We will not lay off any more staff, on any account.
   On no account _____ .
2 The bank will not extend the loan under any circumstances.
   Under no circumstances _____ .
3 I haven't worked so many hours since I did my finals at university.
   Not since _____ .
4 You don't often meet people who have such a clear vision of what they want to do.
   Rarely _____ .
5 The business had just been set up when the impact of the recession was felt.
   Hardly _____ .
6 They are only now beginning to make a profit from the company.
   Only now _____ .

2 Complete the text using only one word in each gap.

◉ Browsing blogs

My first business idea came about when I was about eight. All my friends were mad about water bombs, so not **(1)____** did I promise to sell one to most of the school, **(2)____** I made a huge profit because I found a wholesale supplier and didn't have any overheads.

No **(3)____** had I sold all the water bombs than I increased my product range to include fireworks. Then we grew up and nobody wanted my stuff anymore.

As soon as I left school, I went into property. **(4)____** no circumstances was I prepared to do a job unless I was making a lot of money. I've sacrificed relationships for my work but **(5)____** no account would I be where I am today if I'd put them first. I'm very competitive, but only now **(6)____** I realise how unusual I am and wonder how long I will continue to have this kind of energy.

Emphasis through fronting parts of the sentence

3 It is possible to move parts of a sentence or clause to the front of the sentence
   • for emphasis
   • to provide a clear link with what came before.

a Look at these sentences and decide which part has been emphasised. Re-express them without the emphasis, making any necessary changes.
   Example:
   The door opened and out they came.
   The door opened and they came out.

1 'He's going to resign.' 'That I find hard to believe.'
2 Difficult it may be but impossible it isn't.
3 The restaurant serves excellent lunches. Even better are their dinners.
4 Such has been the response to the competition that we have extended the deadline.
5 Try as we might, we'll never be able to match that achievement.
6 Just when we were losing hope, along came the train.

b Rewrite these sentences to make them more emphatic.

1 The atmosphere was so tense that tempers flared.
2 They tried hard. However, they were unable to get a loan.
3 We rented new premises. There was a park opposite.
4 There was a pause and the actor walked into the room.
5 The impact of the crash was such that the car was not worth repairing.
6 It may be famous but it's very expensive too.

c Work in pairs to complete these sentences about your own lives.

1 Down came the snow, ____ .
2 Try as I might, I ____ .
3 Not since ____ have I ____ .
4 Not only have I ____ , but ____ .
5 Even better than ____ are ____ .
6 Under no circumstances ____ .

Writing 1 Using a range of language

1a Read two versions of an opening paragraph. They are from descriptions of a successful restaurant which was set up by a French businessman.

1 Why is the restaurant unusual?
2 Which opening paragraph do you prefer, and why?

A Does the idea of dining in total, absolute darkness tempt you? Would you like to be served by blind or visually impaired waiters and be left in the dark about what you are eating too? If so, *Dans le Noir* will be right up your street! The first (wildly successful) restaurant opened in Paris but branches are now popping up all over the world. I went to one as part of my research into unusual business ventures.

B If you like the idea of dining in darkness, served by blind or partially sighted waiters, then go to *Dans le Noir*. This successful restaurant first opened in Paris but has now got branches all over the world. I went to one as part of my research into unusual business ventures.

b Read the rest of the description and match the words or expressions in *italics* to a–o.

(1) *Tucked away* down a side street, yet (2) *only a stone's throw* from the fashionable (3) *heart* of the city, the restaurant looks fairly (4) *nondescript* from the outside. It is a shock to the system to (5) *stumble* into the pitch-black dining area, but don't worry – blind waiters are (6) *on hand* to guide you! It is also a fascinating concept to sit in the darkness and try to (7) *establish the whereabouts of* the cutlery, glasses and plates, (8) *not to mention* the people you are with and other diners! Be prepared to (9) *fumble about*, drop things and spill your drinks, to the accompaniment of (10) *good-natured* laughter. Having to guess the composition of each forkful of food is really (11) *intriguing*. In the absence of sight, your other senses are offered (12) *a wealth of* new sensations.

For the 'pleasure' of the experience, the bill came to an incredibly (13) *steep* 45 euros per head and the portions were not large (14) *by any stretch of the imagination*. The food, which has been described as 'innovative', is actually (15) *mediocre*. Is it worth trying once for the experience? Maybe. But I won't be doing it again!

a	walk unsteadily	i	at all
b	unusual and interesting	j	situated in a quiet place
c	centre		
d	expensive	k	not far away from
e	friendly	l	find
f	ordinary	m	not very good
g	a great many	n	handle awkwardly
h	close by and ready	o	as well as

c Find examples of some of these techniques for descriptive writing in the text.

1 specific, rather than general words
2 intensifying adverbs
3 short sentences for effect
4 a range of simple and complex structures
5 direct or indirect speech
6 punctuation devices
7 rhetorical questions
8 giving a personal view

EXPERT STRATEGY

In certain types of writing you need to use techniques to capture the reader's interest. For example:
• a catchy title if appropriate (in reviews, articles, etc.)
• an engaging opening paragraph
• a range of interesting language.

2 Look at the notes below and replace the words and expressions in *italics*. Use the words and phrases from the box or any others you can think of.

charming ambience   cramped   deafening
exorbitantly priced   insubstantial   nibbled
offhand   quirky   packed out

1 The already *small* restaurant *was overcrowded*.
2 I just *took very very small bites of* the food.
3 The décor was certainly very *unusual*.
4 The waiters were *unfriendly*.
5 The restaurant had a *lovely feel*.
6 The food was *expensive*.
7 The music was *very loud*.
8 The portions were *too small*.

3 Work in pairs.

1 Think of an innovative idea for a restaurant or of a restaurant which you have loved or hated. Make notes.
2 Write a paragraph for a travel website, using a range of language. Use the techniques in Exercise 1c and some of the language from Exercises 1b and 2.
3 Exchange your descriptions with other pairs.

8B A means to an end?

Listening 2 (Paper 3 Part 1)

Discussion

1 Discuss these questions.

1 What different ways are there of becoming rich?
2 Which of the people in the pictures most deserves their wealth? Why?

2 Read Exercise 3. What are you going to hear about?

Multiple choice: short extracts

3 🎧 55 Read the strategy on page 170, then do the task.

You will hear three different extracts. For questions 1–6, choose the answer (A, B or C) which fits best according to what you hear. There are two questions for each extract.

Extract One
You hear part of an interview with a rich man who disposed of all his possessions.

1 Why did he choose to do it?
   A He was unsuited to a wealthy lifestyle.
   B He had never been interested in worldly goods.
   C He wanted to use the money to help his family.

2 He decided to set up a charity because he wanted
   A to protect what was left of his money.
   B to provide handouts for the poor.
   C to help poor people to make a profit.

Extract Two
You hear two people comparing their experiences of inheriting large sums of money.

3 They both found that as a result of their inheritance
   A they wanted to become politically active.
   B they had to pretend they weren't well-off.
   C they had little sense of purpose in life.

4 What does the man think about leaving money to his children?
   A It will all depend on what kind of people they turn out to be.
   B Even a little might make them unambitious.
   C A modest amount will give them a good start in life.

Extract Three
You hear a woman telling a colleague about her lottery win.

5 She regrets it because
   A she became obsessed with money.
   B it damaged the relationship with her friends.
   C her life was turned upside down.

6 What has she learnt from winning the lottery?
   A to feel contempt for money
   B to value a simple life
   C to expect little from life

EXPERT WORD CHECK
basics   come into (a fortune)
cost the earth   despise
handle (v)   inundate   so-called
transform   trust fund
work ethic

Task analysis

4 Compare and discuss your answers. What should a candidate be careful of when doing this task?

Discussion

5 Which of the speakers do you agree/disagree with? Would you have done the same in their position? Give reasons.

What might the people find challenging about each of these situations?

Speaking (Paper 4 Part 2)

Vocabulary: spending, investing and giving

1 a Look at the photos. In which of these situations might you: *haggle, dip into your savings, buy stocks and shares, beat someone down, pay in full*?

b What do these expressions mean?
1 *have money to burn*
2 *scrape by*
3 *live beyond your means*
4 *put your money where your mouth is*

c Are you a *spendthrift* or a *saver*? Do you buy *on impulse* or *shop around*? Do you often *go window shopping* or *go on a shopping spree*? Compare ideas with a partner and give examples.

2 a Circle the correct words to complete the text.

Even people who struggle to (1) *make ends meet / live beyond their means* during (2) *crisis / hard* times are quite happy to (3) *chip / cut* in and (4) *carry / support* a good cause by (5) *contributing / granting* a regular (6) *sum / total* each month to their favourite charity. Charity (7) *savings / funding* dropped for a few years after damaging stories appeared about their management. Private (8) *subscribers / donors* didn't like the idea of (9) *pitching in / dipping into* their pockets when charity bosses were earning very high salaries and too much money was being spent (10) *in / on* administration. But recently the charitable sector has regained trust, and many people are happy to (11) *raise / make* money for them, for example, by asking friends and local organisations to (12) *sponsor / subsidise* them in a fun run or a marathon.

b Underline the stress on these words.

contribute/contribution   subscribe/subscription   luxury/luxurious
subsidise/subsidy

c How necessary are charities in the modern world? What are the best ways of helping them, do you think?

What might they have to do to deal with the situations differently?

C

Sample answer

3a What does the interlocutor ask you to do in Part 2 of the Speaking test? Find five mistakes in these instructions.

'In this part of the test, I'm going to give you three pictures. I'd like you to describe each one in detail for about two minutes. It doesn't matter if you stop – if you run out of things to say just describe, don't speculate. Your partner might interrupt you if they have something to say but they will need to listen to you because they are asked a short question at the end. You will need to produce a wide range of language.'

b 🎧 56 Listen to these extracts from Part 2. What are the strengths and weaknesses of each candidate's answer?

Long turn

4a Work in pairs. Take it in turns to do the task. Use a different combination of photos. The person who is not doing the task should time the other one.

b Look at all three photos again and decide together who might be the happiest at the end of the transaction.

c Look at the photos on page 206 and take it in turns to do the task.

Task analysis

5 Review each other's performance based on your conclusions in Exercise 3b.

Discussion

6 Discuss these questions.

1 Have you ever been in similar situations to those in the photos? How did you feel? If not, how *might* you feel?
2 Would you be happier spending, investing or giving money to others? Give reasons.

Language development 2

Comparatives and superlatives

> EXPERT GRAMMAR p.185

1a Read the text and correct the six mistakes.

Each year the United Nations spends $202 million on the protection of human rights, which is much the same than Australians spend on their Easter eggs and far less than Europeans spend on their pets. It is also nowhere near the combined income of the top twenty celebrities under 30 ($690 million). Last year, one of the best paid star was the footballer Cristiano Ronaldo, who became a great deal rich after he signed some big sponsorship deals totalling $38 million, and the tennis player Roger Federer, already wealthy, who became even more prosperous after earnings totalling $47 million. However, the income of the sports stars was nothing as Lady Gaga's, which was a staggering $90 million. And think too of what some people spend on clothes. Although by far the less expensive shoes ever bought cost $3 million, this is considerably fewer than the £12 million spent on a wedding dress with 150 carats of diamonds! Have we got our priorities right?

b Find examples of the following:

1 comparative structures (Does it express a higher, lower or the same degree?)
2 superlative structures
3 a word/phrase that modifies a comparison

c What do you spend your money on? How does it compare with three years ago? What things are more expensive/cheaper? Match words from columns A and B to make sentences.

Examples: *I spend a great deal more on petrol.*
Meat is considerably more expensive than it used to be.

A	B
	like as (much/expensive)
a lot	of the (most expensive/
far/considerably	cheapest)
nowhere	near as (much/cheap)
nothing	deal (more/cheaper)
by	as (cheap/expensive) as
just	(more/cheaper)
one	far (the most expensive/
somewhat/slightly	cheapest)
(not) nearly as	same (as)
a great	less (money/expensive)
much the	about (the cheapest/
	most expensive)
	(most/the most
	expensive)

I spend (Food) is

d Compare life in your town now with how it was a generation ago. If you don't know, guess! You could talk about people's earnings, their standard of living, what they spend their money on, how they dress, what there is to do or anything else that interests you. Give reasons for any possible changes.

Example: *My neighbourhood is far livelier than it was ten years ago. That's because …*

Other ways of making comparisons

2a Circle the correct words to complete the sentences.

1 Some people say they are much *too / so* busy to check their bank statements.
2 It isn't *such a / a such* bad idea to check your balance online.
3 Making ends meet is getting *more and more / the more* difficult.
4 *The least / Least / The fewer / Fewer* shops you go into *better / the better* if you want to avoid temptation.
5 I think he's *tighter / more tight* than careful with money.
6 This is not *as / so much / such* dangerous *that / as / than* it is frightening.
7 Some people work *like / as* slaves all their life and end up *like / as* beggars on the street.
8 *Bigger / The bigger* the banks got, *less / the less* socially responsible they became.
9 I *prefer / 'd sooner / rather* keep my money under the mattress *that / than / as* put it in a bank.
10 It's *a great deal / hardly any* easier said *than / as* done.

b Rewrite the following sentences using the expressions in brackets.

1 As people worry more about banks, they increasingly use cash. (*the more*)
2 I'm not getting as good a rate of interest at this bank. (*such*)
3 Banking is increasingly being done online. (*more and more*)
4 Some people no longer bank online because of their fear of fraud. (*too afraid*)
5 I am more relieved than happy that I got my money back. (*not so much*)
6 I think that I'd prefer to use smart cards everywhere than carry cash. (*sooner*)

3 Work with a partner and compare two people: your two best friends; two members of your family; your two favourite artists (musicians/ singers, actors, writers, etc.). Use expressions from Exercises 1 and 2.

Use of English 2 (Paper 1 Part 4)

Key word transformations

1a Look at the example and correct the answer.

0 You'll never make such an important investment in your life as this one.
FAR
This investment _is the far most important_ that you'll ever make in your life.

b Read the strategy on page 168, then do the task.

Complete the second sentence so that it has a similar meaning to the first sentence, using the word given. **Do not change the word given.** *You must use between* **three** *and* **six** *words, including the word given.*

1 As she examined her accounts, Lucy became increasingly concerned.
THROUGH
The longer Lucy spent looking ____ she became.

2 Designer clothes haven't sold quite as well this year as last year.
SLIGHTLY
This year's designer clothes ____ they did last year.

3 Keiran and I both had the same salaries last year.
MUCH
Keiran earned ____ last year.

4 Steve had expected his credit card bill to be much higher.
NEAR
Steve's credit card bill was nowhere ____ he had expected.

5 I'm sure that we are much happier when we work hard.
HARDER
There's no doubt in my mind that ____ we are.

6 In my previous job, I couldn't save anywhere near as much as I do in my current job.
DEAL
In my current job I am able ____ than I did in my previous job.

Task analysis

2a Answer these questions.

1 What comparative structure can you use to suggest *increasingly*?
2 Which of the expressions are used to express
   a a small degree?   b a large degree?

b You are going to give advice to a candidate new to Key word transformations in Cambridge *Advanced*. What can you say under these headings?

1 the types of items tested
2 the number of changes necessary
3 what you can put in the gap
4 contracted words

Writing 2 Review (Paper 2 Part 2)

Lead-in

1 Discuss these questions.

1 How often do you read reviews of books, TV programmes, films, music albums, etc.? Where do you read them? If you don't read reviews, whose opinion do you listen to when choosing what to watch, read or listen to?

2 Does reading a review ever influence your decision to buy a book, film, etc.? Why/Why not?

3 Have you ever posted your own review of something on a website? Give reasons.

Understand the task

2 Read and analyse the task below. What are the main questions you need to ask yourself before you start the task? (e.g. *Who am I writing the review for?*) What are the answers?

You have bought a book after reading some reviews on an internet shopping site. You decide to write your own review of the book to post on the website. In your review, you should:
- *briefly explain what the book was about*
- *explain whether or not you enjoyed it and why*
- *give reasons for whether or not you would recommend it to other readers.*

Write your review.

Plan your review

3a Decide on a book you will review. Will it be fiction (e.g. novel/book of short stories), a biography (e.g. musician/sportsperson) or non-fiction (e.g. about wildlife/'how-to')? What kind of things will you say about it?

b Make a plan for your review. Will you talk about the style? Will you compare the book to any other books? If it's about a work of fiction, will you mention the plot and the characters? Decide how many paragraphs you will need.

c What will you include in each paragraph? Work with a partner and make some notes.

Language and content

4a Read these review extracts. Match each extract with a part of the task required in Exercise 2 above. (Read the sentence beginning: *In your review you should …*)

Today's Book Reviews

1 ***How I lived on just a pound a day*** *Kath Kelly*

As someone who has a wardrobe bulging with clothes I never wear and a fridge full of out-of-date food, I found *How to Live a Year on Just a Pound a Day* inspiring and informative, with some great ideas for anyone looking to save a little money or do something 'green'. The tone of the book is upbeat and heartwarming, which makes it absorbing and highly readable. The writer's style is modest and engaging, although I found it a bit patronising at times. The main message is that living on a pound a day is time-consuming and entails a lot of hard work even if your rent and utility bills are pre-paid, as hers were.

2 ***Low-cost living: Live better, spend less*** *John Harrison*

So all in all, *Low-cost Living: Live Better, Spend Less* is an absolute must for anyone on a low budget. I love the hints and tips for doing things the old-fashioned way, from growing your own vegetables to baking your own bread. If you want to save energy and save on your bills at the same time, this is the book for you.

3 ***Not buying it – a year without shopping*** *Judith Levine*

It's time we got over our obsession with shopping. That's the message of *Not Buying It*, one of several books in recent years which encourage us to spend and consume less for both personal and environmental reasons. *Not Buying It* is about one New Yorker's attempt to call a halt to her spending for a year, with the exception of a few basic food stuffs (but no processed food), medicine and toiletries. This means doing without new clothes, buying music or going to the cinema. The book tracks her ups and downs as she and her partner pursue their careers. On the way, she asks the big questions like, 'Can the economy survive without shopping?' At the end of the year she saved up enough money to pay off a huge credit card bill and she claims her spending will never be the same again.

b Underline expressions which:
  1 indicate that the book fits into a genre
  2 indicate that the reviewer is explaining what it is about
  3 praise the book
  4 qualify the reviewer's praise
  5 recommend the book

c These are some words and phrases which can be used to make evaluations in a review. Decide which are positive and which are negative and write them in the appropriate column below.

(a bit) repetitive	(rather) flat
(entirely) predictable	a gripping (read)
(quite) witty	couldn't put it down
(truly) original	well worth reading
(really) lively	hard to follow
(excruciatingly) boring	(vastly) overrated
(totally) unconvincing	(particularly) memorable
thought-provoking	(thoroughly) implausible
(profoundly) moving	(too) far-fetched
(thoroughly) tedious	(absolutely) hilarious
(refreshingly) different	compelling
(beautifully) written	

POSITIVE | NEGATIVE

d Which of the phrases in the box could you use in your review? Match them to the sentence parts below.

(get) bogged down
the great strength
(give) the background
the ideas confusing
action-packed
(be) a bit of a letdown
my only criticism
(set) the scene
slow-moving
the best read
(recommend/not recommend) this book to anyone who
writer (go off) at a tangent
spine-chilling
(explain) the rationale
(move) at a brisk pace
(summarise) the main points
the ideas challenge the reader to think about
the characterisation (be) impressive/weak

Describing
The opening chapters ... The last chapter ...
The story ...

Balancing an opinion
I found ... , but .../However, ...
Although ...
Even so, ...
Despite this/In spite of this/And yet ...
On the other hand, ...

Summarising
All in all .../Quite simply ... (this is ...)
... of (the book) is that ...

Write your review

5 Now write your review in 220–260 words, using some of the ideas and language above.

Check your answer

6 Edit your work using the checklist on page 190.

Review

1 Choose the correct word or phrase to complete the sentences.

1 I have to do two jobs to make __ meet.
A things   B ends   C money   D costs

2 The government is targetting a 50 percent __ of digital radio over the next two years.
A network   B downturn   C deadline
D takeup

3 William is hard up right now, so let's __ and help him out.
A chip in   B scrape by   C dip in   D bring out

4 The company is __ its operations in the Far East and relocating.
A beating down   B pitching in   C winding up
D living beyond

5 I suggest you think things __ before you give away so much money!
A up   B through   C back   D about

6 European officials are __ with the government over the latest bailout.
A haggling   B supporting   C advancing
D implementing

7 You pay the __ monthly and they'll send you the magazine.
A subsidy   B handout   C subscription
D sponsorship

8 I'm going to put my __ where my mouth is and not buy any new clothes.
A money   B idea   C wallet   D words

2 Complete the second sentence so that it has a similar meaning to the first.

1 The tablet had only just gone on sale when another company brought out an even better model.
Hardly _____ .

2 As I think about the problem more, I become more worried about it.
The more _____ .

3 It's a bad idea to disclose your business plan to anyone at this stage.
On no account _____ .

4 The decision wasn't as easy as I thought it would be.
It wasn't such _____ .

5 We were so exhausted we couldn't move.
We were too _____ .

6 No English writer has written so well about the poor since Charles Dickens.
Not since _____ .

7 James' brother isn't quite as tall as James.
James is slightly _____ .

8 Liam gives far more to charity than I do.
I give nowhere _____ .

9 This ring isn't as pricey as the other one.
The other ring is somewhat _____ .

10 I'm more depressed than angry about losing my wallet.
I'm not so much _____ .

3 Complete the sentences with a suitable form of the word in CAPITALS.

1 The singer grew up in a pretty rough ____ . NEIGHBOUR

2 His elegant and very ____ hotel is a favourite haunt of film stars. LUXURY

3 My main areas of ____ include macro-economics and regional development. SPECIAL

4 There is a widespread ____ that the whole business is corrupt. PERCEIVE

5 Some very ____ organisations have become active in our country. PHILANTHROPY

6 People's ____ over Europe has increased in recent years. SCEPTIC

7 Rachel was accused of ____ by her boss. LOYAL

8 Discussing problems openly can often ____ a couple's relationship. STRONG

4 Complete the text with one word in each gap.

Jay-Z, **(1)**____ he calls himself, is a popular freestyle rapper, but when he started out, **(2)**____ as he might, he couldn't get a contract with a major record company. Once a high school dropout and street hustler, he decided that the only way forward was to go **(3)**____ business and set **(4)**____ his own record label. After great success, more **(5)**____ he had ever believed possible, he **(6)**____ another huge gamble and created his own clothing brand. In 2007, he became a great **(7)**____ richer when the company had an annual turnover **(8)**____ over $700 million in retail sales alone. After that, he embarked **(9)**____ other business ventures **(10)**____ as an entertainment company and a sports agency. Jay-Z claims that if you want to stay **(11)**____ business, the recipe **(12)**____ success is simple: it's all **(13)**____ to determination, focus and being prepared to work **(14)**____ a horse. Not **(15)**____ has Jay-Z achieved huge success **(16)**____ an artist and businessman, **(17)**____ in 2008 he married Beyoncé Knowles and they became America's richest celebrity couple.

9 The world of science

Overview

9A
> **Reading and Use of English:** Gapped text (Part 7); Word formation (Part 3)
> **Vocabulary:** Expressions connected to space; Ways of seeing; Word formation: science; Idioms with *like*
> **Listening:** Sentence completion (Part 2)
> **Language development:** Reported speech: Patterns after reporting verbs; Impersonal report structures
> **Writing:** Sentence skills: Accuracy

9B
> **Listening:** Multiple choice (Part 3)
> **Speaking:** Vocabulary: The mind; Collaborative task (Part 3)
> **Language development:** Nouns, adjectives, verbs + prepositions; Preposition + *-ing* verb; Confusing pairs
> **Reading and Use of English:** Cross-text multiple matching (Part 6)
> **Writing:** Essay (Part 1)

Lead-in

1a Ask each other these questions.

SCIENCE QUIZ

1 Which planet is the nearest to Earth? Ⓐ Venus Ⓑ Mars Ⓒ Mercury
2 How many years old is Earth? Ⓐ 3.5 million Ⓑ 4.6 billion Ⓒ 10 billion
3 When did man first land on the Moon? Ⓐ 1962 Ⓑ 1965 Ⓒ 1969
4 How much does the average human brain weigh? Ⓐ 1.5 kg Ⓑ 2.2 kg Ⓒ 3 kg
5 Where was radium discovered? Ⓐ China Ⓑ Italy Ⓒ France
6 In which century was the printing press invented?
    Ⓐ the fourteenth Ⓑ the fifteenth Ⓒ the sixteenth
7 What did Marconi invent? Ⓐ the radio Ⓑ the telephone Ⓒ the television
8 How many planets orbit the Sun? Ⓐ seven Ⓑ eight Ⓒ ten

b Check your answers on page 206.

2 Discuss these questions.
   1 Is it better to study an arts or science subject at university? Why?
   2 What do you think are the main dangers of current scientific advances?
   3 Who is the most famous scientist in your country? What is he/she famous for?

135

Reading (Paper 1 Part 7)

Before you read

1 Read the title and introduction to the article. How would you feel about being part of this crew? What challenges would there be? (Think about the effects of the lack of gravity, the absence of normal nights and days, etc.)

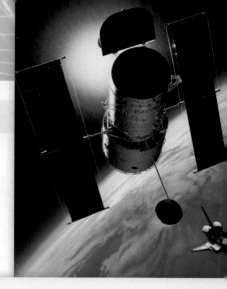

The men and women hurtling around the planet

The first crew entered the International Space Station in 2000. What is it like to be aboard a big tin can travelling at 17,500 mph?

Few people will have noticed a small bright light which appears low in the night sky from time to time before vanishing into the darkness. However, for a handful of people, that dot on the horizon is a place called home. What looks like a wandering star is sunlight reflecting off the International Space Station, 220 miles above Earth.

1

Only a couple of hundred people have first-hand knowledge of life on the largest orbiting spacecraft ever built and only a fraction have stayed more than six months. The longer the stint, the closer these veterans come to perfecting the art of life in freefall. The footage of floating astronauts chasing food through the air makes it seem as if the space station is free from the pull of gravity.

2

Getting to the space station takes two days, flying at more than 30 times the altitude of a cruising jumbo jet and at a breakneck 17,500 mph. The shuttle approaches from below and performs a graceful backwards roll as it approaches. The docking procedure is as slow and cautious as you might expect, given the price tags on the spacecraft (£1.1bn for a shuttle and around £64bn for the space station). Once they are locked together it takes half an hour or so to equalise the pressure and finally open the hatches that separate the crews.

3

That said, even the most welcome visitors can cause chaos if they are inexperienced. There is a subtle art to moving around without crashing into anything (or anyone) or knocking computers, equipment and other objects off the walls, to which they are attached with Velcro pads. One shuttle pilot confesses to leaving a trail of laptops behind him the first time he tried to fly from one room to another. 'You are like a bull in a china shop at first,' he said.

4

In such close quarters, personal hygiene is a must but the weightless environment makes washing difficult. Living in such conditions also does strange things to the body. Body fluids move up to the head, leaving astronauts with thin, weak-looking legs and swollen faces, which has the happy side-effect of erasing wrinkles and making space station crews look years younger, if only temporarily.

5

It takes the space station one and a half hours to fly around the planet, making for 16 complete laps every day. As a result, although the visual effect is spectacular, the continual assault of daylight and darkness would play havoc with astronauts' body clocks. To avoid this, a shutters-down schedule is imposed by mission controllers.

6

'Short visits to the space station are hectic but easier to cope with psychologically than longer ones. If you are there for a week or two, you are basically on a high the whole time,' says a Belgian astronaut. 'It's not the same when you are there for six months. You need to manage your mood and motivation. What you really miss is the contact with your family and friends.'

EXPERT WORD CHECK

altitude   assault (*n*)   hatch (*n*)   hurtle   hygiene   orbit (*v*)
play havoc with   speck   subtle   veteran

Gapped text

2 Complete the task below.

*You are going to read a newspaper article about life on the International Space Station. Six paragraphs have been removed from the extract. Choose from the paragraphs **A–G** the one which fits each gap (**1–6**). There is one extra paragraph which you do not need to use.*

A In time, people can perfect the skill and glide down the length of the station, straight as an arrow, without touching anything except with their fingertips. People sit next to each other in mid-air, tapping at computers, with only a toe hooked under a wall strap to anchor themselves.

B From down here there is little more to see, but close up the speck takes on a more complex form: a shiny hulk of interconnecting tubes, metal frames and giant wing-like panels. As roomy as a five-bedroomed house, these are the most extreme living quarters ever built.

C Each of the crew has a cupboard-like cabin where they can hook a bag to the wall and snuggle down into it. Unsurprisingly, this arrangement can take some getting used to. Just as you are nodding off, you can feel as though you've fallen off a building.

D 'You see these pale faces on the other side and they're always excited to see you,' says astronaut Piers Sellers. The space station has a permanent crew of six so a new arrival is a cause for celebration.

E However, for the exceptional views, you need to step outside. Space walkers see whole continents, mountain ranges, cities and ships crossing oceans. Though you're hurtling through space, the senses are rarely aware of the speed.

F In fact, nothing could be further from the truth. The orbiting outpost is forever falling to Earth and would crash-land were it not moving so fast as to maintain a gentle curve around the planet. In orbit, things are weightless simply because they are all falling at the same speed.

G On the downside, many astronauts lose their sense of smell and taste. 'All our meals taste like cardboard,' says one astronaut. With no gravity exerting itself on the body, both bones and muscles begin to waste and, on long stays, crews try to spend at least two hours a day exercising.

Task analysis

3a Work with a partner. In your opinion, what is the 'best order' to do the following?

- Underline pronouns, etc. to help you make links between paragraphs.
- Predict what kind of information would fit in each gap.
- Check that the 'distractor paragraph' does not fit into any of the gaps.
- Read the base text quickly first to get an idea of the general meaning.
- Check that the text makes sense with your chosen options in the gaps.

b In which way(s) could you do the task more effectively next time?

Discussion

4 In a recent cosmology journal, more than 1,000 people said they would be willing to go on a one-way journey to Mars, with no guarantee of returning. Discuss these questions.

1 Would you be willing to spend thousands of pounds on a return shuttle trip into space?
2 Why do we explore space: for practical or other reasons? Is it a good thing?
3 How dependent are we on space exploration for things such as GPS navigation?
4 What would be the consequences for civilisation if we discovered life on other planets?

Vocabulary

Expressions connected to space

1a Read the sentences and match the phrases in *italics* with the definitions a–f.

1 *Many moons* ago, when I was young, I used to be a dancer.
2 I only ever go to a restaurant *once in a blue moon*, when I'm celebrating.
3 Sorry I forgot – I've just got back from South America and still feel *spaced out*.
4 She doesn't seem to worry about money. It's as if she is *living on another planet*.
5 Come on, concentrate. I'm sure we can do it – it's not *rocket science*.
6 Prices of oil are sure to *rocket* if there is unrest in the area.

a a long time
b very complicated to understand
c very rarely
d go up very quickly
e different from the rest of us
f unaware of what is going on

b Discuss these questions.

1 In what situations do you feel *spaced out*?
2 When do prices *rocket*?
3 What do you only do *once in a blue moon*?
4 What did you use to do *many moons ago* that you don't do anymore?
5 Do you know anyone who acts as if they *live on another planet*?

Ways of seeing

2 Choose the correct word to complete the sentences.

1 I took a close __ at the night sky.
  A glance B look C view D glimpse
2 I sat for a while __ the scenery from the space station.
  A scanning B regarding C observing D spotting
3 I know the rest of the crew by __ .
  A view B sight C vision D look
4 I didn't __ him until he spoke to me.
  A witness B regard C notice D watch
5 You get an excellent __ of the Earth from here.
  A sight B glance C oversight D view
6 Space walkers only manage to __ whole continents as they rush by.
  A note B glimpse C gaze at D look at

Word formation: science

3a Complete the table below and underline the stress on each word.

job	science	adjective
1 chemist	____	____
2 ____	physics	____
3 zoologist		____
4 ____	genetics	____
5 engineer	____	✗
6 astronomer	____	____

b Write the verb, noun or adjective related to these words. Underline the stress on each word, noticing how it sometimes changes according to the part of speech.

verb	noun	adjective
1 discover	____	✗
2 invent	____	____
3 ____	analysis	____
4 explore	____	____
5 ✗	atmosphere	____
6 experiment	____	____

c Discuss these questions.

1 Which science subjects have you studied/would you like to study? (e.g. sociology, biology)
2 What kind of careers in the sciences would you find interesting?
3 Which careers are the most important in the 21st century?

Idioms with *like*

4a Match 1–6 with a–f to make sentences.

1 The pilot flew around the space station *like a bull*
2 At the party I felt *like a fish*
3 What Tom said to me was *like a red rag*
4 When he argues, Conor is *like a dog*
5 They look exactly the same – *like two peas*
6 I told them off but it was *like water*

a off a duck's back.
b in a pod.
c with a bone.
d out of water.
e in a china shop.
f to a bull.

b Substitute the words in *italics* with an idiom from Exercise 4a, then ask each other the questions.

1 Do you know any twins who are *identical*?
2 When people criticise you, is it *normal to be unaffected by it*?
3 What topic of conversation is *likely to make you very angry*?
4 Are you *always bumping into things*?
5 Do you ever feel *as if you don't fit in*?
6 In arguments, are you *the type of person who won't let things drop*?

Use of English 1 (Paper 1 Part 3)

Word formation

1 Read the title and skim the text quickly. Why was Delia Strand inspired to invent the Chargem?

2a Decide which part of speech fits into each gap. Write the gap numbers under these headings: *noun(s), adjective(s), verb(s), adverb(s).*

b Write *singular* (*s*) or *plural* (*pl*) next to each noun. Write *negative* (*neg*) next to any adjectives which need a negative prefix.

3 For questions **1–8**, read the text below. Use the words given in capitals at the end of some of the lines to form a word that fits in the gap **in the same line**. There is an example at the beginning (**0**).

An instinct to invent

Inventor Delia Strand says it was **(0)** <u>laziness</u> that gave her the idea for the Chargem, because she likes to find the quickest way of doing things. She explains that without an electronic device, such as a laptop, phone or MP3 player as a **(1)**_____ , she would have found her daily train journey to work totally **(2)**_____ . The problem was she could never find all her chargers when she needed them.	LAZY DISTRACT BEAR
In a moment of **(3)**_____ , Delia decided that she was going to invent something which would be easy to **(4)**_____ and yet could power six electronic devices at any one time, **(5)**_____ of where in the world you were.	INSPIRE HAND REGARD
Her idea finally got off the ground when she found an **(6)**_____ who agreed to put money into it. Delia set up her own business intending to come up with other **(7)**_____ designed to make people's lives easier. She says her next gadget will be something to help protect people's personal **(8)**_____ .	INVEST PRODUCE BELONG

Discussion

4 Discuss these questions.

1 What is the most difficult personal challenge you have set yourself?

2 Which inventions do you think have been the most important for our lives? Think about medicine, transport, communications, etc.

Listening 1 (Paper 3 Part 2)

Before you listen 1 Read the title of the listening task below. Why do you think someone would want to invent this?

Sentence completion 2 🎧 57 Listen and do the task.

You will hear an extract from a radio programme about an American woman called Frances Gabe, who invented a self-cleaning house.
For questions 1–8, complete the sentences with a word or short phrase.

The self-cleaning house

Before becoming an inventor, Frances ran a (1)____ business.

Frances was mainly thinking of (2)____ people when she invented her self-cleaning house.

The speaker mentions a (3)____ to give us an idea of how the house functioned.

The (4)____ is an example of a domestic appliance which Frances hoped to make irrelevant.

The fact that the house didn't provide a good level of (5)____ prevented it from becoming a commercial success.

The equipment in Frances's house was damaged by a serious (6)____ in the area.

When not inventing, Frances always enjoyed (7)____ as an outlet for her creativity.

The decision to have low (8)____ at the entrance of her house was an example of Frances's unusual behaviour.

Discussion 3 Discuss these questions.

1 Are labour-saving devices a good thing? Do they also have a downside? Give reasons.
2 Do you think a totally self-cleaning house, like the one Frances Gabe dreamt up, would ever take off? Why?/Why not?

EXPERT WORD CHECK

ashes   break the mould   encased   equal measure   grab
nozzle   out of the question   precious   redundant   sector

Language development 1

➤ EXPERT GRAMMAR p 185

Reported speech: patterns after reporting verbs

1 Look at these statements. Which is the reporting verb? How would you report what Frances's father said using *say*, *tell*, *encourage*, *suggest* and *recommend*?

'Reach out and grab life!'
Frances's father advised her to reach out and grab life.

2a Cross out the option that doesn't fit the sentence. How would you say each sentence using the option you have crossed out?

1 She __ him about the train strike.
   A complained   B reminded   C warned
   D told
2 Helen __ having lost my keys.
   A admitted   B denied   C confessed
   D regretted
3 The lawyer __ that I should contact him immediately.
   A insisted   B requested   C recommended
   D told
4 My mother __ to write the letter for me.
   A agreed   B offered   C discussed   D refused
5 Carla suggested __ you.
   A texting   B that I text   C to text   D I text
6 Several people __ on what good company she was.
   A commented   B noticed   C remarked
   D agreed
7 The report __ people to have more meals together.
   A suggested   B urged   C advised
   D persuaded
8 They objected to __ the phone.
   A our using   B us using   C using   D use

b Look at sentences 1–4. How would you say each one in direct speech? For example: 1A *'I'm really fed up with the train strike.'* 1B *'Don't forget about the train strike, will you?'*

3a Match the verbs in the box to what the people say below. Then report each statement, using the best pattern from Exercise 2. There is sometimes more than one possibility.

admit   apologise   blame   explain   regret
remind

1 'I'm sorry I was late for the biology lesson.'
   Emily _____.
2 'I reckon it was Delia who copied my idea!'
   Claudio _____.
3 'Jim, don't forget to meet us at the science museum.'
   Stella _____.

4 'I shouldn't have given up my medical studies.'
   Zak _____.
5 'It's true, I did really badly in that chemistry paper.'
   Joanna _____.
6 'The reason why I became an anthropologist was a book I read.'
   Gary _____.

b Work in pairs. Take turns to make statements expressing the functions: *reminding, apologising, regretting, explaining, admitting* and *blaming*. Then report what your partner said, using the patterns from Exercise 3a.

Impersonal report structures

4a Which of the sentences are impersonal report structures? In which contexts are impersonal report structures used most?

1 a The government should support inventors more.
  b It is suggested that the government should support inventors more.
2 a Massachusetts Institute of Technology (MIT) has a big influence on innovation.
  b MIT is known to have a big influence on innovation.

b Look at the examples in Exercise 4a and complete this information about impersonal report structures.

1 *it* + passive + ____ + clause.
2 subject (MIT) + passive + ____

c Report these comments using an impersonal form and the words in *italics*. In some cases, two structures are possible.

1 People allege that engineering is still a largely male-dominated career.
   a *It …*   b *Engineering …*
2 Academics have argued that more emphasis should be placed on science in schools.
   It …
3 Some people think that space exploration is a waste of money.
   a *It …*   b *Space exploration …*
4 Many people fear that satellite navigation is close to breakdown.
   a *It …*   b *Satellite navigation …*
5 Some scientists have claimed that it is imperative to take carbon out of the atmosphere.
   It …
6 People believed that we would be using flying cars by now.
   It …

d Use the reporting verbs in Exercise 4c to talk about stories currently in the media at the moment. Which ones do you find most interesting?

Writing 1 Sentence skills: accuracy

1a Identify and correct the errors in each extract. The mistakes are coded (*p* = punctuation, *sp* = spelling and *gr* = grammar). The last extract has no coding.

INVENTIONS THAT CHANGED THE WORLD

1

gr	GPS technology were originally developed
p	by the united states military as a
p gr	navigation system uses a network of satellites
p	around the earth to pinpoint the
sp	exact position of a reciever anywhere on
p	the planet. since it was developed in
p p gr	1978 its used in cars, aircraft and boats.
	These days it's also used by geologists
p p	and conservation scientist's among others.

2

p	Nightclub owners dont like them but
p	trainer's have changed fashion and the feet
gr	of generations of people. They haven't taken
p	off until the 1970s although the technique
gr	of melding rubber to cloth first used in
p	1892 by the goodyear Metallic Rubber shoe
	company.
sp gr	With the help of celebreties as sporting
p	superstars they stopped being just practical
sp	clotheing and became a fashion item. The
	army reports that young people now grow
	up without ever wearing leather shoes and
sp	there feet are now too soft to wear
	traditional military boots.

3

Food 'on the go' has been around since the time of ancient greece but convinence food really took off in the 1970's and changed the high street our health and the way familys eat meals.

Traditional family dinners round the tables dissappeared and pre pacaged ready meals many of which were frozen became the norm.

The popularity of processed food however is also blame for the obesity crisis. With high fat salt and sugar content the diet of people in the west has worsened.

b Compare the corrections you made.

2a Do you agree that the inventions in Exercise 1 changed the world? Give reasons.

b Discuss which invention *you* think has changed the world most in the last hundred years. Here are some ideas.

- the microwave
- social networking
- text messages
- electronic money
- Velcro
- cling film
- the computer
- x-ray

3a Plan and write your answer to this task.

You have been asked to write an article for an English magazine on an important invention made in the last hundred years. Cover the following points:
· *who invented it, and when*
· *what you admire about it*
· *the impact it has had on our lives.*
*Write your **article** in **220–260** words.*

b Edit your work carefully, focusing on punctuation, spelling and grammatical accuracy.

4 In which areas do you think you could benefit from doing more work? If necessary, look at the sections on punctuation and spelling on pages 199–200.

Listening 2 (Paper 3 Part 3)

Before you listen

1 Discuss these questions.

1 In what ways do you think teenagers behave differently from
  a adults?
  b children?

2 What are some typical problems that teenagers have? What should the role of the parents be?

Multiple choice

2 🎧 58 Do the task opposite.

Task analysis

3 What is the most useful strategy when doing this task?

Discussion

4 Discuss these questions.

1 How far do you agree with Tom's conclusions?

2 At what age do you think teenagers are at their best/at their worst? Why?

3 Do you think teenage behaviour is different now from what it used to be? In what ways?

EXPERT WORD CHECK

accepted wisdom   acute
deficit   hold out against
impulse   out of synch
reckless   surly   sensory

---

*You will hear an interview with a parenting advisor called Tom Willis and a sociologist called Jane Thompson. They are talking about the reasons for unacceptable teenage behaviour. For questions 1–6, choose the answer (**A**, **B**, **C** or **D**) which fits best according to what you hear.*

1 Tom feels that recent research into the teenage brain has
  A failed to reach a convincing conclusion.
  B confirmed what adults had always thought.
  C provided him with an explanation for certain types of behaviour.
  D shown that previous studies may have been misinterpreted.

2 In Jane's opinion, many Western teenagers behave badly because
  A parents pay little attention to their social development.
  B they're obliged to carry out domestic duties which they hate.
  C they're under pressure to conform to the norms of other teenagers.
  D formal education includes too few practical subjects.

3 Tom thinks that teenagers sometimes do things they shouldn't because
  A they have a natural urge to rebel against their parents.
  B they're unaware that they could hurt themselves and others.
  C they feel an irresistible need to impress their friends.
  D they're unable to stop themselves experimenting.

4 When asked about teenage sleep patterns, Tom and Jane disagree about
  A whether the school day should be organised around these.
  B whether all teenagers actually share the same ones.
  C how long teenagers should sleep on average.
  D how much lack of sleep affects learning.

5 Jane thinks the key difference between teenagers and adults relates to
  A how adaptable teenagers are.
  B how easily influenced teenagers are.
  C how well teenagers can resist temptation.
  D how easy teenagers find it to break a bad habit.

6 Tom believes that teenagers learn best when their parents
  A provide them with good role models.
  B establish suitable routines for them.
  C co-operate with their teachers.
  D trust them to be independent.

Speaking (Paper 4 Part 3)

Vocabulary: the mind

1a Write these words and expressions under the headings below, according to their meaning. Use a dictionary if necessary.

able to think on (one's) feet   all at sea   at a loss   brainy   dense
dim   disorientated   feeble-minded   gifted
have a good head on (one's) shoulders   have a high IQ   knowledgeable
muddled   perplexed   precocious   quick-witted   slow on the uptake

A clever/bright	B not clever/not bright	C confused

b Circle the correct prepositions to complete the text.

Subject: Damon

Damon has a good brain, but sometimes I think he's too clever **(1)** *in / by* half. He knows a lot **(2)** *about / of* a lot of things but he's often preoccupied and you wonder what's going **(3)** *on / along* in his head. He told me this morning he was trying to think **(4)** *across / through* a difficult mathematical problem and all sorts of questions were running **(5)** *through / over* his mind. I suggested he slept **(6)** *in / on* the problem overnight and weighed **(7)** *along / up* possible solutions in the morning when his mind was fresh.

c Choose from the words in brackets to complete the sentences.

1 Telephone numbers are easily _____ . When you've got a mind like a sieve as I have, you need something to jog the _____ . (*forgotten/memory/head/mindless*)

2 Lists should serve as a _____ when you go shopping, but I always _____ the list. (*remembrance/remember/forget/reminder*)

3 If I _____ rightly, his birthday is on 5th May. It's etched in my _____ because it's the day I got married. (*head/remember/memory/think back*)

4 I have no _____ of her at all. Some faces are _____ , but this picture doesn't ring a bell. (*unforgotten/remembering/recollection/unforgettable*)

5 Can you _____ me how the film ends? I've got a complete _____ block about it. (*remind/unforgettable/mental/remember*)

6 I find that some smells and songs are particularly _____ . The smell of lavender, for example, always brings to _____ my childhood holidays in France. (*mind/memory/memorable/mindful*)

2   Discuss these questions.

1 What information is it important for you to remember (e.g. names, numbers, dates, things to buy, song lyrics, lines for a play, words in a foreign language)? Make a list. Which do you find easiest/most difficult to remember and why?

2 What techniques have you got for remembering them (e.g. visual images, acronyms, rhymes, grouping, repeating)? Why are they useful? Which helps best with long-term memory?

3 How do you study for exams (e.g. memorising information, making notes, last-minute cramming)? What are the advantages/ disadvantages?

Collaborative task

3a Look at the spidergram and work in pairs to do this task. Time yourselves. You should take about two minutes.

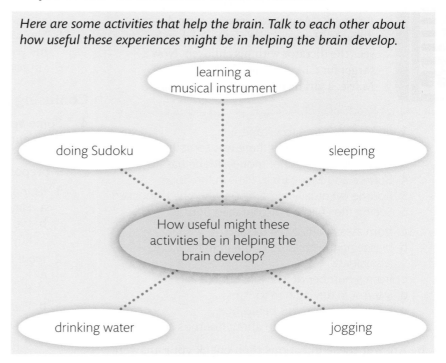

Here are some activities that help the brain. Talk to each other about how useful these experiences might be in helping the brain develop.

learning a musical instrument

doing Sudoku

sleeping

How useful might these activities be in helping the brain develop?

drinking water

jogging

b   Now you have a minute to decide which two activities are the most beneficial. Then tell the class briefly what you decide.

Task analysis

4   Discuss these questions.

1 Decide whether all of the following are important when doing this task in the exam. Which are the most important?
  · inviting your partner to give an opinion
  · coming to a conclusion
  · agreeing with the other person
  · negotiating
  · keeping the conversation going
  · organising your ideas
  · sharing the interaction

2 How would you assess your performance in Exercise 3?

Developing the discussion

5   Work in pairs. Take turns to ask and answer the questions. Give reasons for your answers.

1 When do you think is the best time in life to develop your brain?
2 Do you think it is possible to be *too* clever?
3 Do you think the way we live affects our brains in any way?
4 Do you think society as a whole takes mental health and mental illness seriously enough?

Language development 2

Nouns, adjectives, verbs + prepositions

1a Read the film review then match 1–6 with a–f to make sentences. Mark the word + preposition combinations.

> *The Bourne Identity* is about a young amnesiac (someone who can't remember anything) trying to discover his true identity. Eventually, he finds out that he was part of a secret US Central Intelligence Agency (CIA) plot to assassinate an African dictator. However, the plot fails when he sees the dictator with his children. Now a target for CIA assassins, he is helped by Marie, a girl he meets at the US Embassy.

1 Bourne manages to escape
2 At first, Marie thought there was something
3 Until Bourne gives her money, Marie has no
4 Bourne and Marie go to Paris in the hope
5 Bourne eventually remembers when he is shocked
6 Seeing the children discouraged Bourne

a from assassinating the dictator.
b by seeing the children of the man he was to assassinate.
c from a number of assassins sent to kill him.
d interest in driving him to Paris.
e suspicious about his behaviour.
f of finding out the truth about Bourne's past.

b Answer these questions then check your answers in the grammar reference on page 186.

1 Does a verb/noun/adjective + preposition always have an object?
2 What form of the verb follows a preposition?
3 Is possessive + *-ing* form found in formal or informal English?

2 Complete the sentences with a preposition if necessary.

1 The scientist aimed his remarks ____ politicians and blamed ____ them ____ the lack of funding.
2 They discussed ____ the use of animals in research but were nervous because they were unaccustomed ____ debating the subject in public.
3 They resorted ____ raising funds ____ appeals on television.
4 What's the point ____ having research ____ mental health if it's not properly funded?
5 The head apologised ____ parents ____ not taking students' needs seriously enough.
6 The union representative quarrelled ____ the head ____ his approach.

Preposition + *-ing* verb

3 Rewrite the sentences using a preposition + *-ing* verb.

EXAMPLE:
He's always keen *to find* new techniques for memorising vocabulary.
He's always keen on finding new techniques for memorising vocabulary.

1 I was annoyed *to find* the dictionary missing.
2 I'd like to borrow another one but I'm nervous *to ask* again.
3 My teacher advised me *not to use* a bilingual dictionary.
4 She insisted *that we worked out* the meaning of words from the context.
5 She suspected *that I wasn't keeping good records* in my vocabulary notebook.
6 I'm sorry *that I lost* the dictionary.

Confusing pairs

4 Some verbs and adjectives can be used with different prepositions with a change of meaning. Complete the sentences with the correct word + preposition combination in the correct form.

1 *hear of/hear about*
   a Have you ____ the latest Bourne film?
   b I've ____ Jeremy Renner, but I've never seen any of his films.
2 *shout to/shout at*
   a I ____ her name ____ you, but you couldn't hear with all the noise.
   b Please don't ____ me, it wasn't my fault.
3 *throw to/throw at*
   a A protester ____ a stone ____ the car and damaged a window.
   b ____ the ball ____ me. It's my turn to bowl.
4 *anxious for/anxious about*
   a Families of the survivors hadn't heard anything, so they were ____ news.
   b I'm ____ Tom – he doesn't look well.
5 *care for/care about*
   a The only thing he ____ is money.
   b I don't ____ much ____ those friends of his.
6 *laugh at/laugh about*
   a We ____ it when we got home, but it wasn't funny at the time.
   b You shouldn't ____ him, he can't help it.

5 Discuss with a partner what life might be like if you suddenly lost your memory. Use some of the noun, verb, adjective + preposition combinations above.

Reading and Use of English (Paper 1 Part 6)

Cross-text multiple matching

> EXPERT STRATEGIES page 168

1 Do you think adults are better or worse learners than children? Why?

2 Complete the task below.

You are going to read four blogs on the subject of adult learning. For questions 1–4, choose from the bloggers (A–D). The bloggers may be chosen more than once.

Adult learning

A

It's true that recent studies have made a persuasive case for the contribution the environment and the learner's attitude can make when it comes to learning a foreign language. However, this doesn't really contradict my main point that humans have this inbuilt facility to acquire language up to a certain age. A child's brain has a separate area, known as a 'speech centre', for each language it hears, which means immigrant kids, for example, pick up a new language as easily as breathing, while their parents, who no longer have this inborn ability, often have to learn in a conventional teaching situation and unfortunately tend to struggle. True, some older adults have a special facility for learning languages but that's down to an unusual talent and shouldn't be seen as typical.

B

In my view, the idea that the mind seizes up with age is overrated. If there was a critical period for learning say a language or a musical instrument, everyone would be affected equally, but they're not. Even as the brain ages, it possesses amazing powers to adapt quickly to a learning experience. In terms of language, what most people forget is that a child's whole social network is organised around the language and people are more likely to speak to them in clear simple sentences, exaggerating key points. And yet older adults shouldn't be discouraged. They can learn, for example, a musical instrument or even a language conventionally, and do even better than younger learners if they immerse themselves in the experience, focus on where they need to improve – something children are reluctant to do – and practise small bits at a time until they get them right.

C

You often hear it said that there is a critical period in childhood in which complex skills are best learnt, but what often stops adults progressing is their desire to be perfectionist. Instead of throwing themselves into tasks, observing and copying others, taking risks, too many of them break their learning into segments and worry about their weaknesses, and when they fail, they lose heart and give up. And yet they are always much more effective as learners when they look more at their overall performance. Golfers, instead of worrying about the position of their hands, should focus on their swing, and singers on the tone of their voice rather than the position of their tongue. In other words, adult learners need to shift their mindset and their teachers need to give them praise and general feedback, not over-detailed analysis.

D

I don't know why some people are so negative about the mental skills of older adults. It's true that as our nervous system starts to weaken so our ability to learn is more restricted, but even the very aged can improve the performance of their brain, which is a much more flexible organ than people think. Mental skills respond very well to improved physical fitness, which adults need to build up bit by bit. Even walking can make our minds more alert and improve our attention span. Children are much more physically active than adults and if we are to match them mentally, we need to get closer to matching them physically. Of course, early skills training, for instance in sports, music or languages, is much more effective early in life because certain aspects of a child's mental capacity are more responsive to change at this age and can absorb things more readily. Personal qualities such a willingness to take risks also play a role, probably much more than environmental factors, like the learning situation.

Which blogger

expresses a similar view to Blogger A about the advantages that children are born with in relation to learning? **1** ☐

expresses a less positive view than the others about the ability of adults to learn? **2** ☐

disagrees with the others about the relative advantages children have when learning? **3** ☐

has a different opinion from Blogger B regarding the way in which adult learners could improve their potential for learning? **4** ☐

Task analysis

3 Answer these questions.

1 Did you read the question prompts before you read the texts?
2 Did you skim read all of the texts first and try and answer the questions, or read the first one very carefully first?
3 Did you mark key points in the text?

Discussion

4 Which of the blogs above do you most agree with? Give reasons.

Writing 2 Essay (Paper 2 Part 1)

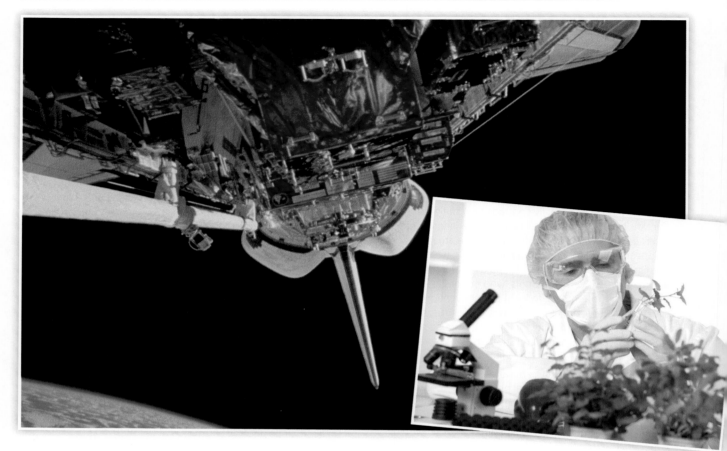

Lead-in **1** Discuss these questions.

1 What areas of scientific research are shown in the photos?
2 Which do you think should receive priority for government funding, and why?

Understand the task **2** Read the task and answer these questions.

1 What type of essay is it?
2 What must you include? What will you have to invent?
3 What style will you use?

Your class has attended a seminar on areas of scientific research that need increased government funding. You have made the notes below:

> Areas of scientific research that need
> increased government funding:
> • space
> • medicine
> • food production

> Some opinions discussed in the seminar:
> 'Without space exploration there would
> be no satellite TV.'
> 'We can't afford endless research into
> disease prevention.'
> 'Genetically modified crops will feed an
> increasing world population.'

*Write an essay for your tutor discussing **two** of the areas in your notes. You should **explain which area you think needs most funding**, **giving reasons** in support of your answer.*
You may, if you wish, make use of the opinions expressed in the discussion, but you should use your own words as far as possible.

Plan your essay

3a Make some notes which answer the question and decide on your point of view. Make sure you give reasons and examples where appropriate.

b Make a paragraph plan for your essay.

c Choose from your notes in Exercise 3a what you will include in each paragraph.

Language and content

4a Read the strategy about introductions and conclusions. What is the purpose of these sentence openings? Complete them for the introduction. Which verb forms will you need? (active or passive? present simple/continuous/perfect? future or past?)

1 It is a commonly held view that …
2 In this essay I …
3 Increased government funding …

> **EXPERT STRATEGY**
>
> The introduction of an essay can provide
> - a 'thesis statement' (a sentence that gives the main point of the essay and which the 'body paragraphs' then explain).
> - a statement of what you intend to write about.
> - background to the topic.
>
> The conclusion of an essay can
> - summarise the main points/ restate the thesis statement in different words.
> - give your point of view about the main idea.

b These are sentence openings which could be used for the 'body paragraphs'. Put the verbs in the correct form and complete the sentences. Use a modal verb if necessary.

1 One of the most important benefits of ____ is that it not only ____ (**hold out**) the hope of ____ but also ____ .
2 Who ____ (**imagine**) life now without ____ ?
3 However, ____ is certainly expensive and ____ (**not/carry out**) without ____ .
4 Indeed, opponents say that scarce resources ____ (**deploy better**) on ____ .
5 There can be no doubt that ____ ____ (**make**) us ____ .
6 However, the downside is that ____ ____ (**be**) also costly ____ .

c Read the strategy again. What is the purpose of these sentences? Complete them for the conclusion. What verb form will you need?

1 Nevertheless, in my view, funding ____ .
2 Finally, unless there ____ .
3 Can you imagine (the situation) if ____ ?
4 As has been discussed, ____ .

d Go back over the sentences you have written in Exercises 4a–c. Check their grammatical accuracy. Could the vocabulary be more varied (e.g. by including phrases like *highly controversial, vast array of, take for granted*)?

Write your essay

5 Now write your essay, using some of the ideas and the language above. Write your answer in 220–260 words in an appropriate style.

Check your answer

6 Edit your essay.
Make sure:
- each paragraph is coherent and develops logically (e.g. Have you used a topic sentence to start a paragraph? Is there a supporting sentence?)
- you have used appropriate linking devices
- you have used a wide range of complex structures
- the style is consistent and appropriate.

Review

1 Complete the sentences with one word in each gap.

1 The boys thought some of the girls were too clever ____ half.
2 He showed great interest ____ doing research ____ bird migration.
3 Tina seems a little slow ____ the uptake this morning.
4 The university is anxious ____ a quick response ____ the government ____ funding.
5 I'm tired and spaced ____ . Do you blame me ____ wanting a holiday?
6 You've never commented ____ my blog. Don't you like it?
7 Criticism doesn't bother me. It's like water ____ a duck's back.
8 Tom quarrelled ____ his mother ____ something she said.
9 This author's new to me. I've never heard ____ him before.
10 Craig has been terrified ____ you ever since you lost your temper.

2 Circle the correct alternative to complete the sentences.

1 Seeing the Earth from space was an *unforgotten / unforgettable* experience.
2 When she caught *sight / view* of him, she went pale.
3 I'm like a *red rag to a bull / dog with a bone* if a cause is worth fighting for.
4 I remember the incident but it happened *many moons ago / once in a blue moon*.
5 Their child has the *precocious / brainy* self-assurance of an adult.
6 The scientist gave them a *glance / glimpse* of what life might be like in the future.
7 The class looked *all at sea / woolly-headed* when she began to explain the detail.
8 Clara *objected / regretted* to her daughter marrying someone so poor.

3 Rewrite the sentences in reported speech using the verbs in brackets.

1 'It was the fault of the service provider. They cut us off,' said our team leader. (**blame**)
2 'OK, Chris. I'll contact the press for you,' said Olivia. (**agree**)
3 'Open your bags,' the customs official said to us. (**insist**)
4 'Don't be late for college, Ryan,' said his mother. (**warn**)
5 'Listen, girls. I want you all to co-operate,' said the teacher. (**try/persuade**)
6 'It's true. I was driving carelessly,' said Darren. (**confess**)
7 'Why not try a new approach, Sam?' Liam said. (**suggest**)
8 'Don't rule out any of the options,' Mark told us. (**advise**)
9 'We never get enough money for research,' said the head of department to the principal. (**complain**)
10 'I think it was Peter that caused the accident,' said Eli. (**suspect**)

4 Complete the sentences using the words in brackets. Add any other necessary words.

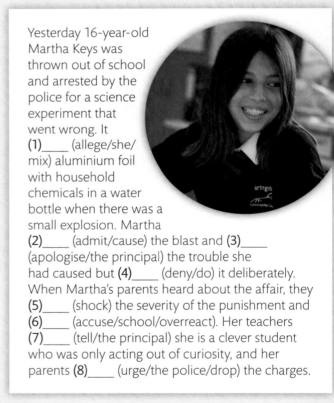

Yesterday 16-year-old Martha Keys was thrown out of school and arrested by the police for a science experiment that went wrong. It (1)____ (allege/she/mix) aluminium foil with household chemicals in a water bottle when there was a small explosion. Martha (2)____ (admit/cause) the blast and (3)____ (apologise/the principal) the trouble she had caused but (4)____ (deny/do) it deliberately. When Martha's parents heard about the affair, they (5)____ (shock) the severity of the punishment and (6)____ (accuse/school/overreact). Her teachers (7)____ (tell/the principal) she is a clever student who was only acting out of curiosity, and her parents (8)____ (urge/the police/drop) the charges.

Overview

10A
> **Reading and Use of English:** Multiple matching (Part 8); Multiple-choice cloze (Part 1)
> **Vocabulary:** Health and fitness: Word formation, similar words; Sport and fitness metaphors
> **Listening:** Multiple choice: short extracts (Part 1)
> **Language development:** Participle clauses; *To*-infinitive clauses
> **Writing:** Sentence variety: using a range of structures

10B
> **Listening:** Multiple matching (Part 4)
> **Speaking:** Complete Paper 4
> **Language development:** Modals and semi-modals (Part 2); Certainty, willingness and characteristic behaviour; Modal revision; Alternatives to modals
> **Reading and Use of English:** Open cloze (Part 2); Key word transformations (Part 4)
> **Writing:** Proposal (Part 2)

Lead-in

1a Which of these are the most important in life? Choose the five most important.

physical strength and flexibility   a stable family life   good physical and mental health
a clear purpose   secure and loving relationships   having a good group of friends or colleagues
a hobby/playing or taking part in a sport   a job which satisfies you   financial stability
someone to talk to   an optimistic and positive temperament   a good night's sleep
being able to choose your own lifestyle   high energy levels

b Which most affects our sense of well-being?

c Compare your ideas.

2 Discuss these questions.

1 As a society are we fitter or less fit than we've ever been? Why?
2 Do you think we are too obsessed with our own health?
3 What part do these play in our health: our upbringing, our education, economic circumstances, genetics?

Reading (Paper 1 Part 8)

Before you read

1 Read the title and introduction to the article. What kinds of contribution would be needed from a support team? Why would teamwork be essential?

Multiple matching

2 Complete the task.

> *You are going to read a magazine article about the team which supports the Formula 1 driver Sebastian Vettel. For questions 1–10, choose from the sections of the article (A–D). The sections may be chosen more than once.*

Which team member

admits getting a sense of personal satisfaction from Vettel's success? ___1___

appreciates Vettel's unusual willingness to be honest? ___2___

feels he occasionally needs to restrain Vettel from being over-ambitious? ___3___

has encouraged Vettel to analyse his own performance? ___4___

appreciates Vettel's mental strength? ___5___

admits that there was only a limited amount he could teach Vettel? ___6___

mentions how crucial it was to generate funds for Vettel? ___7___

sees one of his roles as preparing Vettel for sudden emergencies? ___8___

believes Vettel is aware of how vital teamwork is to achieving victory? ___9___

praises Vettel's emotional maturity? ___10___

Task analysis

3 Read the strategy on page 169. Tick the advice about the multiple matching reading test that is correct.

1 Read the text before the options. ☐
2 Skim the text quickly the first time. ☐
3 Underline key words in the options. ☐
4 Similar ideas may come up in more than one text, so be careful. ☐

Discussion

4 Discuss this question.

What sort of team support is necessary for professional individual sports (e.g. tennis, cycling)? How does this compare with team sports such as football, ice hockey, water polo?

EXPERT WORD CHECK

awash (in)   data   dimension   lap (*n*)   nail down   refreshing
sponsor (*n*)   stall (*v*)   unflappable   worn (tyres)

Team Vettel

Even a racing driver as talented as Sebastian Vettel has to learn and be nurtured. We talk to members of Sebastian Vettel's support team.

A The special adviser

'It wasn't until 2004 that I nailed down seventeen-year-old Sebastian with a contract and went on to guide his career. In his first year at Formula BMW, he won 18 out of 20 races before going into Formula 3. He had a difficult first half-season, but the second half was good after we'd made quite big changes in the team on Sebastian's insistence. He can be extremely determined when he feels he needs to be. Sebastian always knew that driving is only a part of motor racing and that if you don't have the right knowledge and the right support, then you won't be a regular winner. Over the years, I've had to slow him down a bit because he's wanted to do too much too soon. But we've always had a very good working relationship and I'm a great admirer of his courage and powers of concentration, which are unbelievable.'

B The race engineer

'They call me his "second brain". At the track, I'm the team's "face" for him. During a race weekend, essentially I make sure the car is set up to his liking. There's also the human dimension, as I help him with motivation and how to deal with the inevitable ups and downs. When his car blew up while he was leading in the final stages, he was able to deal with it because we'd rehearsed exactly that type of scenario. To do my job, you have to be as unflappable and confident as possible. If the highs are too high and the lows are too low, then it can become difficult. Generally an understanding of the phrase "There's only so much you can control," and an ability to rationalise things, only comes with age, but Seb has that already. It helps that we talk a lot; what you see at a race track is the putting into place of everything we've discussed by phone and email since the last race.'

C The technical director

'Nobody made Vettel. He made himself. But I remember when I was watching him once, I saw him do a lap which was extraordinarily fast even with worn tyres and a heavy fuel load. When we spoke about it and he looked at the data, he wasn't quite sure how he'd done this, so I told him to go away and give it some thought. The next day he told me "I know what I did." But I didn't ask him exactly what that was. That's for him to know. It's his secret of being fast, if you like. I just wanted him to think about how he actually did it and register it mentally. Something else that we gave him as a team was our complete trust, and that enabled him to trust us too. In his first race for us, he made a mistake in qualifying and immediately said, "I made a mistake." Normally, the racing driver's book of excuses is longer than *War and Peace*, so this was refreshing.'

D The mentor

'He caught my attention even as a toddler on my go-kart track because he was very good at what he was doing. The Vettel family wasn't awash in cash – quite the contrary – and I felt I had to try and prevent his career from stalling in the event of him running out of money, so I helped find him sponsors. I rented out my go-kart business so I could have time to fully support his career, when he was only 10. When he entered Formula 3, I realised it was time for me to step aside. As soon as he got involved in bigger teams, I wasn't able to actively contribute anymore so I went back to karts. I knew he was in good hands. When he took his first Formula 1 title, it was the greatest gift to me I could think of because it was the perfect acknowledgement that I hadn't been wrong about him.'

Vocabulary: health and fitness

Word formation, similar words, etc.

1 Quickly skim the extracts in Exercises 2a–c, which are all connected to Formula 1 driving. Match these headings to the extracts.

Diet   Why do drivers have to be fit?   Physical training

2a Complete the extract with the correct form of the words in brackets.

People new to F1 racing are (1)_____ (*vary*) astonished to learn that its drivers are some of the most highly conditioned athletes on Earth, their bodies (2)_____ (*specify*) adapted to its exacting requirements. The stamina required is greater than in any other type of motor racing, as (3)_____ (*endure*) driving for two hours puts an (4)_____ (*exception*) strain on the body. Added to this is the amount of adrenalin being pumped around the body, which causes an (5)_____ (*expect*) high heart rate, equivalent to a marathon runner crossing the finishing line. Because of cornering in a race, drivers must (6)_____ (*sure*) that their neck has the strength to support 24 kg. To (7)_____ (*able*) them to control the car during longer races, powerful arm muscles are also (8)_____ (*essence*).

b Circle the correct alternative to complete the extract.

In order to (1) *build / raise* up physical strength drivers have to (2) *undergo / go under* a personalised fitness (3) *event / programme*. This centres on (4) *tense / intensive* cardiovascular training over a period of time – usually running or swimming. Core strength and resistance work, using (5) *actions / activities* such as rowing and weightlifting, is also incorporated into their exercise regime, (6) *despite / moreover* the danger that the drivers will get too big. F1 cockpits are very small and don't (7) *accommodate / fit* someone with the (8) *figure / build* of a weightlifter.

c Complete the extract with one appropriate word in each gap.

In terms (1)_____ nutrition, F1 drivers eat much (2)_____ athletes, carefully regulating their protein and carbohydrate intake to keep their weight (3)_____ check. (4)_____ , in the lead-up to a big race they'll usually stuff (5)_____ with a huge bowl of carbohydrate, such as pasta, for energy. Just before the race, and sometimes (6)_____ the race itself, drivers absorb large (7)_____ of water, without (8)_____ they could suffer dehydration through sweating and through the extreme heat in an F1 cockpit.

3 Use words and expressions from Exercise 2 to discuss how you could improve your health and fitness.

Sport and fitness metaphors

4a Explain what you think the expressions in *italics* mean in the context.

1 Julia *skated around* the subject of her marriage, obviously trying to avoid mentioning it.
2 Tim *sailed through* his exam as effortlessly as ever.
3 I had to *rein in* her spending – it was getting out of control.
4 It *took the wind out of her sails* when I admitted straightaway what I'd done.
5 Carly is very much *on the ball* at work and knows exactly what's going on.
6 I thought I was right to leave at five, but they'd *moved the goalposts* – we were expected to work until six.

b Use the metaphors to talk about events in your own life.

Use of English 1 (Paper 1 Part 1)

Lead-in **1** Discuss these questions.

1 What is meant by team spirit? Can teams succeed without talented individuals?
2 When can individuals with outstanding talent ruin a team performance?

Multiple-choice cloze **2a** Read the text below. Do you agree with what it says?

b For questions **1–8**, decide which answer (**A**, **B**, **C** or **D**) best fits each gap. There is an example at the beginning (**0**).

Team spirit

Doing sport obviously has a (**0**) _B_ number of health benefits for young people. It is also an ideal opportunity to (**1**)__ technology aside for a while. In addition, team sports such as rugby have an excellent (**2**)__ for encouraging youngsters to work with others towards achieving a common goal. Many schools acknowledge that such sports encourage transferable abilities. For example, players often need to be (**3**)__ of making a decision on the spur of the moment and learn to (**4**)__ with conflict.

Then there are the social benefits: team sports continue to play an important role throughout many people's lives, helping them to relax and form friendships that may (**5**)__ a lifetime.

One of the most interesting facts about team sports is that (**6**)__ successful teams tend to be those which work really well together. When joining a team, it is essential that people make a strong (**7**)__ to give their all; any personal differences have to be (**8**)__ for the good of the team.

0	A wide	B great	C heavy	D broad
1	A put	B place	C forget	D stand
2	A distinction	B esteem	C respect	D reputation
3	A skilled	B competent	C capable	D qualified
4	A deal	B handle	C treat	D concern
5	A keep	B last	C live	D remain
6	A greatly	B deeply	C fully	D highly
7	A dedication	B allegiance	C commitment	D assurance
8	A put away	B set aside	C left out	D given up

Task analysis **3** Which of these language areas are NOT a main test focus in a multiple-choice cloze?

1 fixed expressions (e.g. phrasal verbs/collocations)
2 grammatical words such as relative clauses, auxiliary verbs, articles
3 linking words
4 words with similar meanings
5 idioms

Discussion **4** Do you prefer doing team sports or individual sports? Why?

Listening 1 (Paper 4 Part 1)

1 Read questions 1–6 below.

Multiple choice: short extracts

2 🎧 59 Listen and do the task below.

*You will hear three different extracts in which people are talking about stories or experiences connected to teamwork. For questions **1–6**, choose the answer (**A**, **B** or **C**) which fits best according to what you hear. There are two questions for each extract.*

Extract One
You hear two friends talking about a group of miners who were trapped underground for 70 days.

1 The woman thinks the main reason for the miners' survival was
   A their willingness to co-operate with one another.
   B a determination to save as much food as possible.
   C the fact that they were able to remain optimistic.

2 When talking about the miners' leader, the man is
   A reinforcing the woman's opinion.
   B justifying his previous viewpoint.
   C admitting he misunderstood the situation.

Extract Two
You hear part of an interview with a member of a ballet company.

3 How does she feel about always being part of a group?
   A She wishes there was a greater variety of people to dance with.
   B She accepts she's not ambitious enough to become a principal dancer.
   C She says there are both advantages and disadvantages.

4 She admits that she likes the idea of
   A being the centre of attention.
   B being given more demanding roles.
   C being appreciated more by the company.

Extract Three
You hear a doctor telling a colleague about some advice his hospital received.

5 The hospital was seeking advice about
   A how to improve patient safety during operations.
   B how surgical teams could work better together.
   C how to select the best staff to support surgeons.

6 What main failing was identified in the hospital's procedures?
   A basic mistakes were not being noticed.
   B there was inadequate staff training.
   C nobody had overall responsibility.

Discussion

3 In which other jobs or situations is it essential to work as a team? Would you say you were a team player or more of an individualist? Give reasons.

> **EXPERT WORD CHECK**
>
> bond (*v*)   come to terms with   fatal   (7 seconds) flat
> glamorous   maintain   stuck with   thereabouts   typecast
> unity

Language development 1

Participle and *to*-infinitive clauses

> EXPERT GRAMMAR p 187

Participle clauses

1a Work in pairs. Student A: Look at the grammar reference on page 187. Student B: Read out sentences 1–5. Work together to match the highlighted participle clauses to their uses.

1 Having been underground for 69 days, the miners were finally rescued.
2 Knowing I would never become a soloist, I left my dance company.
3 On hearing the news, I sat up all night, worrying about what to do.
4 He contacted the Formula 1 team, determined to get some advice from them.
5 Given the time, he'd be very happy to help.

b Say the sentences in Exercise 1a, using finite verbs (i.e. verbs with a tense). Why might you want to use participle clauses instead?

c Rewrite these sentences, replacing the parts in *italics* with a suitable participle clause. Make any other changes necessary.

1 The young Romanian became a household name after *she'd won* a gold medal for gymnastics.
2 *I flicked through the magazine and* found an article on my favourite footballer.
3 *Alex is tall and slim, so he's* the ideal build for a runner.
4 *Maya trained for* 15 years as a dancer, *so she's* very fit.
5 *If the shoes are taken care of, they* should last for years.

to-infinitive clauses

2 Which of these sentences expresses a *purpose*, a *condition*, a *result* or an *unexpected consequence*?

1 To watch him, you'd never guess he wasn't professional.
2 I went back into the house to get my trainers.
3 He turned up for the marathon, only to find out it had just been cancelled.
4 I've played rugby often enough to know that I'm useless at it.

3a Combine these sentences using a suitable participle or *to*-infinitive clause. Make any other changes necessary.

1 I couldn't afford the ticket. Therefore, I didn't go to the cup final with my friends.
2 I really enjoyed the Pilates classes. That's why I enrolled for the next course.
3 She decided to go shopping. She needed to get some suitable clothes for her yoga session.
4 You should see Laura playing netball. You'd think she'd been playing it for years.
5 He switched on the TV. Then he sat down to watch the news.
6 I was surprised how high Tim could jump. You'd never believe it from looking at him.
7 I've watched the England team play often enough. As a result, I know they'll lose on penalties.
8 I bought my brother a new squash racket. I know he's lost his.

b Read the text and use participle and *to*-infinitive clauses to rewrite the parts in *italics* more economically. You may need to cut a word.

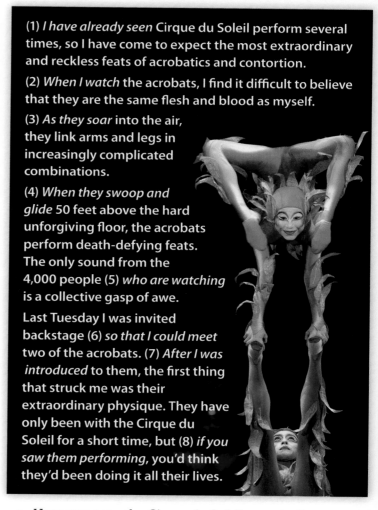

(1) *I have already seen* Cirque du Soleil perform several times, so I have come to expect the most extraordinary and reckless feats of acrobatics and contortion.

(2) *When I watch* the acrobats, I find it difficult to believe that they are the same flesh and blood as myself.

(3) *As they soar* into the air, they link arms and legs in increasingly complicated combinations.

(4) *When they swoop and glide* 50 feet above the hard unforgiving floor, the acrobats perform death-defying feats. The only sound from the 4,000 people (5) *who are watching* is a collective gasp of awe.

Last Tuesday I was invited backstage (6) *so that I could meet* two of the acrobats. (7) *After I was introduced* to them, the first thing that struck me was their extraordinary physique. They have only been with the Cirque du Soleil for a short time, but (8) *if you saw them performing*, you'd think they'd been doing it all their lives.

c Have you seen the Cirque du Soleil or any other acrobatic performance? Do you/Would you find this kind of performance exciting or too frightening to watch? Why do you think people watch performances like this?

Writing 1 Sentence variety: using a range of structures

1a Look at the main sentence patterns of English on page 202 and then do Exercise 1b.

b Combine each set of sentences into one sentence, using a variety of patterns and making any changes necessary. Try to avoid simple conjunctions such as *and*, *but*, *so*. Make sure your punctuation is correct. There is more than one right answer.

1 I am a risk-averse kind of person in my daily life. However, I do enjoy skiing and rugby. This means that I have had quite a few injuries.

2 Many people say that Messi is the most talented footballer in the world. Even Ronaldo agrees that this is the case. Messi was born in Argentina but lives and works in Spain.

3 My brother was useless at team sports at school. The reason for this is probably because he has very little co-ordination. He does, though, excel at long-distance running and cycling.

4 My daughter has been working towards the Duke of Edinburgh's Award all year. To get this, students have to show evidence of working at a physical activity and another skill. They also go on expeditions. These test navigation skills, teamwork and resourcefulness.

5 Riding is expensive. This is especially true if you have your own horse. It can also be dangerous. The risk increases when you get the horse to jump and do cross-country activities.

c Work in pairs to write some of the sentences, using different structures to those in Exercise 1b.

2a Read this task and mark the points you have to include in your answer.

You have received an email from a younger friend who needs your advice. You have decided to write an email to your friend, responding to the points made in this extract:

> Sorry I haven't been touch for a while – I've been spending far too much time recently in front of a screen doing work for college. As a result, I feel very unfit. I know you're very active. What kind of sport do you think would suit me? Preferably outdoors, so I can get some fresh air at the same time. I'm not as sociable as you, remember, but there must be something I could do, preferably that doesn't take up too much time.

*Write your **email**.*

b Now edit part of one student's answer by combining some of the sentences so that there is a greater variety of sentence patterns. Make sure you link the ideas clearly, using appropriate linking expressions. You may change the order of the sentences.

> (1) I'm not sure I'm the best person to be giving you advice. (2) This is particularly true as I haven't seen you for quite a while. (3) I'm not very fit myself these days. (4) This is mainly because I don't have as much time as I used to. (5) I've got kids now! (6) We are also different because I'm quite a gregarious person, as you say. (7) This means that I like team sports a lot. (8) I have a feeling these may not appeal to you as much. (9) I really enjoy getting together with a group of mates for a kickaround. (10) We usually follow it with a curry and a drink in our local Indian restaurant.

3a Complete the sample answer in Exercise 2b or plan and write your own answer to the task.

b Exchange your work with a partner. Edit each other's work for range of sentence structures.

Listening 2 (Paper 3 Part 4)

Before you listen

1 Read the task below. Then read the instructions for Task One again and look at items D and H in the first list A–H. What kind of activities could give benefits like these?

Multiple matching **2** 🎧 60 Listen and do the task below.

You will hear five short extracts in which people are talking about leisure activities.

TASK ONE

*For questions **1–5**, choose from the list (**A–H**) the main benefit each speaker gets from the activity.*

TASK TWO

*For questions **6–10**, choose from the list (**A–H**) what problem related to the activity each speaker mentions.*

While you listen you must complete both tasks.

A being able to demonstrate your skills
B getting away from a daily routine
C having a chance to
   re-establish contact
D spending time with more
   educated people
E meeting strangers who share
   your feelings
F gaining a sense of
   achievement
G learning something new
H developing a skill which will last a lifetime

Speaker 1 | 1
Speaker 2 | 2
Speaker 3 | 3
Speaker 4 | 4
Speaker 5 | 5

A periods of depression
B people not turning up
C people without talent
   joining in
D inexperienced newcomers
E an attempt by someone to
   dominate
F people not doing what
   they're supposed to
G the unexpected expense
H people unable to get over
   negative feelings

Speaker 1 | 6
Speaker 2 | 7
Speaker 3 | 8
Speaker 4 | 9
Speaker 5 | 10

Task analysis **3** Compare and discuss your answers. How do you prefer to do this task? When you listen the first time, do you prefer to do the first task only or do both tasks quickly? What do you do during the second listening?

Discussion **4** Discuss these questions.

1 What do the activities above all have in common? Which do you most identify with and why?
2 What sort of feel-good activities do you enjoy? Do you prefer to be on your own or with others in your spare time? Why?

EXPERT WORD CHECK

disparate   drag (n)   enlightening   euphoria   gain
get caught up in   gifted   go off at a tangent
let (one's) hair down   resentment

Speaking (Complete Paper 4)

Paper 4 quiz

1a Can you answer these questions about the Speaking paper?

1 How many candidates normally take the Speaking test together?
2 How many examiners are there? What are their roles?
3 How many parts are there, and how long does each one take?

b For each part of the Speaking test

1 what do you have to do?
2 what criteria are you assessed on?
3 what is the most useful strategy?

c Check your answers in the Exam reference on page 171. How much did you know?

Part 1: Social interaction

2a Work in groups of four and choose a role.

Interlocutor: Ask *some* of the questions on page 207. Stop the discussion after two minutes.
Candidates A and B: Respond to the interlocutor.
Assessor: Listen and evaluate the candidates' performance.

b Change roles so that everyone has a turn at answering the questions.

Part 2: Long turn

3 Work in the same group as Exercise 2 and change roles, or form different groups. Look at the photos opposite.

Interlocutor: Give Candidate A the instructions on page 207.
Candidate A: Follow the interlocutor's instructions. (*about one minute*)
Interlocutor: Give Candidate B the instructions on page 207.
Candidate B: Follow the interlocutor's instructions. (*about one minute*)
Assessor: Listen and evaluate the candidates' performance.

Part 3: Collaborative task

4 Work in the same group as in Exercise 3 and change roles, or form different groups. Look at the spidergram below.

Interlocutor: Give Candidates A and B the instructions on page 207.
Candidates A and B: Follow the interlocutor's instructions.
(*about four minutes*)
Assessor: Listen and evaluate the candidates' performance.

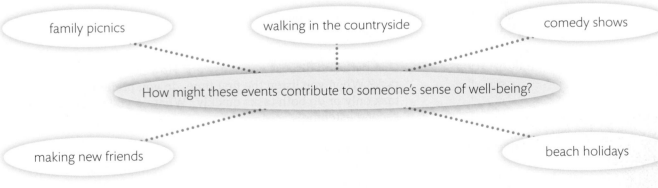

family picnics — walking in the countryside — comedy shows — How might these events contribute to someone's sense of well-being? — making new friends — beach holidays

Part 4: Extending the discussion

5 Work in the same group as in Exercise 4 and change roles.

Interlocutor: Ask Candidates A and B the questions on page 207.
Candidates A and B: Answer the interlocutor's questions.
(*about five minutes*)
Assessor: Listen and evaluate the candidates' performance.

Task analysis

6 Use your list of criteria from Exercise 1b to assess each other's performance.

Why might the people have chosen to do these things?

How relaxing might it be to do the activities?

How might people benefit from these activities?

How might the people be feeling?

Language development 2

Modals and semi-modals (Part 2)

1a Work with other students to answer this quiz.

> **Modal quiz**
>
> **1** True or false?
>   A Modal verbs are auxiliary verbs. We have to use them in conjunction with other verbs.
>   B Modal verbs express a speaker's attitude to an event or situation.
>   C Modal verbs come before the main verb in affirmative and negative statements. In questions, they come before the subject.
>   D Modal verbs must agree with the subject of the sentence.
>   E When modal verbs talk about the past, we use the past form of *have*.
>
> **2** Which **modal verbs** can you think of?
>
> **3** Which **semi-modals/verbs with modal meanings** (e.g. *need*, *have got to*) can you think of?
>
> **4** Match one of your answers in 2 and 3 with each of these meanings: *requesting, offering, giving permission, advising, suggesting, inviting, expressing certainty.*

b Check your answers in the grammar reference on page 188.

Certainty, willingness and characteristic behaviour

2a What is the difference in meaning between these sentences?

  1 a If you spend all the time texting, you'll miss the gig.
     b If you will spend all the time texting, of course you'll miss the gig.
  2 a Don't worry, it'll be Nick on the phone.
     b No matter the time of day, it would be Nick on the phone.

b Complete the sentences using *will, won't, would* or *shall.*

  1 When I was young, at weekends I _____ spend the whole time on my game console.
  2 Have you seen the new stadium? It _____ hold at least 50,000 spectators.
  3 It _____ start raining just as we are about to go out, _____ it?
  4 I'll pick you up at eight o'clock, _____ I?
  5 _____ you mind giving me a hand setting up an email account?
  6 What's the matter? Why _____ you talk to me?
  7 She _____ insist on uploading every single personal photograph. I think she does it to annoy me.
  8 I _____ have thought you'd be pleased I'd got a job as a model.

c Match the meaning of the modal in each sentence with these functions.

  annoyance   certainty   insistence   offer   refusal   request   surprise   typical behaviour

Modal revision

3 Rewrite the two sentences as one sentence, using a modal to express the meaning in the second sentence.

  1 They're not here yet. It's possible they've had an accident.
  2 Clara drove to work. It wasn't necessary.
  3 You didn't go to bed early last night. That was silly of you.
  4 Tom always leaves the door open. It's an annoying habit.
  5 They're there by now. I'm sure of it.
  6 I don't remember exactly what time we left. I'm sure it was around seven.
  7 He said he was 40. I don't believe he was telling the truth.
  8 We've been invited to a party. It's not necessary to go if we don't want to.

Alternatives to modals

4a Rewrite the sentences using one of the structures from the box and the register in brackets. There may be more than one possibility.

  be advisable to   be forbidden to   feel obliged to
  be required to   be + *to*-infinitive   be supposed to
  be under no obligation to   had better

  1 Oh, Tom, you should have got a licence for that TV. (*Informal*)
  2 Visitors must report to reception on arrival. (*Formal*)
  3 I think I should phone home and tell them I'm going to be late. (*Informal*)
  4 Remember, you don't have to answer any questions. (*Quite formal*)
  5 All DVDs out on loan must be returned by the end of term. (*Very formal*)
  6 I thought I had to invite my cousins to the wedding. (*Quite formal*)
  7 Mobile phones must not be used in this part of the hospital. (*Formal*)
  8 We tell our customers that they should take out insurance when travelling abroad. (*Formal*)

b Think of different real-life situations where these structures could be used. Make a sentence for each situation.

Use of English 2

Lead-in **1** How are optimists different from pessimists? How would you describe yourself?

Open cloze (Paper 1 Part 2) **2a** Read the title and text below quickly. (Ignore the gaps at this stage.) What are the disadvantages of being optimistic?

b If necessary, read the strategy on page 167, then complete the task.

For questions 1–8, read the text below and think of a word which best fits each gap. There is an example at the beginning (0).

The optimism bias

We think of ourselves as rational creatures and yet **(0)** *in* the main we expect things to turn **(1)**____ better than they end up being and underestimate the likelihood of negative events. Indeed, a tendency to look on the bright side may be **(2)**____ closely linked with human survival that evolution must have made us that way. Research findings show that optimists live longer and are healthier, **(3)**____ if their hopes are irrational and result **(4)**____ unwanted outcomes. In order to reach our goals we have to visualise success. However, some people argue that ceaseless optimism makes for a greater shock when things **(5)**____ wrong and that optimists need constant reassurance, which can increase anxiety. **(6)**____ than rejecting uncertainty and insecurity, they say it's better to imagine the worst. If you think you might lose something, you start to appreciate its value. It **(7)**____ the Stoics of Ancient Greece who believed that we should not avoid negative emotions. To them, the ideal state of mind was **(8)**____ of complete acceptance of any emotions, positive or negative.

3 Discuss these questions. Give reasons.
1 Do you think optimism creates happiness or anxiety?
2 How would you deal with a failure? (e.g. not getting a job)
3 Are some cultures more optimistic than others?

Key word transformations (Paper 1 Part 4) **4** Complete the second sentence so that it has a similar meaning to the first sentence, using the word given. **Do not change the word given.** You must use between **three** and **six** words, including the word given.

1 Mary regrets not having kept her appointment at the dentist's yesterday. **TURNED**
Mary wishes she ____ at the dentist's yesterday.
2 The specialist says I should have slightly less salt in my diet. **AMOUNT**
According to the specialist, I should cut ____ salt I have in my diet.
3 Alice would only go to the gym for a workout if I accompanied her. **INSISTED**
Alice ____ her to the gym when she went for a workout.
4 It's likely that the ambulance is stuck in a traffic jam somewhere. **PROBABLY**
The ambulance will ____ up in a traffic jam somewhere.
5 Thanks to the success of the treatment, Jake was cured of his illness. **LED**
The success of the treatment ____ of his illness.
6 I hate being shouted at by instructors in the middle of a session. **WHEN**
I hate ____ in the middle of a session.

5 What, in your view, are the most important factors for a healthy life?

Writing 2 Proposal (Paper 2 Part 2)

Lead-in

1 a Which of the activities in these advertisements would you like to see in a good up-to-date leisure centre? What other things can you think of?

b Do you take part in activities like these? Do you belong to any clubs or societies or attend any leisure centres regularly?

c If you were asked to promote a leisure centre to the local community, how would you go about it?

A

Apart from the usual sports and fitness facilities you'll find peace and tranquillity at our volunteer-run meditation workshops.

- LEARN simple techniques to develop balance in your life. Reduce stress and anger and deepen your understanding of what meditation can do for you.

- EXPAND your horizons and continue on a journey of self-discovery during our summer festival devoted to all aspects of modern Buddhism.

- CHILL OUT in our World Peace Café and enjoy our delicious vegetarian food.

B

How can we improve your fitness and give you a healthier lifestyle?

Sports

High-quality, inclusive and affordable sports, whether it is a swim in the pool, a game of squash or a run round the track. Tennis coaching available. Regular tournaments.

Workout

A workout in a fully equipped state-of-the-art fitness suite under the watchful eye of our fitness coaches and highly knowledgeable personal trainers.

Classes

A range of classes in our dance and exercise studios led by experts in the field to leave you feeling exhilarated.

C

We have a holistic approach to your well-being and we encourage you to take a balanced approach to your mind and body.

Sauna and steam rooms

Relax and unwind following your workout in the sauna or steam room available poolside.

Therapies

Take advantage of a range of sports, beauty and natural therapies, such as Indian head massage, aromatherapy and physiotherapy.

How are we different?

Understand the task

2 Read the task below. What questions must you consider? Think of such areas as: purpose, content, style, presentation.

> *You are employed as a senior administrator in a local sports and fitness leisure centre.*
>
> *The managing director of the centre has asked you to write a proposal recommending low-cost ways in which the centre's activities could be extended **and** suggesting how best to promote them.*
>
> *Write your **proposal**.*

Plan your proposal

3 Write a plan for your proposal. What will it consist of? What steps must you follow? What will you need to consider?

Language and content

4a Compare these two possible introductions to the proposal. Which is the better answer and why?

> **A** What low-cost ways are there to extend the centre's activities? In this proposal I'll give some ideas and say how best to promote them.

> **B** The aim of this proposal is to suggest what activities might be added to the centre's portfolio and how we should promote them. Having looked at customer feedback received in recent months, a clear picture emerges.

b Choose a phrase from the list below to begin these sentences. In some cases there is more than one possibility. Then match the sentences to your paragraph plan.

1 ... that there is no café where customers can meet their friends.
2 ... franchised out to a local café to run.
3 ... must be put on our website.
4 ... welcome meditation workshops.
5 ... the above measures are adopted.
6 ... invite local journalists to the launch.
7 ... appreciate our superb facilities.
8 ... our website is in need of an overhaul.
9 ... the treatment is professional and effective.
10 ... addition of therapies such as Indian head massage.
11 ... tennis coaching.

Reporting what has been said
It is clear that our customers ...
Many say they would ...
There have been many requests for ...
A constant complaint has been ...
Customers have commented that ...

Recommending
I would suggest that we ...
The facility could be ...
Another low-cost option would be the ...
Customers would be prepared to pay if ...

Urging action
If the centre is to develop, it is vital that ...
Obviously, all developments ...

Write your proposal

5 Read the strategy on page 170, then write your proposal in 220–260 words using some of the ideas and language above.

Check your proposal

6 Edit your work using the checklist on page 190.

Review

1 **Choose the correct word or phrase to complete the sentences.**

1 I still want to play for the team __ having been dropped at the weekend.
A regardless   B however   C nevertheless
D despite

2 The mechanics change the tyres in no time, which shows they're highly __ what they do.
A qualified in   B skilled at   C able to
D fit for

3 Sarah has a working-class background, __ my own.
A same as   B much like   C close to
D quite as

4 This is a tricky situation. I'm not sure how to __ it.
A handle   B deal   C treat   D cope

5 The project's going well over budget. We must __ the costs.
A rein in   B sail through   C skate around
D scrape by

6 The __ was held in a huge arena in the centre of London.
A programme   B episode   C event
D occurrence

7 You've got three hours or __ before the race starts.
A estimated   B close   C thereabouts
D approximate

8 Jo's very loyal. She's __ me through thick and thin.
A stuck on   B stuck with   C stuck to
D stuck at

2 **Complete the sentences with the correct form of the words in CAPITALS.**

1 The dancers were a joy to watch. They seemed to perform so _____ . **EFFORT**

2 I learnt a lot from reading your book – it was a truly _____ experience. **LIGHTEN**

3 _____ , it's the younger teachers who come up with the best ideas. **VARY**

4 We don't harbour any sort of _____ towards the manager. **RESENT**

5 My exercise regime has fallen apart because of time _____ . **CONSTRAIN**

6 It's _____ to see someone so cheerful in the mornings. **FRESH**

7 We need to act _____ if we are to get the job done. **COLLECT**

8 Quite a surprise! I found the whole book _____ uplifting. **EXPECT**

3 **Complete the second sentence so that it has a similar meaning to the first.**

1 I'd take singing lessons if I had half a chance.
Given _____ .

2 Tim always talks while I'm trying to work.
Tim will _____ .

3 Facing up to the truth must have been hard for her.
It couldn't _____ .

4 He's over 60, but if you look at him you wouldn't think so.
To look _____ .

5 Are we required to work together as a team?
Do we _____ .

6 I couldn't get the tickets because I didn't have enough time.
Not _____ .

7 I realised the class had been cancelled when I saw there was no one there.
Seeing _____ .

8 We set off after we'd got our things together
Having _____ .

4 **Circle the correct alternative to complete the text.**

◎ **Browsing blogs**

My friend Bob told me that taking line dancing classes **(1)** *must / would* help me relax after work, and I've known him long **(2)** *time / enough* to trust him. Also, **(3)** *having been / on being* quite a good disco dancer in my time, I thought it might be the perfect pastime for me. **(4)** *To know / Knowing* that you **(5)** *are not allowed to / had better not* make physical contact with the other dancers and simply have to follow a series of steps in unison, I thought that learning how to do it **(6)** *wouldn't be / needn't have been* a problem. Little did I know! **(7)** *On discovering / Discovered* that everyone was so much older than me, I was determined **(8)** *put on / to put on* a good show and so threw myself into the dance, **(9)** *finding / only to find* that I kept getting the steps wrong! I soon realised it **(10)** *might have been forbidden / would have been advisable* to stand back and watch the others first. The whole experience could **(11)** *have been / had been* a disaster if it hadn't been for a very kindly old lady, who I'm sure **(12)** *must be / must have been* doing it for years. She told me to slow down and not try so hard!

Exam reference

Paper 1: Reading and Use of English (1 hour 30 minutes)

There are eight parts to this paper, with a total of 3,000–3,500 words.

- Part 1: four-option multiple-choice cloze – one short text with eight items
- Part 2: open cloze – one short text with eight gaps
- Part 3: word formation – one short text with eight gaps
- Part 4: key word transformations – six separate items
- Part 5: four-option multiple choice – one long text with six questions
- Part 6: cross-text multiple matching – four short texts with four questions
- Part 7: gapped text – one long text from which six paragraphs have been removed and jumbled
- Part 8: multiple matching – one long text or several short texts with ten items

There are 56 questions overall.

- Parts 1–3: each correct answer gets one mark
- Part 4: each correct answer gets up to two marks
- Parts 5–7: each correct answer gets two marks
- Part 8: each correct answer gets one mark

Total number of marks = 72 marks.

EXPERT TASK STRATEGY (ALL TASKS)

- For all text-based tasks, read the titles and skim the text quickly to get a general sense of what it's about and how it's organised before you begin.
- Read the instructions carefully and be aware of the time constraints. Make sure you answer all the questions.
- Before choosing an option in a text-based task, read the part of the text it relates to very carefully.
- Notes can be made on the question paper, but your answers must be transferred to the answer sheet before the end of the test.

Part 1: four-option multiple-choice cloze

This is a four-option multiple-choice task with eight gaps. The focus is on awareness of vocabulary and an understanding of the text, both at a phrasal/sentence level and with longer stretches of text. Even if the option fits grammatically, it may not be appropriate in the context. Collocations (e.g. *spend time*), complementation (e.g. *made her go*), idioms (e.g. *jump on the bandwagon*), phrasal verbs (e.g. *turn up*), linking expressions (e.g. *Despite that*) and different shades of meaning (e.g. *gaze* vs. *glance*) may all be tested.

EXPERT TASK STRATEGY

- Look at the sentences before and after the gap and think about what kind of word or phrase fits each gap. Some words have similar meanings but the choice will depend on the words they collocate with (e.g. a preposition or direct object), as well as the context.
- Think carefully about the exact meaning and use of each option before making a decision about which one fits the context. If you aren't sure, cross out the answers which you know are incorrect, and then make a guess depending on what sounds right to you.
- Read the whole text again with your chosen options to make sure they make sense and fit grammatically.

Part 2: open cloze

You have to read a text with eight gaps (one gap for each missing word). The focus is on awareness and control of grammar and lexico-grammatical items. The missing words are usually grammatical and may include articles (e.g. *the*), pronouns (e.g. *that*), prepositions (e.g. *against*), verb forms (e.g. *running*), auxiliaries (e.g. *have*), conjunctions (e.g. *after*), set phrases (e.g. *in a while*), etc. Some will form part of phrasal verbs and fixed phrases.

EXPERT TASK STRATEGY

- Read the text quickly first to get an idea of what it is about.
- Look at the context and the words around each gap. What kind of word is needed to fit the meaning and the grammar?
- Put only one word in each gap. Don't use contractions.
- Read the text again to make sure it makes sense and that your spelling is correct.

Part 3: word formation

This is a text with 8 gaps. At the end of some of the lines, you are given the base form of a word. You have to put it into the correct form to fit the context of the gap in that line. This task's main focus is vocabulary, in particular the use of prefixes and suffixes, internal changes and compounds, although an understanding of structure is required.

EXPERT TASK STRATEGY

- Read the line with the gap in the context of the paragraph and the whole text.
- Work out what part of speech the missing word is (e.g. noun, verb, adjective, adverb).

- Check if a negative or plural form is needed. Think about which affixes will be needed to change it so that the word fits the context.
- If the stem has more than one possible derivative (e.g. two different noun forms), look carefully at the context to ensure you choose the right one.
- Change the form of the base word in capitals so that it fits the meaning. More than one change may be needed to the stem.

Part 4: key word transformations

In this part of the test, you are given six lead-in sentences. Each one is followed by another sentence, to which you are given the beginning and the end. You are also given a key word. You have to complete each gapped sentence in three to six words so that it has a similar meaning to the first sentence. You must include the key word, which should not change in any way. Contracted words (e.g. *she'll*) count as two words.

The focus is on grammar, vocabulary and collocation. You are tested on your ability to express the same idea using different grammatical forms and patterns. There are always two testing points for each sentence (e.g. a change to the word from the input sentence and a change to the word order to create a new sentence pattern).

EXPERT TASK STRATEGY

- Read both sentences carefully so that you understand the meaning of what is missing from the second sentence.
- Identify what the key word is (e.g. noun, verb, etc.) and how it will fit into the gapped sentence.
- Read your completed sentence to check that it reflects the meaning of the first sentence, it makes sense and it is spelt correctly.
- Make sure you have included all the elements of the first sentence. Your answer may include words that are not in the first sentence, but which express the same idea. However, avoid 'over-transforming' in any way (e.g. adding words which aren't necessary).

Part 5: multiple choice

The text in this section is followed by six four-option multiple-choice questions in the same order as the information in the text. The task tests detailed understanding of the writer's opinion, attitude, tone and purpose, as well as inference and features of text organisation. Close reference to the text is needed in order to eliminate similar answers. The final question may require interpretation of the text as a whole.

EXPERT TASK STRATEGY

- Read the text first to get an idea of the overall context.
- Read all the stems (questions or unfinished sentences) and underline the key words.
- For each question, find the relevant part of the text that relates to it and read it carefully.
- Try to answer the question (or complete the unfinished statement) in your own words before looking at the options.
- Look at the four options and decide which one is nearest to your own answer. This will require close reading of the text as there may be very similar views expressed elsewhere. However, only one will match the option exactly.
- If you are not sure of the answer, try to eliminate the ones that can't be correct.

Part 6: cross-text multiple matching

In this part of the test, you are given four short texts on a related theme, followed by four multiple-matching question prompts. You have to read all the texts and understand the opinions and attitudes expressed so that you can identify where the opinions of the four writers are the same and where they are different.

EXPERT TASK STRATEGY

- Read the instructions carefully.
- Read the question prompts and underline the key words.
- Read the texts quickly to identify the parts which directly refer to the opinions and points of view of each writer.
- Read these sections again very carefully to make sure you fully understand them.
- Read all the texts again to find where the other writers talk about the same issues. Which of the other three sections is the question referring to? This will require careful reading as the opinions will be expressed in different ways.
- Some questions may ask you to identify the writer who has a different opinion from the other three. To do this, go through the texts and underline the sections where the issue is discussed. Then read the texts again to see who has a different opinion.
- Mark your answers and read through one more time to check.

Part 7: gapped text

In this task, there is a text from which six paragraphs have been removed and placed in jumbled order. You have to decide where in the text they fit. (There is one extra paragraph which does not fit anywhere in the text.) The task focus is on understanding of the text as a whole, and how the argument or narrative is developed and is organised. Careful reading is required and an ability to recognise linguistic devices such as reference words (e.g. *despite this, they*) and near-synonyms. This will help you to follow the logical development of the text and locate where the missing paragraphs fit.

EXPERT TASK STRATEGY

- Read the base text carefully to see how the overall theme is developed and to get a feel of the overall structure. For example, how do the ideas develop? Is the use of different tenses, linking words, etc. helpful in following this?
- Read the text around each gap carefully and try to predict what kind of information is missing. Look for clues such as reference words (e.g. pronouns), time references (e.g. *earlier*), verb forms and parallel phrases.
- Read the missing paragraphs and think about the purpose they serve. Are they adding information to develop an argument? Are they referring back to an event? Are they contrasting a point of view? Underline topic links, grammatical links (tenses, pronouns, articles, linkers, etc.) and lexical links (e.g. parallel phrases) to the main text.
- Choose the best option to fit each gap.
- Read the whole text again in sequence. Does it make sense? Are you sure the 'distractor paragraph' cannot fit anywhere?

Part 8: multiple matching

This part of the paper contains either a continuous text divided into paragraphs, or several short texts, preceded by ten multiple matching questions. You must match each question to an element or section of the text. This part tests your understanding of detail, opinion, attitude and specific information and your ability to locate it quickly.

EXPERT TASK STRATEGY

- Read the questions and mark the key words before reading the text.
- Scan the text section by section to find information or ideas which match the questions. It is not necessary to read every word. Use parallel phrases and ideas in the questions and text to help you find the information you need.
- Read the section of text you choose again carefully to make sure it has exactly the same meaning as the question. Be careful because there may be similar ideas expressed in different sections.
- If you are unsure, go on to the next question. It will be easier to answer when you have dealt with more questions.

Paper 2: Writing (1 hour 30 minutes)

There are two parts to this paper, and one task in each.
- Part 1 is a compulsory essay.
- Part 2 consists of a choice between three tasks. You will be asked to write a letter, proposal, report or review.

Each task carries equal marks. The instructions clearly specify the type of writing, the target reader and the purpose for writing. Candidates should read the instructions carefully, as all relevant information must be included.

EXPERT TASK STRATEGY (ALL TASKS)

For all task types, you should:
- answer the question and include all relevant points.
- consider the target reader carefully so that you use the appropriate register.
- spend time thinking about and planning your writing.
- organise your answer in a way that is appropriate to the task type.
- use a wide range of vocabulary and sentence structures, including some more complex language.
- use discourse markers effectively.
- engage the reader's interest.
- leave enough time to check your answers.
- try to keep approximately within the recommended word limit. If you write too much, you run the risk of including irrelevant information and repetition of ideas. If you write too little, you may not cover all the required points.

Part 1

Part 1 is based on input material in the form of notes made during a seminar, lecture or panel discussion. You have to write an essay developing and supporting an argument on a particular topic in 220–260 words. You can choose from the points made in the input texts or use your own ideas. However, if you use ideas from the input texts, they must be in your own words as far as possible.

EXPERT TASK STRATEGY

- Read the instructions carefully to check how many parts there are to the question. Decide which of the input notes you are going to write about and make sure you are clear about the points to include. Process and combine the information before you start to write.
- Make a paragraph plan showing how the essay will be structured. Make notes of key points that you will include in the introduction, conclusion and other paragraphs in the body of the text.

- Decide how you will back up and exemplify the key points. Make sure each paragraph focuses on a different topic.
- Check that you have used a range of language and that your register is consistent.
- Check for spelling and punctuation mistakes.

➤ **EXPERT WRITING** pages 191–192

Part 2

In Part 2, you have to choose one of three tasks. You are provided with a clear context, topic, purpose and target reader for your writing. You must write between 220 and 260 words.

Letter
- Identify the purpose of the text, for example, making a complaint, giving advice, asking for information, etc. There may be a narrative element or factual information required.
- Make sure that you write it at the appropriate level of formality depending on your target reader.
- Conventions such as an opening salutation, clear paragraphing and closing phrasing are important.
- Link ideas together into paragraphs, each with a clear focus.

Proposal
- Make sure you write in a style appropriate to, for example, a superior or a peer group.
- Plan your proposal carefully, making notes of suggestions, supported by factual information, in order to persuade the reader of a course of action.
- Decide how you will organise your points. (e.g. under headings)
- Think carefully about how to make polite recommendations or suggestions.

Report
- Ensure you address all the points in the question.
- Organise your report into paragraphs with sub-headings and bullet points.
- Make sure your report is worded in a suitably formal and impersonal style.
- Make your points clearly and succinctly.
- The introduction should state the aim of the report and the report should end with a recommendation.

Review
- Think about the kind of language you will need to write the review. Will it include narrative, description or evaluation, for example?
- Think of vocabulary connected to the review. Include adjectives and adverbs to express praise and criticism.
- Plan your review and order the points.
- Think of a title.
- Remember to conclude with a recommendation.

➤ **EXPERT WRITING** pages 193–197

Paper 3: Listening
(approximately 40 minutes)

This paper has four parts.
- Part 1: three-option multiple choice – three short extracts with two questions each
- Part 2: sentence completion – a monologue with eight questions
- Part 3: four-option multiple choice – an interview or discussion with six questions
- Part 4: multiple matching – five themed monologues with ten questions

Each part is heard twice. The instructions, which are recorded as well as printed on the page, are followed by a pause, giving you time to read through the task for that section. Notes can be made on the question sheet during the exam, but at the end you are given time to transfer your answers to the answer sheet provided. Each correct answer gets one mark.

EXPERT TASK STRATEGY (ALL TASKS)
- Read and listen to the rubrics carefully, so you know what you are going to hear.
- In the time provided, read through the task to help you predict the content/missing information.
- Remember that you won't hear exactly the same sentences or words as in the questions or options. They will be expressed in a different way.
- You will hear each extract twice, so check your answers during the second listening.
- When transferring your answers to the answer sheet, check that your answers make sense and fit grammatically, the key words are spelt correctly and your handwriting is legible.

Part 1: multiple choice: short extracts

In this section, you will hear three unrelated extracts from exchanges between interacting speakers. They could be extracts from conversations, radio broadcasts, etc. Each extract lasts about a minute and has two three-option multiple-choice questions. You may need to identify the speaker's feelings, attitude or opinion, and whether the two speakers agree or disagree with each other. You may also need to listen for gist and purpose as well as detail.

EXPERT TASK STRATEGY
- Before you listen, read the context sentences carefully to establish the situation and who will be speaking.
- Read the questions and mark the key words.
- Predict what you will be listening for.

- Listen for the answers to the questions. Remember you will often be listening for the opinions or attitudes of the speakers.
- Listen again and decide which option is nearest to your answer.

Part 2: sentence completion

In this section, you will hear a monologue of around three minutes such as an extract from a radio broadcast, a lecture, speech, etc. You will have to complete eight gapped sentences which summarise the stated information you hear. The items follow the order of information in the text and you have to complete the gaps with one to three words, usually concrete nouns or noun phrases. This part tests your ability to follow the structure of a text and extract specific information and stated opinion.

EXPERT TASK STRATEGY

- Read the rubric and each question carefully to understand the context and predict the information or words that you might hear.
- The words you need to write are on the recording. You do not need to change them.
- You may hear other words that would fit grammatically, so make sure that the word/words you have chosen make sense in the context.
- Listen for discourse markers to help you follow the structure and topic shifts of the talk.
- Check and complete your answers during the second listening.

Part 3: multiple choice

In this section, you will hear an interview or discussion of around four minutes between two or more people. There are six four-option multiple-choice questions and the focus is on the attitudes and opinions of the speakers.

EXPERT TASK STRATEGY

As for Part 1, but also listen for:
- discourse markers and other cues which signal a change of topic, agreement, disagreement, etc.
- words and phrases that have a similar meaning to the options but which are expressed in a different way.

Part 4: multiple matching

In this section, you will hear five short monologues of around 30 seconds, each on a related theme. There are two tasks (One and Two) and ten questions in all. In each task you have to select the correct five options from a list of eight possibilities. The task focus is to listen for gist and main points and identify and interpret information about the context, the speakers and their opinions and attitudes.

EXPERT TASK STRATEGY

- Before you listen, read the rubric and options carefully so that you understand the context and what you have to listen for.
- Read the eight options (A–H in both tasks) and mark the key words.
- When you listen, match the gist of what you hear to the ideas in the prompts. Choose one option from Task One and one from Task Two for each speaker.
- When you listen again, check your answers. If you haven't already completed Task Two, then do that now. Remember there are three options in each task which you do not use.
- Only one of the options will match what each speaker says but you will hear similar ideas expressed.
- If you are not sure of an answer, make a guess.

Paper 4: Speaking
(approximately 15 minutes)

This paper is divided into four parts, each of which focuses on a different type of interaction. You take the test with a partner. The standard format is two candidates and two examiners: the interlocutor, who asks the questions and assesses, and the assessor, who listens and assesses but does not take part. In a few situations, there are groups of three candidates, in which case more time is allowed.

Each part is designed to encourage a range of spontaneous language based on prompts. It is important to speak as much as possible in order to demonstrate your ability to use a range of language, but it is equally important to include your partner where appropriate and encourage his/her contribution. Examiners can only assess you on the language you produce, so you will not do well if you do not contribute. Note: they only assess your language, not your ideas.

Assessment is based on performance in the whole of the speaking test, using the following criteria:

- range of appropriate vocabulary
- control of a range of simple and some complex grammatical forms
- comprehensible pronunciation of individual sounds, accurate stress and appropriate intonation
- ability to produce and manage an extended stretch of language, including the use of discourse markers and cohesive devices to organise ideas
- ability to maintain and develop interactive communication with others

The assessment scales for *Advanced* Paper 4 are based on the C1 *Common European Frame of Reference for Languages* (CEFR) and range from Band 5 (the highest) to Band 1.

EXPERT TASK STRATEGY (ALL PARTS)

- Listen to the examiner's instructions carefully so that you know what you have to do.
- Don't be afraid to ask him/her to repeat anything, if necessary.
- Use a wide range of structures and vocabulary. This is your chance to show your command of spoken English.
- Avoid repeating yourself.
- Speak clearly so that the examiners can hear.
- Give yourself thinking time by using expressions such as *Let me think* or *I haven't given that much thought before, but I suppose* (although these should not be over-used).
- Paraphrase if you can't think of a word.
- In Parts 1, 3 and 4, participate fully but don't dominate – encourage your partner to speak as well.

Part 1: social interaction

This is a short social interaction of about two minutes between the interlocutor, yourself and another candidate on general topics relating to your interests, experiences, plans for the future, etc.

EXPERT TASK STRATEGY

- React naturally – don't use prepared answers.
- Expand your answers as fully as you can. Give extra information or a reason.
- Avoid being monosyllabic – invent ideas if necessary.
- Keep talking – don't leave long pauses.
- Don't repeat language the other candidate or examiner uses. Use a wide range of grammar and vocabulary, and try to sound lively and interesting.

Part 2: long turn

In this task, you have to talk for about a minute without interruption. You are given three pictures around a particular theme and you have to compare and react to two of them. The prompt is also written above the pictures. You need to compare, contrast, give opinions, speculate and hypothesise, rather than simply describe the pictures. You are also asked to comment briefly for about 30 seconds after your partner has spoken.

EXPERT TASK STRATEGY

- Make sure you don't just describe the pictures.
- Keep talking until the examiner says *Thank you.* Try not to repeat yourself.
- Organise your ideas so that you answer both parts of the question, and try to express yourself coherently and with enthusiasm.
- Don't leave long pauses. Paraphrase if necessary or use 'fillers'.

- When your partner is speaking, listen but don't interrupt. You will have to give a view on what he/she says later.

Part 3: collaborative task

In this section of the speaking test, you and your partner are given written prompts on a spidergram. You are asked to collaborate on making a decision or solving a problem, although there is no one correct answer. In the first part of this task, you and your partner are expected to discuss the five prompts on the spidergram in order to answer the question which is also printed there. After two minutes, you are given the second part of the task and you have a minute to reach some kind of conclusion, although you do not have to agree. You then have to report on and justify the outcome of your discussion.

This task requires a range of communicative skills such as expressing and justifying opinions, agreeing and disagreeing, eliciting ideas, suggesting, speculating, evaluating and reaching a decision. It also requires you to be able to keep the conversation going by using strategies such as paraphrasing, asking for clarification and using conversational 'fillers'.

EXPERT TASK STRATEGY

- Be ready to initiate and give your opinions, but it's essential not to dominate.
- Invite your partner to contribute and follow up on what he/she says.
- Be aware of the time limit. Give opinions and move on.
- Use as wide a range of language as you can.
- Don't rush to come to a decision in the last minute – you will not be penalised for failing to reach a negotiated decision.

Part 4: follow-up discussion

In the last part of the speaking test, the examiner leads a discussion which develops the issues raised in Part 3 in a broader, more abstract way and in more depth. You may be asked to respond to the same or different questions. The task is a three-way discussion in which you have an opportunity to exchange information, give and justify opinions, and agree and disagree. You have about five minutes for this.

EXPERT TASK STRATEGY

- Take full part in the discussion, avoiding very short answers.
- Respond to and develop the points made by your partner.
- Do not interrupt or dominate the discussion.
- If you have no opinion on the issues, invent them! There are no 'right' answers.

Expert grammar

Module 1

1 Verb forms – present and past (page 13)

A Continuous forms

1 **Used to talk about temporary events**

I'm studying in the USA at the moment. (present continuous)
I was backpacking around Peru this time last year. (past continuous)

2 **Used to show an event is ongoing**

He's been working here for two weeks (and he still is). (present perfect continuous)
I was having a bath when the phone rang. (past continuous: event in progress)

3 **Used to focus on the action/situation**

She's always leaving the door open. (present continuous: characteristic behaviour – often not wanted)
I've been cooking all day. I'm exhausted. (present perfect continuous: leading to present result)

Notes
- Some verbs are not normally used in the continuous. These are:
  – verbs that describe states of being, e.g. *appear, be, deserve, doubt, exist, hate, mean, own*
  – verbs used to describe the speech being 'performed', e.g. *agree, apologise, promise*
  – verbs of sense and perception, e.g. *smell, taste, think*
  When these verbs are used in the continuous they change their meaning:
  I'm thinking of going out. (= I'm considering)
- Some verbs which describe physical feelings, e.g. *feel, hurt*, can be used in the simple or continuous form with little or no difference in meaning: *How are you feeling/do you feel?*

B Perfect forms

We use perfect forms to talk about things which happen before or leading up to another time/event:
I've been a novelist for a long time. (present perfect: time up to the present).
Listen, I've found out something very interesting about this university. (present perfect: past event/action with present relevance)
I'd already met J.K. Rowling, so she knew who I was. (past perfect for a prior event in the past)

Note
for = a period of time, e.g. *for six weeks*
since = a point of time, e.g. *since last June*

C Verb forms often confused

1 **Present simple and present continuous**

- Present simple
  The sun rises in the East. (= general truth; fact)
  She lives in France. (= long-term situation)

He (often) watches TV in the evenings. (= habit)
I like coffee. (= state, e.g. feeling/opinion)
I'll see you when you get back. (= future time after when/as soon as/after)

- Present continuous
  Look! The sun's rising.
  (= event in progress/changing situation)
  She's living in France for the summer. (= temporary situation)

2 **Present perfect and past simple**

- Present perfect (= thinking of past and present together)
  Oh, no! I've left the tickets at home. (a past action with present relevance)
  The president has arrived. (recent past)
  I've been all over the world. (general experience)
  I've lived here for three years. (an unfinished time period)

- Past simple (= thinking only of the past)
  I left the tickets on the table when I left. (completed action at a specific time in the past)
  His plane landed at 10 o'clock. (completed action)

3 **Past continuous and past simple**

- Past continuous (= long temporary action/state not complete at a time in the past)
  At six o'clock I was driving home.

- Past simple (= short completed action)
  As I was driving home, I had an accident.

4 **Present perfect simple and present perfect continuous**

- Present perfect simple (= completed actions when we are interested in the result)
  No, thanks. I've read that book three times.
  Present perfect continuous (= interested in the action or to emphasise how long)
  I've been reading this book for over a month and still haven't finished it.

5 **Past perfect simple and past perfect continuous**

- Past perfect simple (= to stress that one event finished before the other began)
  I'd finished my dinner before she got there.

- Past perfect continuous (= for a longer/continuous period up to a specified time in the past)
  Before I came to London I had been working in Paris.

6 *used to* **and** *would*

- *used to* (habits/states that are no longer true)
  She used to live in London. (= discontinued state)

- *would* (habits/actions that are no longer true)
  He would read the newspaper every morning./
  He used to read the newspaper every morning.
  (= discontinued habit)

Note
Would is not used for discontinued states.

2 The passive (page 18)

A Use

1 We use a passive construction when:
- we don't know who or what did something:
  *Our school **was broken into** last night.*
- it is obvious who the 'doer' is or it is not important at the time of speaking:
  *I **was given** a new contract yesterday.* (obviously by my employer)
- we don't want to say who the 'doer' is:
  *Some mistakes **were made** in the preparation of the report.* (We don't want to say who made the mistakes – possibly to protect them or ourselves!)

2 When we wish to focus on who or what did something, we use *by* + the 'doer':
*My husband was badly injured **by a lorry**.* (The new information (*a lorry*) is brought into focus by putting it at the end of the sentence.)

3 The passive is more common in writing than speaking and can sound formal and impersonal. It is often used
- in orders and rules:
  *All money **must be paid** by the end of the week.*
- to talk about events and achievements:
  *The school **was founded** in 1978.*
- to talk about processes:
  *First, strips of wood **are put** through the machine.*
- in academic and scientific English.

Note
The passive cannot be used with:
- intransitive verbs (verbs with no direct object): *It ~~was arrived~~.*
- state verbs (e.g. *be, have, seem*): *A bath ~~is being had by Jane~~.*

B Form

1 Active versus passive forms

	Active	Passive
modal verb (present) → modal verb + *be* + past participle	*All students **must take** an entrance exam.*	*An entrance exam **must be taken** by all students.*
modal verb (past) → modal verb + *have been* + past participle	*They **should** not **have elected** him.*	*He **should** not **have been elected**.*
make, see, hear, help → *be* + past	*They **made** me **do** it.*	*I **was made** to **do** it.*
participle + *to*-infinitive	*They **heard** him **shout**.*	*He **was heard** to **shout**.*
let → no passive form	*They **don't let** candidates use dictionaries.*	*Candidates **are not allowed**/**permitted** to use dictionaries.*

2 Passive -*ing* forms and infinitives

When verbs are followed by an -*ing* or infinitive form, these forms can be made passive:

- verb + passive infinitive
  *The film star **agreed to be photographed**.*
- verb + -*ing* form
  *I'm tired of **being lied to**.*

3 *need* + -*ing* can have a passive meaning
*The cups **need washing**.* = *The cups **need to be washed**.*

C Impersonal passive structures

The following structures can be used with reporting verbs:
- subject + passive verb + *to*-infinitive
  *He is **considered/said/thought to be** the greatest writer ever.*
  *They are **believed/reported/thought to have become** extinct.*
- *It* + passive verb + *that* clause
  *It is **thought/expected/said/understood that** the weather will get worse.*
- *There* + passive verb + *to be*
  *There are **thought/expected/said/known to be** huge food shortages.*

D *have/get* + object + past participle

We can use this structure:

1 to talk about something which someone else does for us because we have asked them to (*get* is more informal than *have*):
*Have you **had** your hair **cut**?*
*I want to **get** the house **redecorated**.*

2 like the passive, for things that happened by accident or unexpectedly, usually something unpleasant; it is fairly informal:
*How **did** your car **get damaged**?*
*I've **had** my bike **stolen**.*

Module 2

1 Relative clauses (page 29)

A Relative pronouns and adverbs

1 A relative pronoun can be the subject of a relative clause:
*I talked to the producer **who/that** made Dream School.*
(I talked to the producer. **She** made *Dream School*.)
*Tania, **who** is very romantic, is always falling in love.*
(Tania is always falling in love. **She** is very romantic.)
*Judy's the woman **whose** parents have just retired.*
(Judy's a woman. Her parents have just retired.)
*This is the car **which/that** has broken down.*
(This is the car. **It** has broken down.)

Note
We cannot:
- use a subject pronoun after a subject relative pronoun:
  I talked to the producer who ~~she~~ made Dream School.
- omit a subject relative pronoun:
  I talked to a woman made Dream School. ✗

2 A relative pronoun can be the object of a relative clause:
*Lionel Messi, **who** I met once at a party, is a very nice man.*
*Lionel Messi, **whom** I met once at a party ...* (formal)
(Lionel Messi is a very nice man. I once met **him** at a party.)
*Some of the goals **which/that** he scores are amazing.*
(He scores goals. Some of **them** are amazing.)

Note
We cannot:
- use an object pronoun and an object relative pronoun in the same relative clause:
*The goals **which** he scores ~~them~~ are amazing.*

3 Relative adverbs include *where* (places), *when* (times) and *why* (reasons). They can be the subject or object of a relative clause. Alternatives to *where, when* and *why*:
*This is the place **where/in which** we spent our honeymoon.*
*1986 is the year **when/in which** he was born.*
*I know the reason **why/that** they came here.*

4 The relative pronoun *which* can be used to refer to a whole sentence, not just the subject/object:
*He was very quiet, **which** is unusual for him.*
*He arrived at nine, **which** was when he was expected.*

We can also say ..., which was how/why/what/where ...
*The train was delayed, **which was why** he was late for work.*

B Defining relative clauses

These identify or classify a noun/pronoun. They are necessary for the sense of a sentence. We do not use commas:
*He is someone **who** is generally very punctual.*

We can omit the defining relative pronoun if it is an object:
*He's the man **(who/that)** I met when we were volunteers together.*

C Non-defining relative clauses

These add extra information and are not necessary to the sense of a sentence. The extra information is separated by commas. Non-defining relative clauses are more common in written English than spoken English.
*The phone, **which had been quiet all evening**, suddenly rang.*

Notes
- We cannot omit the relative pronoun.
- We cannot use *that* instead of *which*.

D Words used with relative pronouns

1 Prepositions and prepositional phrases
- A preposition can go at the end of a relative clause or before the relative pronoun:
*It's a mystery **which** there is no explanation **for**.*
(less formal)
*It's a mystery **for which** there is no explanation.*
(more formal)

Note
After a preposition, we use the pronoun *which* (not *that*) for things and *whom* (not *who*) for people:
*Is this the place **which/that** we used to eat in?* (less formal)
*Is this the place **in which** we used to eat?* (formal)

- Prepositional phrases are often used in non-defining relative clauses:
*It might rain, **in which case** we'll have to go home.*
*We waited for him until seven, **at which point** we gave up.*
*Facebook was founded in 2004, **since when** it's become a worldwide phenomenon.*

2 Words such as *all, both/neither, some, many of* are often used before the relative pronoun in non-defining clauses: *There are 500 people outside, **many of whom** have waited for several hours.*

3 The following words may be used before a relative pronoun in defining relative clauses with *who* (not *whom*) and *that* (not *which*): *someone/something, anyone/anything, everything, some, all, many, little, much, those*
***Anyone who** saw the young Elizabeth Taylor said how beautiful she was.*
*I disagreed with **much that** was said.*

E Replacing relative clauses

1 We can often reduce a relative clause by omitting the relative pronoun and the auxiliary verb:
The man ~~who was~~ living next door ... (active meaning)
The wall ~~which was~~ built during Roman times still stands. (passive meaning)

2 We can sometimes replace a relative clause containing a modal with a *to*-infinitive:
*There's no-one here **to speak to**.* (= that I can speak to)

F Nominal relative clauses

In these clauses, the whole relative clause functions as a noun. Nominal relative pronouns include: *what, whatever, whoever, whichever, when, where, who, how, why*
*Tell me **what** you did yesterday.* (= the things that you did)
***Whatever** he did must have been terrible.* (= whatever things)
*You can invite **whoever** you want.* (= any person who)
*This is **where** I was born.* (= the place where)
*That's **why** I like it.* (= the reason why)
*You're not **who** I thought you were.* (= the person who)

2 Nouns, articles, determiners and pronouns (page 34)

A Uncountable nouns

1 These refer to things we think of as a 'mass', rather than individual, countable things. They usually have no plural form and are used with a singular verb:
accommodation, advice, clothing, equipment, food, flu, luggage, patience, weather, etc.
*Progress **is** very slow.*

2 We do not normally use the indefinite article (*a/an*) with uncountable nouns. Instead, determiners like *some, any,* etc. may be used:
Here is ~~an~~ some advice.
There isn't ~~an~~ any evidence.

3 We can use the definite article with uncountable nouns when we are talking about a specific example of something:
*Can you give me back **the** money I gave you?*
However, we do not use the definite article to talk about things generally:
***Money** is the root of all evil.*

4 To make uncountable nouns countable, we use phrases like these:
***a bit of** help, **a piece of** evidence/information, **a pile of** rubbish/books, **a slice of** bread/cake, **a spoonful/two spoonfuls of** (sugar)*

B Countable or uncountable nouns?

1 Many nouns can be countable or uncountable depending on the context:

Uncountable	Countable
***Life** here is very good.*	*Many **lives** were saved.*
***Time** is short.*	***Times** were hard.*
*Don't stay out in the **cold**.*	***Colds** are common in winter.*
***Science** is not a popular subject.*	*The **sciences** are squeezed of funds.*

2 Some uncountable nouns can be used with the indefinite article. They are usually qualified by an adjective or phrase:

Uncountable	Countable + adjectival phrase
***Knowledge** is power.*	*He has **a good knowledge** of the area.*
*I've got no **time**.*	*Have **a good time**.*
***Tolerance** is a virtue.*	*He showed **a great deal of tolerance**.*

C Subject–verb agreement

1 Uncountable nouns ending in *-s* are followed by a singular verb: *aerobics, athletics, genetics, maths, news, physics, politics,* etc.
*No news **is** good news.*

2 These nouns are always followed by a plural verb:
- Nouns ending in *-s*, usually clothes and tools:
pyjamas, shorts, trousers;
glasses (= spectacles), pliers, scissors
To make these singular, we usually use *a pair of*:
a pair of trousers
- Nouns made up of many 'parts':
the authorities, belongings, cattle, contents, goods, (the) people, (the) police, remains

3 The noun *whereabouts* can be followed by a singular or plural verb:
*His **whereabouts is/are** unknown.*

4 Collective nouns (nouns referring to groups)
- These may be used with a singular verb if we think of them as a **single unit**, or with a plural verb if we are referring to **members of the group**. We use *the* with these nouns:
***The staff is** excellent.* (= thinking of an impersonal unit)
***The staff are** excellent.* (= thinking of the people who work there)
*The media **is/are** very powerful.*
Other examples include: *army, audience, choir, committee, headquarters, orchestra, press, public*
- We generally use a singular verb after *a/an* + collective noun:
***An** army of volunteers **is** on its way.*
- We generally use a plural verb after the following expressions when they are followed by *of* + plural noun: *the majority/minority (of), a number (of), a couple (of)*
*Only a minority of people **support** the new law.*
*A number of people still **cling** on to the old beliefs.*
Compare:
*A small minority **disagree/disagrees** with the ruling.*

5 If a plural subject describes a single unit, e.g. an amount or quantity, we usually use a singular verb:
***Thirty kilometres is** a long way.*
***Five euros is** not much.*
***Six per cent is** a big increase.*

D Determiners, pronouns and quantifiers

1 Before nouns
- With a countable or uncountable noun:
some/any, (not) enough, half/all (of), a lot of/lots of, more/most, no, plenty of
- With a countable noun:
a few (= some), few (= almost no), (not) many, one/both (of), each (of), every, either/neither (of), several
- With an uncountable noun:
a little (= at least some), little (= almost none), (not) much, less, the whole

2 Determiner or pronoun?
Most of the words in the above section can be used as determiners (before a noun) or pronouns (on their own).
***Most people** enjoy sport.* (determiner)
***Some of your ideas** are crazy.* (pronoun)
*'Which one do you want?' '**Either** is OK.'* (pronoun)

Notes
- *no* and *every* are determiners, never pronouns.
- *none* is a pronoun, never a determiner.

3 each, every

- We use *each* to talk about two or more things or people, considered separately:
  *She held a bag in **each** hand.*

- We use *every* to refer to all the people or things in a particular group (more than two):
  ***Every** road in the centre was blocked.* (= all roads)

- In some contexts, we can use *each* or *every* interchangeably:
  ***Each/Every** person in the group joined in.*

- We can use *each* (not *every*) as a pronoun:
  *We **each** have our own skills.*
  ***Each** of us went our own way.*

- We can use e*ach/every + one of*:
  *We played several games and lost **each/every one of** them.*

- *Each* and *every* are followed by a singular verb:
  ***Each** of us **has** a job to do.*

4 all, both

- We use *both* to talk about two people, things, etc. together, and emphasise that each is included:
  ***Both** films were boring.* (determiner)
  *'Which one shall I buy?' 'Why not get **both**?'* (pronoun)

- We use *all* to refer to the whole of an amount, thing, or type of thing, or every one of a number. We don't usually use *all* as a pronoun on its own:
  *I haven't seen him **all** week.* (determiner)
  *'Which one do you like?' 'I like **all** of them.'* (pronoun)

5 the whole (adjective, noun)

We use *(the) whole* to refer to all of something, often instead of *all of*:
*We wasted **the whole day** looking for it.*
*Climate change affects **the whole (of the) planet**.*

6 either, neither

We use *either* and *neither* to refer to one or the other of two things or people. Strictly speaking, they are followed by a singular verb, but a plural verb is common in spoken English.
*'You can have **either** tea or coffee.' '**Neither**, thank you.'*
*I wouldn't want to do **either** of these jobs. **Neither** of them is very interesting.*

7 no, none

No is a determiner, *none* is a pronoun. In formal English, they are followed by a singular verb, but a plural verb is more common:
*'For those who believe, no explanation is necessary. For those who do not, **none** (= no explanation) will suffice.'*
***None** of us is/are perfect.* (= not one of us, for a group of three countable nouns or more)

Module 3

1 Future forms (page 45)

A Verb forms often confused

1 *will/going to*

will
*Tom **will fail** his driving test.* (prediction based on personal opinion)
*Wait. **I'll help** you.* (spontaneous decision, offer)

going to
*Look at those clouds. It's **going to rain**.* (prediction based on evidence)
*I'm **going to get** a new job.* (plan: decision already made)

2 Present simple and present continuous for future reference

- Present simple
  *The bus **leaves** at 7.35.* (timetables and programmes)

- Present continuous
  *We're **leaving** the country very soon.* (personal arrangement already made)

3 *will* and future continuous

*I'll **see** you next lesson.* (inevitable event)
*Next week, we'll **be sitting** on the beach.* (temporary event in progress in the future)

4 Future perfect and future perfect continuous

*William **will already have left** by the time we **get** there.* (future perfect for something completed before a specific time in the future)
*Next Christmas I'll **have been teaching** for ten years.* (future perfect continuous to say how long something will have continued by a certain time)

5 Present simple or present perfect for future time

We use the present simple or present perfect, not *will*, for future time after time conjunctions, e.g. *after, as soon as, once, until*:
*I'll phone you **as soon as I check/I've checked** in.*

B Expressions with future meaning

1 For fixed/planned events

- *be to + infinitive* to talk about official, formal arrangements, e.g. in a radio commentary
  *The Prince **is to meet** everyone concerned with the charity.*

- *be due to + infinitive* (*due* = expected to happen at a particular time)
  *The ceremony **is due to start** at 9.00 a.m.*

2 For events that will happen very soon

- *be about to + infinitive*
  *She looks as if she's (just) **about to burst** into tears.*

- *be on the point/verge of + -ing/noun*
  *The talks were **on the point/verge of collapsing/collapse**.*

3 To talk about probability

- *be likely/unlikely to* + infinitive
  The country's **likely to get** poorer next year.

- *expect (somebody/something) to* + infinitive
  We **expect** the country **to get** poorer.

4 To talk about certainty

- *be bound/sure to* + infinitive
  Don't lie to him. He's **bound to/sure to find out**.

C Future in the past

1 To talk about the future from a viewpoint of the past, we can use: *was/were going to* + infinitive
  I **was going to phone** you yesterday, but I forgot. (unfulfilled intention)

2 We can transfer any verb/expression with future meaning to the past using: *was/were about to, was/were due to, would (have), was/were to have*
  I **was about to go out** when you called.
  We **were due to go out** at six.
  I thought you **would finish/would have finished** before now.
  The Queen **was to have come** down the Mall. I don't know what went wrong.

2 Modals and semi-modals (Part 1) (page 50)

A Obligation and necessity: *must/have (got) to, need to*

Modal verbs (*can, must, should,* etc.) are used to express an opinion/attitude or to control a possible action:
They **must** have finished. They've been there for ages. (strong opinion about a fact)
You **can** go if you've finished. (controlling possible action – giving permission)

Semi-modals (*dare, had better, need, ought to, used to*) are in some ways formed like modal verbs and in some ways they are like main verbs:
He **needn't** worry. (no third person -s, like a modal verb)
He **doesn't need to** worry. (using do, like a main verb)

1 *must/mustn't*

- Used to express strong obligation when we impose this on ourselves:
  I **must** go to the doctor's.
  I **mustn't** forget to take out insurance.

- Used to express a strong opinion:
  We **must** all do our bit for the environment.

- Used to give instructions, usually in writing:
  This appliance **must** be earthed.

2 *have to/need to*

  have to or *need to* for an obligation imposed by someone else
  This report **has to/needs to** be finished by Monday.

3 *must/have to/need to*

  must, have to and *need to* to express general necessity
  Everyone **needs to** take a holiday at least once a year.

B Lack of necessity: *not have to, need not, not need to*

You **don't have to/needn't/don't need to** get up early today. (It's not necessary.)

Note
Need has two past forms with different meanings:
She didn't need to take a coat. It wasn't cold. (We don't know if she took a coat or not.)
She needn't have taken a coat. (She took one, but it wasn't necessary.)

C Prohibition and criticism: *mustn't, shouldn't, can't, couldn't, may not, should/shouldn't have*

1 *mustn't* or *shouldn't*

- Used for prohibition imposed by the speaker:
  You **mustn't** start a fight! (strong prohibition)
  You **shouldn't** be so thoughtless! (weaker prohibition)

2 *can't* or *may not*

- Used for prohibition imposed by someone else:
  You **can't** drive a car yet, you're too young. (= are not allowed to)
  Candidates **may not** leave the room during the exam. (formal)

3 *couldn't*

- Used for prohibition in the past:
  As children, we **couldn't** stay up later than 10 p.m. (= were not allowed to)

4 *should/shouldn't* + *have* + past participle

- Used to express regret or criticism of a past action:
  I **should have become** a doctor, but I didn't. I wish I had. (regret)
  You **shouldn't have done** that. (criticism)

D Advice, recommendation: *must, should, ought to, had better*

1 *must* for strong advice and recommendations:
  You **must** visit the castle.

2 *should/ought to* when the advice is less strong:
  You **should/ought to** protest.
  You **shouldn't** go on strike.

Note
We rarely use *ought to* in questions and negative statements.

3 *had better (not)*
  I'd **better** go and get ready.
  You'd **better not** tell your mother. (= It is not a good idea.)

E Permission: *can, could, may, might*

'**Can** I use your car?' 'Yes, you **can**.'/'No, you **can't**.'
Could I ask you to do me a favour? (tentative, polite)
'**May** I leave the office early today?' (more formal)
'Yes, you **may**.'/'No, you **may not**.'
I wonder if I **might** have a word with you? (formal, polite)

F Ability: *can, can't, could, might, be able to*

1 *can/can't* for general ability in the present and future:
*I **can** sing. I **can't** come tomorrow.*

2 *could* for general ability in the past:
*I **could** play the piano when I was six.*

3 *was able to* for ability in a specific situation in the past:
*I **was** finally **able to** pass my driving test last week.*

4 *wasn't able to* or *couldn't* for negative general and specific ability in the past:
*They **couldn't/weren't able to** make the wedding on time.*

5 *could/might + have + past participle* for a past ability or opportunity not used:
*He **could have gone** to college, but decided against it.*

6 Other ways of expressing ability:
*I **managed to** (was able to) raise some money for charity last week.* (suggests success in the face of difficulty)
*Scientists have not yet **succeeded in** finding a cure for cancer.*

G Possibility, probability: *can, could, may, might, should*

1 *can, could, may* for things that are theoretically possible and happen sometimes:
*Temperatures **can** reach –20°C at night in the desert.*
*These chemicals **could/may** cause cancer.*

2 *could, may, might* for possibility in the present or future:
*It **could** be weeks before he returns.*
*There **may** well be a strike next week.*
*I **might** be late for the meeting.*

3 *could* for theoretical possibility in the past:
*My father **could** be really strict with me when I was young.*

4 *can, could, may, might + have + past participle* for specific past possibilities:
*She **may/might/could have been** held up in traffic.* (It's possible she was.)

5 *could/might (+ have + past participle)* to express criticism/annoyance:
*You **might** at least say 'thank you'.*
*They **could/might have let** us know they weren't coming!*

6 *may, might (well)* to acknowledge something is true, before introducing a contrast:
*He **might (well)** be a good actor, but he can't sing.*

7 *should/shouldn't* for probability/expectation:
*It **should** be a nice day tomorrow.*
*Peter **should** be arriving any moment now.*
*It **shouldn't** be too difficult to find the way.*

H Deduction: *must, can't, couldn't*

1 *must* for something we are sure about because of evidence:
*He **must** be a vegetarian. He doesn't eat meat.*

2 *must + have + past participle* to express a deduction about the past:
*There are a lot of broken windows. There **must have been** a riot.*

3 *can't/couldn't*, not *mustn't*, in negative sentences:
*He **can't/couldn't** be her father. He looks too young.*
*He **can't/couldn't** have phoned. I've been in all evening.*

I Offers, promises, suggestions, requests, orders: *can, could, may, might, will, shall, would*

1 Offers and promises
Can/May I help you? I'll come with you if you like.
Shall I carry that for you?
Would you like a cup of tea?

2 Suggestions
You could join a club.
You might think of taking a gift.
We can/could get a takeaway.

3 Requests
Can/Could you help me?
What shall I bring? (asking for advice)
You wouldn't lend me £20, would you?

4 Orders
All payments shall be made in cash.
Passengers will please proceed to the gate.

Note
In question tags, *shall* is preferred to *will* in first person singular tags: *I'll do that, shall I?*

Module 4

Noun clauses (page 66)

Noun clauses are groups of words that function like a noun in a sentence and can be referred to by *it* or *that*. Like nouns, they can act as the subject, object or complement of the sentence. They normally refer to abstractions (e.g. ideas, processes, facts) rather than people or things. Noun clauses use the following structures.

A *that*-clauses

1 Following nouns, e.g. *danger, evidence, fact, idea, likelihood, opinion, possibility*:
*There is **evidence that** more people are becoming aware of Multiple Intelligence Theory.*

2 Following adjectives, e.g. *clear, interesting, likely, possible, sad, sure, true*:
*It is **encouraging that** more teachers are adopting its ideas.*

Note
With this structure, we usually start the sentence with *It*.
We don't omit *that* except following *It's a shame/pity (that)* …

3 Following thinking and reporting verbs (as object), e.g. *believe, explain, know, say, suggest, understand*:
*Multiple Intelligence Theory **suggests that** people learn differently.*

Note
We often omit *that* after a verb.

Expert grammar

4 *that*-clause as subject
That-clauses can be used as the subject in formal English:
That his theories were revolutionary *is clear.*

B Clauses beginning with a question word

1 As subject of the sentence
What is good for one learner *might not be good for another.*
Whoever wrote this music *is a genius.*

2 As object of the sentence
Do you know ***when he is coming?*** (NOT ~~when is he coming?~~)
I'm always forgetting ***where I've left things***.

3 Following *be*
The question is ***how far intelligence is genetically determined***.

4 Following a preposition
It depends ***on who you know*** *not* ***what you know***.
Have you read ***about how you can improve your memory?***

5 With *to*-infinitive clauses
He showed me ***how to solve the problem***.
I don't know ***what to say***.

6 *if/whether (or not)*
- We use *if* or *whether* in indirect *Yes/No* questions:
  John asked ***if/whether*** *I wanted to go to the cinema.*
- We use *whether* rather than *if* when talking about a choice:
  I didn't know ***whether*** *to go (or not).*
  Whether (or not) *the theory is true is arguable.*
- We usually use *if* when the noun clause is the object of a verb:
  I've often wondered ***if he was genuine***.

C *-ing* and *to*-infinitive clauses

1 As subject
Taking extra classes *might benefit some learners.*
To achieve the best results for everyone *must be the aim of all schools.* (formal)

Note
An introductory *It* structure is more common than a *to*-infinitive as the subject of a sentence in neutral or spoken English:
It *must be the aim of all schools to achieve the best results for everyone.*

2 As object
I enjoy ***being looked after***.
I want ***everyone to be happy***.

3 Following *be*
My ambition is ***to become a neurologist***.
My main worry is ***not being good enough to pass***.

4 Following a noun or adjective
We had some difficulty ***finding the place***.
My plan ***to leave the country*** *failed.*
It is important ***to adopt a variety of approaches***.

5 Adding a subject to a *to*-infinitive clause
When there is a subject in a *to*-infinitive clause, we usually add *for*:
It's impossible ***for me*** *to go with you.*

6 Verb + object + *-ing* clause
When the main verb is followed by an object + *-ing* clause, we use an object, or, in formal language, a possessive form:
I don't mind ***him/Peter (his/Peter's) getting*** *a pay rise.*

Module 5

1 Gradable and ungradable adjectives (page 77)

A Modifying gradable adjectives

Most adjectives are 'gradable' because they describe qualities we can think of in terms of a scale, and therefore can be weaker or stronger.

1 Gradable adjectives, e.g. *important, slow, valuable, vigorous*, can be made stronger using *extremely, incredibly, most* (formal), *pretty* (informal), *rather, really, terribly, very*:
  It's ***pretty obvious*** *that he's not interested.*
  The talk was ***most interesting***. (formal)
  I thought he was ***rather nice***.

Note
We cannot use *absolutely* with gradable adjectives.

2 Gradable adjectives can be made weaker using *a (little) bit, fairly, quite (= fairly), relatively, slightly, somewhat* (formal):
  He's ***quite rich***, *but not a millionaire.*
  We were ***somewhat disappointed*** *with the service.*
  The hotel was ***relatively/fairly cheap***.

B Modifying ungradable adjectives

'Ungradable' adjectives, e.g. *brilliant, correct, disastrous, exhausted, furious, identical, perfect, unique*, indicate extreme or absolute qualities.

1 The extreme/absolute quality can be stressed using *absolutely, completely, quite (= completely), really, totally, utterly*:
  They were ***absolutely furious***.
  This vase is ***quite unique***.

Note
Absolutely cannot be used with all ungradable adjectives. In some cases, *completely, totally* or *utterly* are preferred (see Section D).

2 We can say that something is very nearly in an absolute state using *almost, nearly, practically, virtually*:
  The tank is ***almost empty***.
  The two vases are ***virtually identical***.

C Gradable and ungradable

Some adjectives can be gradable or ungradable, depending on the context:

*The beach was **fairly empty**.*
(gradable = There were not many people.)
*The beach was **absolutely empty**.*
(ungradable = There were no people.)

D Adverb + adjective collocations

Some adverbs tend to collocate with certain adjectives:

bitterly   cold, disappointed, opposed
completely   different, incomprehensible, new, sure
deeply   ashamed, attached, divided, unhappy
entirely   beneficial, different, satisfactory, unexpected
heavily   armed, dependent, polluted
highly   contagious, critical, intelligent, likely, sensitive
painfully   aware, obvious, sensitive, slow
perfectly   balanced, normal, safe, serious
seriously   damaged, hurt, rich, wealthy
totally   harmless, inadequate, unbelievable
utterly   different, disastrous, impossible, useless
widely   available, held, publicised, used

2 Conditionals (page 82)

A Overview

1 Zero conditional: real events/situations, things which are always true

If means the same as *when*.

- present + present
  *If/When I **work** late, I always **get** home tired.*
- past + past
  *If/When the weather **was** bad, we **used** to stay indoors.*

2 First conditional: possible or likely events/situations (future)

If + present + modal verb/present continuous (with future meaning)/*going to*/imperative

*If it **snows** tomorrow, the match **will/may/could** be cancelled.*
*If it **snows** tomorrow, I'**m staying** at home.*

3 Second conditional: unlikely or unreal situations (present or future)

If + past + *would/could/might* + infinitive

*If you **met** your favourite actor on the street (unlikely), what **would** you do?*
*If I **became** president (but I won't), I'**d build** more hospitals. (in the future)*
*If I **were** you (but I'm not), I'**d take** warm clothes. (= advice)*

4 Third conditional: unreal/impossible past situations

If + past perfect + *would/could/might* + *have* + past participle

*If we **had known** about the blizzard, we **wouldn't have set out**. (but we didn't know)*
*If you **had listened** more carefully (but you didn't), you **would have understood**. (= criticism)*

B Mixed conditionals

Mixed conditional structures combine the verb forms from two different conditional patterns. The most common combinations are:

- unreal past + unreal present
  *If we **hadn't got lost**, we'**d be** there by now.*
- unreal present + unreal past
  *If I **were** a more ambitious person (but I'm not), I'**d have become** a politician.*

C Alternatives to *if*

Other conjunctions can be used to introduce conditions:

- *unless* (= *if ... not* or *only if*)
  ***Unless** the weather improves, we will have to cancel the game. (**If the weather doesn't improve** ...)*
  *She won't go to sleep **unless** you tell her a story. (**She will only go to sleep if you** ...)*
- *providing/provided (that), on condition that, as/so long as* (= *only if*)

Note

These conjunctions are not used with the third conditional.

*I'll lend you the money **providing (that)** you pay it back.*
*I'd lend you the money **as long as** you paid it back.*

- *but for* (= *if it had not been for, if ... not*)
  ***But for** your warning, we wouldn't have realised the danger. (If it had not been for your warning,/If you had not warned us, ...)*
- *whether ... or not* (= *it doesn't matter which of these situations*)
  ***Whether** governments like it **or not**, they have to give more aid to the developing world.*
- *suppose/supposing, what if* (used to talk about imaginary situations)
  – The present tense suggests the condition may be fulfilled:
    ***What if** your plan fails, what then?*
  – The past tense suggests the condition is unlikely:
    ***Suppose** you won the lottery, what would you do?*
- *assuming that* (= *in the possible situation that*)
  ***Assuming (that)** you're right, we should turn left here.*
- *in case* (as a way of being safe from something that might happen)
  *Take your umbrella **in case** it rains.*
- *otherwise* (= *if not*)
  *Let's hope the weather improves. **Otherwise** (= If it doesn't), we'll have to cancel the picnic.*

D Omission of *if*

If can be omitted and the auxiliary verb moved in front of the subject (inversion). This structure is formal.

- *should* suggests that the condition is unlikely:
  ***Should** you ever find yourself in Oxford, we would be glad to see you. (If you should ever ...)*

- *were* suggests that the condition is unlikely:
Were the company to collapse, many people would lose their savings. (If the company collapsed ...)

- *had*
Had I known earlier that you wanted to join the team, I'd have put your name on the list. (If I had known ...)
*My horse would have won **had** he not fallen at the final fence.* (... if he had not fallen ...)

Module 6

Verb + *-ing* or infinitive with *to*? (page 98)

➤ See also *Patterns after reporting verbs*, page 186.

A Verbs followed by *-ing*

1 Verb + *-ing*

The verbs marked * can also be followed by an object + *-ing*:
adore*, advise, allow, appreciate*, avoid*, can't bear*, can't help*, consider, contemplate, deny, detest*, dislike*, enjoy* fancy*, finish, forbid, imagine*, involve*, keep, mention*, miss*, permit, practise, recommend, resent, resist*, suggest, understand*
*Have you **considered taking** up yoga?*
*They **forbid/allow/permit** smoking here.*

2 Verb + object + *-ing*

Further verbs followed by object + *-ing* include:
catch, discover, feel, find, hear, leave, notice, observe, see, spot, want, watch
*She **caught** him **cheating** in the exam.*
*I don't **want** you **going** home alone.*

➤ See also Section D on page 183.

Notes
- In more formal style, we can use a possessive form for the object:
*I can't understand **him/John/his/John's** making such a fuss.*
- The verbs *advise, allow, forbid, permit, recommend* are followed by a *to*-infinitive, not an *-ing* form, when they have an object:
*I **advise taking out** insurance for the trip.*
*I **advise you to take out** insurance for the trip.*
*I don't recommend **staying** here.*
*I don't recommend **you to stay** here.*

B Verbs followed by infinitive

1 Verb + *to*-infinitive

The verbs marked * can also be followed by an object + *to*-infinitive.
afford*, agree, appear, arrange, attempt, choose*, dare*, deserve*, expect*, force*, guarantee, help*, hope, intend*, manage, need*, neglect, prepare, pretend, refuse, volunteer, want*, wish*
*He **appeared to be** discovering the truth.*

2 Verb + object + *to*-infinitive

Further verbs followed by object + *to*-infinitive include:
advise, allow, cause, command, compel, encourage, forbid, get, instruct, invite, leave, oblige, order, permit, persuade, recommend, remind, request, tell, urge, warn

Note
for is used before object + infinitive with these verbs: *arrange, long, plan, wait*
*I **long for them** to return.*

3 Verb (+ object) + infinitive without *to*

The following verbs take an infinitive without *to*:
had better, let, make, would rather
*You'd **better** go.*
*Please **let me come** with you.*
*He **made me finish** my report.*

Notes
- *hear, make, see* are followed by infinitive with *to* in the passive:
We were made to walk home.
- *let* is replaced by *be allowed to* in the passive.
- *dare, help, need* can be followed by infinitive with or without *to*:
*Can you **help me (to) carry** this case?*

C Verbs + *-ing* or *to*-infinitive

1 With little difference in meaning

attempt, begin, can't bear, can't stand, continue, hate, like (= enjoy), love, prefer, start
*I **started watching/to watch** the programme.*

With verbs of liking/preference, the *-ing* form tends to refer to general activities, and the *to*-infinitive to a specific activity:
*I **like swimming**.* (in general)
*I **like to swim** every weekend.* (I think it's a good idea.)

Note
We use the *to*-infinitive after *would like/love/prefer*:
'Would you **like to go** out?' 'I'd **prefer to stay** at home this evening.'

2 With a change in meaning

- *forget/remember*
*I **remember/forget bringing** the key.* (looking back)
*Please **remember**/Don't **forget to bring** the key.* (looking forward)

- *go on*
*Please **go on telling** us about it.* (continue)
*He **went on to become** president.* (do something next)

- *mean*
*Managing well **means communicating** well.* (involves)
*We **meant to get** up early.* (intended)

- *regret*
*I **regret leaving** school so early.* (feel sorry)
*I **regret to inform** you that your contract will not be renewed.* (formal: used in official letters or statements)

- *stop*
  She **stopped working** for the gallery ages ago. (no longer do something)
  She **stopped to buy** a programme. (stop and change activity)
- *try*
  Try going for a run. (to see what happens)
  Try to get more exercise. (make an effort)

D Sense verbs: *feel, hear, notice, see, smell, taste, watch*

Sense verbs, or verbs of perception, can be followed by:

1 object + *-ing* form when we are describing an action in progress or a repeated action:
  *I **heard him singing** a great song.*

2 object + infinitive when we are describing a single or completed action:
  *I **heard him sing** a great song.*

Module 7

1 Emphasis: cleft sentences (page 109)

Cleft, or 'divided', constructions can be used to emphasise particular items of information in a sentence by putting them in a separate clause. They are common in spoken English, and can also be used to signal emphasis in writing, where it cannot be indicated by intonation.

A Emphasis with *what, the thing that, the place where, the reason why*, etc.

1 *wh-* clause (with a verb) + a form of *be* + emphasised information. This structure can be used:
- to put emphasis on the subject, object or complement of a sentence:
  Living on your own (subject) *can be lonely.*
  → *What can be lonely is **living on your own**.* (focus on the subject)
  *I like **living on my own**.* (object)
  → *What I like is **living on my own**.* (focus on the object)
  The clauses can be reversed.
  ***Living on your own** can be lonely.*
  ***Living on my own** is what I like.*
- to put emphasis on the action in a sentence. The *wh-* clause must contain a verb. We use a form of the auxiliary *do*. The emphasised part usually contains an infinitive:
  I decided to sell my flat, so I put it on the market.
  → *I decided to sell my flat, so **what I did was to put** it on the market.*

2 This structure can also be used to focus on a thing, person, place, time or reason, but usually with the addition of an introductory phrase, e.g. *the thing that, the person who*, etc. The *wh-* clause acts like a relative clause:

The (one) thing that *(really) keeps you young is being with young people.*
The people who *live next door are very friendly.*
The place where *I go for a workout has got some great classes.*
The reason (why) *I like going back home is that I can spend time with my brother.*
All I'd (ever) wanted to do *was (to) have a family of my own.*
All I know is (that) *my father was very kind.*

B Emphasis with *it + be*

This structure can put emphasis on most parts of a sentence except the verb. It often implies a contrast with the previous statement:
Sarah wanted a job as a travel agent in the capital.
→ *It was **Sarah** who wanted a job as a travel agent.* (emphasising the subject)
→ *It was **a job as a travel agent** that Sarah wanted.* (emphasising the object)
→ *It was **in the capital** that/where Sarah wanted a job as a travel agent.* (emphasising the prepositional phrase)

2 Past tenses for hypothetical meanings (page 114)

We use past tenses after the following expressions to describe situations in the present, past or future which are imagined or unreal:
wish/if only, It's (high) time, would rather/sooner, would prefer, as if/though, suppose/supposing, what if

A *wish/if only*

1 We use *wish/if only* + past when we want a present situation to be different:
  *I **wish/If only we had** more money.* (but we haven't)
  *I **wish I was** (formal: were) a bit taller.* (but I'm not)

2 *wish + would* is used to express a wish for something to change in the present or future.
- We often use it to criticise or complain about someone or something:
  *I **wish** Peter **would** wear smarter clothes.*
  *I **wish** the weather **would** improve.*
- *I wish + would* cannot be used to refer to oneself:
  *I **wish I could** (not ~~would~~) stop smoking.* (but I can't)
- We cannot use *would* for an impossible change:
  If only the earth ~~would be~~ was (formal: were) square.

Note
Notice the difference between *wish* and *hope*. If we hope something will happen, we believe it is possible and likely:
*I **hope** they **will** come.* (= I want them to and I think it's likely.)
*I **wish** they **would** come.* (= I don't believe it's likely.)

3 We use *wish/if only* + past perfect to express regret about a past situation:
  *I **wish we'd had** something to eat earlier.* (but we didn't)
  *If only I **hadn't missed** my appointment.* (but I did)

4 Differences between *wish* and *if only*:
   • *if only* is usually more emphatic than *I wish*.
   • We can put a subject between *if* and *only* for emphasis:
     ***If only you/If you only** knew what I've been going through.*

B It's time

We use this expression to say that something is not happening and it should be:
***It's (high) time you gave up** playing computer games.* (You should give them up!)

C would rather/sooner, would prefer

***I'd rather/I'd sooner** you didn't ask me for any more money.* (Please don't!)
***I'd prefer it if** you didn't ask me for any more money.*

Notes
• If the speaker and the preference are the same, we use an infinitive, not the past tense:
  ***I'd rather/sooner watch** TV.* (not ~~to watch~~)
  ***I'd prefer to watch** TV.* (not ~~watch~~)
• We can also say *I'd prefer you not to go.*

D as if/as though

• We use the past after *as if/as though* to indicate that the situation is unlikely:
  *He acts **as if/though he was** (formal: **were**) a teenager.* (In fact, he's in his thirties.)
• We use a present tense to indicate that something is likely:
  *He **looks as if/though he is** a teenager.* (And he probably is.)

E suppose/supposing, imagine, what if

We use these expressions to ask about an imaginary situation in the present or future, and its possible consequences:
***(Just) suppose/supposing/imagine** you won the lottery, how would you spend the money?*
***What if** you had hurt yourself – what would have happened then?*

Module 8

1 Emphasis (page 125)

A Emphasis using negative introductory expressions

The following expressions can be placed first in a sentence for emphasis. The subject and verb are then inverted. We use *do/does/did* if there is no auxiliary.

• *little, never, rarely, scarcely*:
  ***Never** have I seen so many people.*
  ***Little** did we know that he had followed us.*

• *no sooner ... than, barely/hardly ... when*:
  ***No sooner had** he got the job **than** he asked for a pay rise.*
  ***Hardly** had I got through the door **when** the phone rang.*

• *at no time, under no circumstances, on no account, no way* (informal):
  ***Under no circumstances** should you let anyone in.*

• *not since, not for, not a (person/thing), not only ... (but also)*:
  ***Not since** the 90s has he written such a superb novel.*
  ***Not a soul** did we see on our journey.*
  ***Not only** do they want a pay increase, they **(also)** want reduced hours.*

• *only + time expression or prepositional phrase*:
  ***Only now/after all these years** has the crime been solved.*
  ***Only when I got to the airport** did I realise I had forgotten my passport.*

B Emphasis through 'fronting' parts of the sentence

'Fronting' involves moving elements of a sentence to the front in order to:
• start with the most important information
• provide an emphatic contrast with the previous sentence
• provide a link with what came before by putting known information at the front of the sentence.

Note
In order to avoid ending a clause or sentence with *be* as a result of fronting, we normally invert the subject and verb.

1 Fronting the object or complement
  *I don't know **what we're going to do**. → **What we're going to do** I don't know.*
  *I don't believe **that**. → **That** I don't believe!*

2 Fronting adverbials and verbs of place or movement (+ inversion)
  *And now we are in the market place. **Here** stood the old Corn Exchange building. **Opposite** is the church.*
  *We arrived at our camp. **Then** began the slow process of acclimatisation.*
  ***Into the room** swaggered the Count.*

Note
We don't invert the subject and verb
• if the subject is a pronoun:
  Here stands his statue. Here it stands. ~~Here stands it.~~
• with time phrases:
  ~~At eight o'clock went off the alarm clock.~~

3 Fronting comparative or superlative phrases, *so, such* (when not followed by a noun), *also* (+ inversion)
  *She has made five films to date. Her latest film is **particularly good**. → **Particularly good** is her latest film.*
  *The storm was **so terrible** that the ship sank. → **So terrible** was the storm that the ship sank.*
  *His financial position was **such** that his friends started to worry. → **Such was his financial position** that his friends started to worry.*
  *The house loomed out of the darkness. **Also visible were** several dogs guarding the door.*

4 Fronting *as* and *though*
> Try **as** they might, they could not win the race.
> Exhausted **though** he was, he stumbled on.

5 Fronting noun clauses
> ➤ See *Noun clauses* (Section A4), page 180.

2 Comparisons (page 130)

A Review of comparison

1 Comparative structures

- to a higher degree:
  Boston is smaller/safer than New York.
  Living in the centre is more fashionable these days.

- to the same degree:
  Congestion in London is (just) as bad as it is in Paris.
  He's as good a businessman as his father was.
  Both cities are equally beautiful.

- to a lower degree:
  The city is not as/so safe as it used to be.
  It's not such a safe city as it used to be.
  That's not such a good idea. (implied: *as you might think*)

2 Superlative structures
> *Mexico City is one of the largest cities in the world.*
> *Yoga is the most/least effective way of dealing with stress.*

B Modifying comparisons

1 To express a big difference, we can use:

- *a great deal, (quite) a lot, considerably, far, (very) much* + comparative
  It's much easier to get around today.

- *by far (and away), easily* + superlative
  This is easily the best book I've ever read.

- *nothing like, not nearly, nowhere near as ... as*
  The euro is nowhere near as strong as it used to be.

- *just about* + superlative
  He's just about the nicest person I know.
  (= extremely nice)

2 To express a small difference, we can use:

- *barely, a bit, hardly any, a little, scarcely (any), slightly, somewhat* + comparative
  The house is scarcely bigger than a rabbit hutch.

- *nearly, not quite as ... as, much the same as ...*
  The city is much the same as it was 50 years ago.

C *so/such*; *too/enough* (result)

- *so* + adjective + *that*-clause
  The company was so successful that it had to take on more staff.

- *such a* + adjective + noun + *that*-clause
  It was such a successful company that it had to take on more staff.

- *too* + adjective (+ *for*) + *to*-infinitive
  It was too dangerous (for us) to go out at night.

- (*not*) adjective + *enough* (+ *for*) + *to*-infinitive
  It wasn't safe enough (for us) to go out at night.

D Other types of comparison

1 Repetition of the same comparative form to emphasise increase or decrease:
> *I'm getting colder and colder/more and more anxious.*

2 *the ... the* to say how a change in one thing affects another:
> *The more I see you, the more I like you.*
> *The less you know, the better.*
> *The longer we stand here in the rain, the worse I feel.*

3 To contrast two similar qualities:
> *His behaviour was more strange than suspicious.*
> (*His behaviour was strange rather than suspicious.*)
> *I'm not so much angry as relieved.*

E *as* vs *like*

1 *like* + noun = *similar to*
> *He looks like a bank manager.* (but he's not)

2 *as* + name of job, etc. = role, function
> *He works as an 'extra' in films.* (That's his job.)

F Ways of expressing preferences

We sometimes use comparative forms when expressing preferences:
> *I'd want/prefer to be poor and happy rather than rich and miserable.*
> *I'd (far) sooner/rather live in Chicago than New York.*

Module 9

1 Reported speech, reporting verbs (page 141)

A Review of reported speech

1 Tense changes

To report something said in the past using a past tense reporting verb, we usually use a tense one step further back in the past. This is sometimes called 'backshift'.

> *'We're getting married.'* (present)
> → *He said they were getting married.* (past)

> *'I met Peter recently.'* (past)
> → *He said he had met Peter recently.* (past perfect)

We do not backshift:

- when the reporting verb is in the present tense:
  He says (that) they're getting married.

- when the reporter sees the past events from the same point of view as the speaker:
  He said he was pleased (that) my exam results were good.

- when we report modals *would, should, might, could, ought to*:
  You should learn to swim. → *He said (that) she should learn to swim.*

- with the past perfect:
  'They'd already left.' → *He told me they'd already left.*

We can choose to backshift or not when present and future events are still true:
'Come after lunch.' → *He suggested (that) I came/come after lunch.* (It is not lunchtime yet.)

Note
shall changes to *would* when it refers to the future and *should* when it is a suggestion:
'We shan't see you tomorrow.' → *They said (that) they wouldn't see us the next day.*
'Shall we open the window?' → *They suggested (that) they should open the window.*

2 Changes of pronouns and adverbs

If the person, place or time of reporting is significantly different from the words in direct speech, we change pronouns and adverbs.
'I'll see you here tomorrow.'

→ *He said he would see **me there the next day**.* (spoken three days later in a different place)

→ *He said he'll/would see **me here tomorrow**.* (spoken today in the same place)

3 Word order in reported questions

- To report questions, we use the same order as in statements:
  'When are you going?' → *He asked me **when I was** going.*
  'Have you seen my wallet?' → *She asked him **if he had** seen her wallet.*

- With *what/who/which* questions + *be* + complement, *be* can go before the complement:
  'Which is our bus?' → *She wanted to know **which was our bus/which our bus was**.*

B Patterns after reporting verbs

➤ See *Verbs followed by infinitive*, page 182.

1 Verb + *that*-clause

Some of these verbs can also be followed by a *to*-infinitive or an *-ing* form (see below):
add, admit, agree, announce, answer, argue, claim, complain, confess, decide, deny, expect, explain, hope, promise, repeat, suggest, swear, threaten, warn

2 Verb + *that*-clause (+ *should*)

advise, beg, demand, insist, prefer, propose, recommend, request, suggest
*She **advised** (that) the house **should** be sold immediately.*
*I **recommended** (that) he **should** see a lawyer.*

Note
- In more formal contexts, we can omit *should*:
  *She advised (that) the house **be** sold immediately.*
  *I recommended (that) he **see** a lawyer.*
- In less formal contexts, we use an ordinary tense:
  *I recommended (that) he **saw** a lawyer.*

3 Verb + *to*-infinitive

agree, ask, claim, decide, demand, expect, hope, intend, offer, promise, refuse, swear, threaten
*She **asked to see** the manager.*

4 Verb + object + *to*-infinitive

advise, ask, beg, command, encourage, expect, forbid, intend, invite, order, persuade, recommend, remind, tell, urge, warn
*They **told/warned him** not **to be** late.*
*You **are forbidden to smoke** in the building.*
*I **invited them to stay**.*

5 Verb + *-ing* form

admit, deny, mention, propose, recommend, regret, report, suggest
*They **regretted leaving/having left** so soon.*

6 Verb (+ object) + preposition (+ object/genitive) + *-ing*

accuse sb of, apologise (to sb) about, apologise for, blame sb for, complain (to sb) about, comment on, confess to, insist on, object to
*They **accused me of telling** a lie.*
*He **confessed to stealing** the money.*
*They **insisted on me/my going** with them.*

Note
Some reporting verbs may be followed by a *wh-* clause:
*He **commented on how** tall she'd grown.*

➤ See also *Noun clauses*, page 179.

C Impersonal report structures

The following impersonal structures can be used after verbs of mental processes, e.g. *accept, agree, announce, argue, believe, claim, feel, hint, hope, know, report, repute, say, suggest, think*, to avoid mentioning the agent and/or to focus attention on the last part of the sentence. This structure is generally used in written English, often in newspapers.

1 *It* + passive + *that*-clause

***It is said** (that) he is extremely rich.*
***It is believed** (that) the city was established in Roman times.*

2 Subject + passive + *to*-infinitive/perfect infinitive

***He is said to be** extremely rich.*
***The city is believed to have been** established in Roman times.*

2 Nouns, adjectives, verbs + prepositions
(page 146)

A General rules

1 When verbs, nouns and adjectives are followed by a preposition, the preposition is always followed by an object. This can be a noun, pronoun or the *-ing* form of a verb:
*I'm not interested **in the opera/in going** to the opera.*

2 When we use a subject with the *-ing* form, it can be put in the possessive form in more formal English:
*We depend on **his/him** giving us the money.*

3 Related verbs, nouns and adjectives often take the same preposition:
*We don't **object to** the proposal.*
*We have no **objection to** the proposal.*

Note
Some verbs, nouns and adjectives can be followed by different prepositions with a change in meaning. Compare:
*The other children laughed **at** him. (negative = made unkind remarks)*
*We laughed **about** the incident later.*

B Verb + preposition patterns

A preposition is required after some verbs to link the verb to the object. The combination may give a new meaning.

1 Verb + preposition + noun/-*ing*

agree on sth/with sb, aim for, believe in, care about/for, count on, dream of, hear about/of, laugh about/at, object to, pay for, quarrel with, resort to, shout at/to
*My boyfriend and I don't **agree on** everything.*
*Do you **agree with** increasing taxes?*
*We're **aiming for** a big increase in sales.*
*The rebels **resorted to** violence/committing violent acts.*

2 Verb + direct object + preposition + indirect object

aim sth at sb/sth, blame sb for sth, blame sth on sb, discuss sth with sb, explain sth to sb, save sb from sth
*This programme is **aimed at** teenagers.*

Notes
• The direct object must come before the preposition and indirect object:
I explained ~~to him the problem~~. → I explained the problem to him.
• If the order of the objects is changed, different prepositions are used:
*I **blame him for** the poor results.*
*I **blame** the poor results **on him**.*
*They **presented the actress with** the award.*
*They **presented** the award **to the actress**.*

3 Verb + direct object + preposition + -*ing* form

accuse sb of -ing, advise sb against -ing, discourage sb from -ing, prevent sb from -ing, suspect sb of -ing
*The Foreign Office **advises** tourists **against travelling** to certain countries.*

4 Verb + preposition + object + preposition + object

Verbs used in this pattern are usually reporting verbs.
agree with sb about sth, apologise to sb for sth, complain to sb about sth, depend on sb for sth, disagree with sb about/over sth, quarrel with sb about/over sth, rely on sb for sth
*I **agreed with** the others **about** the need for speed.*
*She **apologised to** him **for** having to leave early.*

5 Verb + preposition + subject + -*ing*

depend on, insist on, rely on sb/sth -ing
*Success **depends on** us/our **getting** the product out on time.*
*Her parents **insisted on** Mary/Mary's **coming** home by 11 p.m.*

C Noun + preposition patterns

amazement at, anger about/at, apology for, belief in, delay in, effect of, increase in, insistence on, point in/of, prospect of, success in, taste for
*What's the **point of going** there now?*
*There's no **point in worrying**.*

Notes
• Related verbs and nouns often take the same preposition:
insist on, insistence on
• Some nouns are followed by a preposition although the related verbs are not:
discuss sth, have a discussion about sth; fear sth, have a fear of sth

D Adjective + preposition patterns

Many adjectives describing feelings and opinions are followed by a preposition.
afraid of, annoyed about sth, annoyed at/with sb, disappointed about/at/with, disappointed in sb, excited about/at/by, interested in, keen on, nervous about/of, proud of, scared of, sorry about sth/for -ing
*She's very **excited about** her forthcoming trip.*
*I was very **excited at/by the prospect of seeing** her again.*
*He was **nervous about** his exams.*
*They were **nervous of** their teacher at first.*

Note
Related adjectives, verbs and nouns often take the same preposition:
be interested in, take an interest in
depend on, be dependent on

Module 10

1 Participle and *to*-infinitive clauses (page 157)

➤ See also Replacing relative clauses (section E), page 175

Participle clauses allow us to express ourselves economically, both in speech and writing.

A -*ing* participle clauses

We can use -*ing* participle clauses:

1 to show that two actions occurred at the same time, or one happened immediately after another:
*I sat there **twiddling my thumbs**.*
(= As I sat there, I twiddled my thumbs.)
***Turning to the crowd**, he smiled and waved.*
(= He turned to the crowd and smiled.)
*He finally resigned, thus **ending days of speculation**.*
(= When he resigned, he ended days of speculation.)

Note
A perfect participle can be used to emphasise that one thing happened before another:
***Having taken off** his shoes, he walked upstairs.*

2 to suggest a cause, reason or result, especially with stative verbs such as *be, believe, feel, have, know, want*:

Feeling ill, I decided to stay at home. (= I felt ill, so I decided ...)

Wanting to become more independent, he left home. (= Because he wanted ...)

He felt at home in the village, *having lived there for many years*. (= ... because he had lived ...)

3 to replace adverbial clauses of time or contrast. The participle clause is introduced by a conjunction:

On seeing her brother, she gave him a big hug. (= When she saw ...)

Before leaving the room, he turned off the light. (= Before he left ...)

While/Although admitting he'd been very stupid, he refused to apologise. (= While/Although he admitted ...)

B -ed participle clauses

These participle clauses have a passive meaning and are more frequent in written English. They can be used to suggest cause, reason and condition:

I applied for the job, *convinced* I could do it. (= ... because I was convinced ...)

Told well, my jokes are as funny as anyone's. (= If they are told well, ...)

The job *successfully completed*, they left. (= The job was successfully completed, so they left.)

Notes
- If the subject of a participle clause is not stated, it must be the same as the subject of the main clause.
- If the subject of a participle clause is stated, it can be different from the subject of the main clause:
  It being high season, **all the hotels** were fully booked. (= As it was high season, all the hotels ...)

C to-infinitive clauses

To-infinitive clauses may be used to express purpose and sometimes consequence, condition or result:

He went back into the house **to get** the tickets. (purpose = in order to get)

I got to the theatre **only to find** the show had started. (unexpected consequence = and found)

I've been there often enough **to know** my way around. (result = and therefore know)

To see him, you'd never think he was 60 years old. (condition = If you saw)

➤ See also *Attitude clauses and phrases* (Section 2), page 201.

2 Modals and semi-modals (Part 2) (page 162)

A Form

1 Modal verbs have only one form. They have no to-infinitive form, -ing form or past form. They do not agree with the subject of the sentence.

2 Modals always go before other verbs (main verbs or auxiliary verbs but not other modals) in a verb phrase.
You **should get** a move on. (NOT ~You should to get ...~ ~You should must ...~)

Affirmative: He **might** be there. (NOT ~He mights~)
Negative: I **can't** hear you. (NOT ~I don't can hear you.~)
Question: **Could** you post this letter for me? (NOT ~Do you could post ...~)

Also:
✓ You won't tell him, **will you**? (NOT ~do you?~)
✓ A: Will you help me?   B: I **might (do)**.
✓ I'll bring a coat, **shall** I? (NOT ~will I?~)

3 We can indicate the past by using a modal verb + *have* + past participle:
He **must have arrived** very late.

B Certainty, willingness and characteristic behaviour: will, won't, would, shall

1 Certainty, decisions, intentions, predictions
- Predictions about the future and intentions:
  I **will pass** (**I'll pass**) that exam! (I'm determined to OR I'm sure of it.)
  I **shall pass** that exam. (With I/we – but more formal)
  Sue and Anna **won't arrive** until this evening. They **will be** tired.
- Past predictions/intentions:
  He said he **would/wouldn't** be late.
- Certainty about the present based on knowledge or expectations:
  'I heard a knock at the door.' 'That **will be** the postman.'
  As you **will have realised**, we are behind schedule.
  They only left two hours ago, so they **won't be** home yet.
- Certainty or deductions about the past:
  I became an apprentice when I left school. I **would have been** 14.

2 Willingness, refusal, promises
  The doctor **will** see you now.
  He **won't** talk to me.
  They **wouldn't** let us into the country. (past)
  You **shall** go, I promise. (formal)

3 Commands in formal contexts
  This door **shall** be kept closed at all times.
  You **shall not** (**shan't**) use any of our software.

4 Frequency, habits, characteristics
- Habits and typical behaviour in the present:
  Accidents **will happen**.
  This car **will do** 0 to 60 in ten seconds.
- Past habits
  He **would sit** for hours watching the birds.
- To express annoyance
  She **will play** music at full volume.

C Alternatives to modals

1 Obligation and necessity

- *be required to + infinitive*
  You **are required** by law **to wear** a seat belt. (formal)
- *be to + infinitive*
  We **are** all **to report** to the principal's office. (very formal)
- *had better + infinitive*
  We'**d better** (**had better**) **leave** before it gets dark. (informal)
- *feel/be obliged + to-infinitive*
  Many parents **feel obliged to support** their children. (quite formal)
- *You* **are obliged to report** *to the police once a week.* (formal)
- *be supposed to + infinitive* (rule, law or custom but often not done)
  We'**re supposed to be** carrying our passports. Let's go back and get them. (informal)
  You **are not supposed to walk** on the grass. (but many students do)
- *be advisable to + infinitive*
  It **is advisable (not) to discuss** the matter with a third party. (formal)
- *under no obligation*
  You **are under no obligation to** buy anything. (quite formal)

2 Prohibition

Smoking is **forbidden/not permitted** here. (formal)

3 Plans

We **are supposed to be** flying (= should be flying) to Rio tomorrow. (informal)
We **were supposed to** fly (= should have flown) to Rio (but the trip was cancelled).

Expert writing

Contents

➤ See EXPERT STRATEGIES on page 169.

Assessment

Cambridge *Advanced* is at Level C1 of the *Common European Framework of Reference for Languages* (CEFR). There are five assessment bands where Band 5 is the highest and 1 is the lowest. An acceptable performance at *Advanced* is represented by Band 3.
Students are assessed on the four subscales below:

Content
This focuses on how well you have done what you were asked to do.
- The content is relevant to the task.
- The target reader is informed.

Communicative achievement
This focuses on whether you have used the conventions of the communicative task effectively.
- The target reader's attention is held.
- Straightforward and complex ideas are communicated.

Organisation
This focuses on whether the text is well organised and coherent.
- A variety of cohesive devices is used.
- Organisational patterns are used effectively.

Language
This focuses on whether you have used:
- a range of vocabulary, including less common lexis, appropriately.
- a range of simple and complex grammatical forms with control and flexibility. Occasional errors may be present but do not impede communication.

Writing checklist

- Have you answered the question and included all the points? Read the exam rubric again to check. Have you avoided irrelevance?
- For Part 1 tasks, have you used your own words and avoided copying from the input?
- Have you organised your writing in accordance with the particular task? For example:
  Essay: Have you divided your writing into paragraphs? Is each paragraph logically organised? Have you used suitable discourse markers?
  Letter: Have you used appropriate opening and closing phrases? Is the register appropriate to the purpose and target reader?
  Proposal: Is your writing persuasive? Have you given a reason for each recommendation?
  Report: Have you organised your writing under the correct headings/ sub-headings?
  Review: have you used suitable descriptive and evaluative language? Have you included recommendations?
- Have you shown a good knowledge of grammar and vocabulary, including collocations, prepositional and verb phrases?
- Have you used complex sentence structures, e.g. use of impersonal structures, conditional sentences, emphasis?
- Have you used the appropriate register consistently (formal, semi-formal, informal)?
- Have you written the correct number of words?
- Does your piece of writing show evidence of good organisation and paragraph use? Does it include an appropriate introduction and conclusion?
- Have you checked for any inaccuracies in your spelling or grammar that might prevent comprehension or lead to lack of clarity?

Part 1: Essay (Sample 1)

➤ See EXPERT STRATEGIES on page 169.

Task

Your class has attended a panel discussion on why working from home might be difficult for employees. You have made the notes below:

> **Reasons why working at home might be difficult for employees:**
> • domestic pressures
> • loss of human contact
> • lack of structure

> Some opinions expressed in the discussion.
> 'You get involved in family issues.'
> 'It can be lonely.'
> 'I like organising my own working life.'

Write an **essay** for your tutor in 220–260 words in an appropriate style, discussing **two of the reasons** in your notes. **You should explain which issue might be the most difficult and provide reasons** to support your opinion.

You may, if you wish, make use of the opinions expressed in the discussion, but you should use your own words as far as possible.

Model answer

As technology has progressed, so it has become easier for people to work from home. Gone are the days when most employees were expected to be in the office every day from 9 to 5. There are many reasons why this change is desirable, such as increased flexibility, less commuting and more involvement in family life.

However, there are many reasons why it might cause difficulty. The first reason is to do with the loss of a clear dividing line between work and home life. Unless you are very focused, it takes a strong person not to turn on the television or get involved in domestic matters, such as picking the children up from school or dealing with a repair man trying to fix your washing machine.

Secondly, many employees need the discipline of being in a particular place at a particular time and being told what to do and when. Working from home demands a lot of self-discipline: you have to organise your own physical working environment and set yourself daily targets and deadlines. It is of no interest to the employer how and when the work is done, as long as the job is finished when required, even if it means the employee working all night.

In my view, the more difficult of the two issues is the second. While most of us will enjoy the independence of working from home, it does require a great deal of personal responsibility, and not all employees are self-starters, able to plan their day's work and stick to it.

Remember you are only asked for two reasons.

Answer all parts of the question.

Show awareness of different points of view.

Invent examples where necessary.

You can use opinions not written in the question.

Your opinion can be different from those in the task notes.

Further practice

You have attended a talk on the best ways to adapt to living abroad. You have made the notes below:

> **Ways to adapt to living abroad:**
> • being realistic about what life will be like
> • embracing the culture
> • making practical plans

> Some views expressed after the talk:
> 'I was charmed by the people at first, then they started to annoy me.'
> 'Lots of the locals spoke my language, which I liked.'
> 'It was better when I got a job.'

Write an **essay** for your tutor in 220–260 words in an appropriate style discussing **two of the ways** in your notes. **You should explain which way might be the most beneficial** and **provide reasons** to support your opinion.

You may, if you wish, make use of the opinions expressed in the discussion, but you should use your own words as far as possible.

Part 1: Essay (Sample 2)

➤ See EXPERT STRATEGIES on page 169.

Task

You have attended a seminar on why the development of nuclear power should be halted. You have made the notes below:

> **Reasons why the development of nuclear power should be halted:**
> - lack of safety
> - radioactive waste
> - cost

> *Some views expressed in the seminar:*
> *'Leaks can occur due to aging or earthquakes.'*
> *'Waste has to be stored for centuries.'*
> *'Other sources of energy are also not cheap.'*

Write an **essay** for your tutor in 220–260 words in an appropriate style, discussing **two of the reasons** in your notes. You **should explain which reason you think is more important** and **provide reasons** to support your opinion.

You may, if you wish, make use of the opinions expressed in the discussion, but you should use your own words as far as possible.

Model answer

Use a formal or semi-formal style.

Use clear connectors and one topic for each paragraph.

Use complex as well as simple and compound sentences.

It is often argued that nuclear power offers an unlimited and 'clean' source of energy. However, despite some attractions, on balance the disadvantages outweigh the advantages.

First, nuclear plants can never be made fully safe. As they get older and less reliable, so they become unstable and leakages can occur. Also, if there is a geological event such as an earthquake, there is a serious danger of leaks and contamination for miles around and a toxic aftermath which can last for decades.

Another safety concern is that the technology is the same as that used for nuclear weapons, which could make plants vulnerable to terrorist attacks and lead to a dangerous proliferation of nuclear weapons.

Next, and in my view the main reason why nuclear power is unattractive, is the problem of radioactive waste and the need to store it underground until it no longer poses a threat, which could be hundreds of thousands of years. The dangers associated with 'safe' storage over such a long period are unknown but it is unlikely that there could ever be complete protection from the threat of earthquakes. Are we not just dumping our problems onto future generations?

To sum up, I feel the issue of waste is probably the main argument against nuclear power and the reason why we need to think of alternatives. We need to develop further renewable and efficient sources of energy using the sun, the wind and the sea. Some countries have made a good start in this direction, but most have done far too little.

Introduce the argument in general terms.

Use a range of vocabulary.

Remember you have been asked to support an argument.

Finish with a logical conclusion.

Further practice

You have attended a panel discussion on what methods can be used to make a closer link between schools and the workplace. You have made the notes below:

> **Methods of linking school to the workplace:**
> - employers in the classroom
> - work placements
> - curriculum changes

> *Some opinions expressed in the discussion:*
> *'There's no point spending two weeks in an office just filing.'*
> *'Employers can help teachers adapt teaching materials.'*
> *'Maths and language skills should be focused on more.'*

Write an **essay** for your tutor in 220–260 words in an appropriate style, discussing **two of the methods** in your notes. You **should explain which method you think is more important** and **provide reasons** to support your opinion.

You may, if you wish, make use of the opinions expressed in the discussion, but you should use your own words as far as possible.

Part 2: Report

➤ See EXPERT STRATEGIES on page 170.

Task

You are on the leisure committee of your college and you have been asked by the town council to write a report on the leisure facilities for young people in the town.

Your report should indicate what facilities young people use, explain whether the facilities are adequate or inadequate, giving reasons, and suggest other ways the town might help young people.

Write your **report** in 220–260 words.

Model answer

List the aims of the report and say where you got your information.

Use clear headings linked to the question.

Use numbers or bullet points for a list.

Save your recommendations for the end.

Don't use the same words as the input.

Use an impersonal formal style.

Make your points clearly and succinctly.

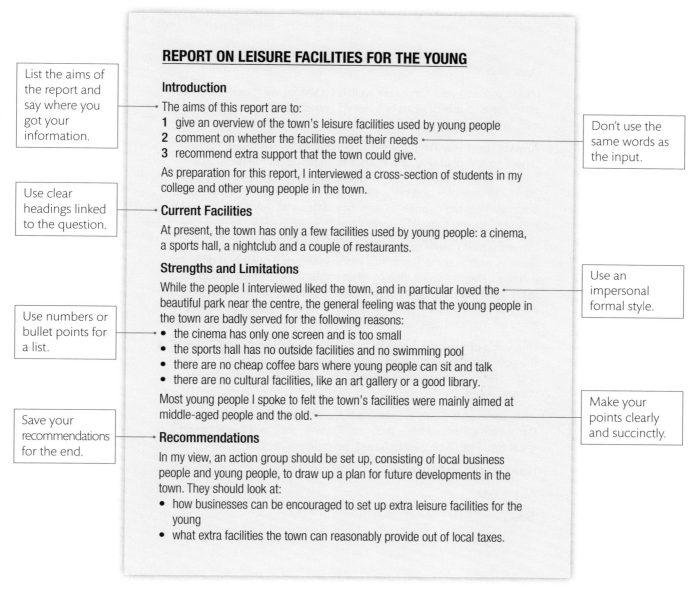

REPORT ON LEISURE FACILITIES FOR THE YOUNG

Introduction

The aims of this report are to:

1 give an overview of the town's leisure facilities used by young people
2 comment on whether the facilities meet their needs
3 recommend extra support that the town could give.

As preparation for this report, I interviewed a cross-section of students in my college and other young people in the town.

Current Facilities

At present, the town has only a few facilities used by young people: a cinema, a sports hall, a nightclub and a couple of restaurants.

Strengths and Limitations

While the people I interviewed liked the town, and in particular loved the beautiful park near the centre, the general feeling was that the young people in the town are badly served for the following reasons:

- the cinema has only one screen and is too small
- the sports hall has no outside facilities and no swimming pool
- there are no cheap coffee bars where young people can sit and talk
- there are no cultural facilities, like an art gallery or a good library.

Most young people I spoke to felt the town's facilities were mainly aimed at middle-aged people and the old.

Recommendations

In my view, an action group should be set up, consisting of local business people and young people, to draw up a plan for future developments in the town. They should look at:

- how businesses can be encouraged to set up extra leisure facilities for the young
- what extra facilities the town can reasonably provide out of local taxes.

Further practice

You are a student in the Information Department of an international college. You have been asked to write a report for an international survey about how the students in your college use the internet.

Your report should indicate how much it is used by students for study purposes and how much by teachers in classes, what the benefits and problems are (if any), and suggest ways it can be further integrated into courses.

Write your **report** in 220–260 words.

Part 2: Letter (1)

➤ See EXPERT STRATEGIES on page 170.

Task

Next summer you are taking a group of teenagers to an English-speaking country and you are looking for a good place to stay. Write a letter to a friend of yours in 220–260 words in an appropriate style explaining:
• the kind of place you are looking for
• how your friend might help you with other aspects of the visit
• why there might be problems with some members of the group.
Write your **letter**.

Model answer

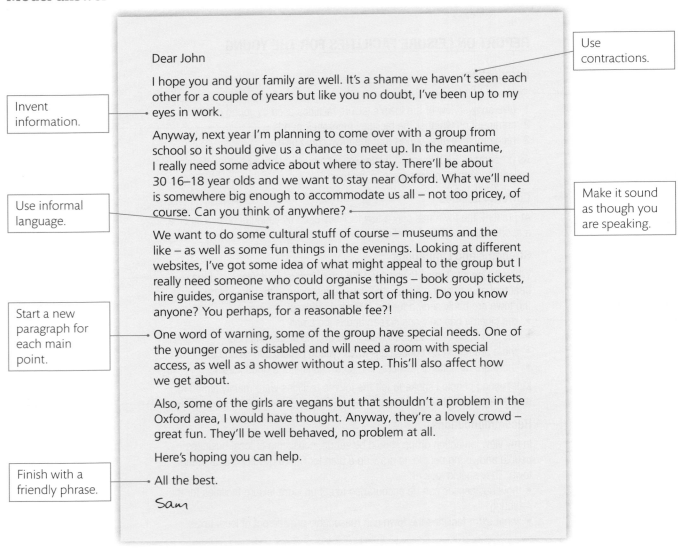

Use contractions.

Invent information.

Use informal language.

Make it sound as though you are speaking.

Start a new paragraph for each main point.

Finish with a friendly phrase.

Dear John

I hope you and your family are well. It's a shame we haven't seen each other for a couple of years but like you no doubt, I've been up to my eyes in work.

Anyway, next year I'm planning to come over with a group from school so it should give us a chance to meet up. In the meantime, I really need some advice about where to stay. There'll be about 30 16–18 year olds and we want to stay near Oxford. What we'll need is somewhere big enough to accommodate us all – not too pricey, of course. Can you think of anywhere?

We want to do some cultural stuff of course – museums and the like – as well as some fun things in the evenings. Looking at different websites, I've got some idea of what might appeal to the group but I really need someone who could organise things – book group tickets, hire guides, organise transport, all that sort of thing. Do you know anyone? You perhaps, for a reasonable fee?!

One word of warning, some of the group have special needs. One of the younger ones is disabled and will need a room with special access, as well as a shower without a step. This'll also affect how we get about.

Also, some of the girls are vegans but that shouldn't a problem in the Oxford area, I would have thought. Anyway, they're a lovely crowd – great fun. They'll be well behaved, no problem at all.

Here's hoping you can help.

All the best.

Sam

Further practice

A friend has sent you a letter asking your advice on organising a farewell party for a work colleague. You have been asked to give some ideas about:
• timing
• catering arrangements
• suitable entertainment.
Write your **letter** in 220–260 words in an appropriate style, giving your advice.

Part 2: Letter (2)

➤ See EXPERT STRATEGIES on page 170.

Task

You have received this letter from a hotel after a recent visit. You have decided to write a letter of complaint to the hotel manager.

Your letter should respond to the points in the letter from the hotel.

> *Thank you for filling out our feedback questionnaire. We are sorry to see that you were not satisfied with your arrival arrangements. Would you be so kind as to provide us with detailed comments and make suggestions for improvement? We trust the rest of your stay was satisfactory and will happily give you one night's free accommodation on your next visit.*

Write your **letter** in 220–260 words.

Model answer

Write 'Dear Mr Stephens'/'Dear Ms Jenkins' if you know the name of the person.

Don't make your language too forceful or you will have a negative effect on the reader.

Try to end on a positive note.

Use a formal ending.

Use formal language.

Say why you are writing.

Explain what the problem was. Give details about what happened. Try to remain factual but polite.

Give further details.

Don't forget to answer all parts of the question.

Dear Sir/Madam

I am writing in response to your letter asking for detailed comments about our stay at your hotel.

When my husband and I first arrived to check into the hotel, we were surprised that there was no one at the reception desk. We rang the bell, but no one took any notice. After a very frustrating wait, a young receptionist appeared. We explained we had been waiting for ten minutes and were surprised by his rather discourteous reply.

Eventually, after an incredibly slow check-in, we were given a key and went to our room, only to find that it had not been cleaned. The bed was unmade, and there were dirty towels on the floor. We went back down to reception to complain, and were given a rather weak apology, and told to wait until the cleaners could be found. We asked to be moved into a different room, but this was refused without explanation. All in all, it was another hour before our room was cleaned and we could settle in.

Clearly, the two problems were staffing and training. There need to be more staff working in reception at the time of day when most guests arrive, and they need to be better trained in dealing with guests. There also need to be more cleaners.

Fortunately, things got better after we had settled in, and the rest of the stay was satisfactory. We appreciate the offer of a free night's accommodation and will gratefully accept the next time we are in the area.

Yours faithfully
A. N. Other

Further practice

Student numbers at the international college where you are studying have been declining in recent years. You have been asked by your student committee to write a letter to the local newspaper. Your letter should explain:
• why your college is losing students
• what the college is planning to do
• how the local council and local businesses could help.

Write your **letter** in 220–260 words.

Expert writing

Part 2: Proposal

→ See EXPERT STRATEGIES on page 170.

Task

You work for a small company, and you see this notice on the staff noticeboard.

> *The company has been informed by government inspectors that it pays too little attention to environmental issues.*
>
> *The chief executive invites you to send a proposal outlining the three main areas in which there are problems **and** to make an overall recommendation for taking the matter forward. Decisions will then be made about a suitable course of action.*

Write your **proposal** in 220–260 words.

Model answer

Have a suitable neutral title.

Make it clear where the proposal is coming from.

Use formal language.

Conclude with your suggestion.

Proposal to improve company environmental policy

Introduction
In the view of many of my colleagues, the government inspectors have made a correct judgement: the company at present does too little to conserve natural resources, reduce pollution in all its activities and influence and encourage others to be more aware of environmental issues.

Efficient use of energy
From our own observations, there is considerable waste in terms of energy, including lighting, water heating and refrigeration. However, at present, staff appear unaware of the need for conservation and to reduce energy consumption.

Environmentally friendly products
The companies that supply detergents and pesticides are at present not encouraged to provide the company with environmentally friendly products, endangering the work environment and the health of the people who work there.

Waste
Little attention is given to ways of reducing waste and making it easier to reuse and recycle paper, glass, aluminium, plastics and other company waste, using the most environmentally friendly means. This indicates a lack of responsibility in such matters and compares unfavourably with other companies we know.

Committee recommendation
We propose that a group of environmental consultants is brought into the company to examine what we do, and suggest ways in which we can make members of staff aware of environmental issues and encourage them to get involved. Some of us have had personal experience of the consultants Johnson and Co., and we believe they would be a suitable choice. We urge the company to take this forward as a matter of urgency.

Break the proposal into sections and include sub-headings.

Be clear, concise and direct.

Use a detached tone.

Use the passive voice to 'distance' the criticisms.

The aim of the proposal is to persuade the reader about your suggestion, so you need to show conviction without being offensive.

Further practice

You work for an international tour company which, in the summer, recruits large numbers of untrained students to work on its campsites in a number of roles: dealing with arrivals and departures, organising children's activities and solving general problems. Your company director has asked you to write a proposal for a training programme indicating:
• the sort of training that will be required
• how long the training will take
• how the company will benefit.

Write the **proposal** in 220–260 words.

Part 2: Review

➤ See EXPERT STRATEGIES on page 170.

Task

The editor of an international student magazine has asked you to write a review which compares two action films you have seen recently **and** gives reasons for these opinions.

Write your **review** in 220–260 words.

Model answer

Catch your readers' attention in the opening sentence.

Make the plot summary very brief: your aim is evaluation.

Include evaluative adjectives as you go along.

If you are reviewing two films, use the language of comparison and contrast.

Best and worst action films

What a difference a good script can make! *World War Z*, an apocalyptic horror film in which one man saves the world, and *A Good Day To Die Hard*, the fifth film in the *Die Hard* franchise, may both be comic book action movies but while one is gripping and well crafted, the other is tired and dull.

At the start of *World War Z*, the Brad Pitt character, a former investigator for the UN, tries to get his family to safety. He is then reluctantly persuaded by his former UN boss to cross the world to try to stop a global zombie uprising. Fortunately, the director keeps the film rooted in a compelling dramatic situation. The set pieces are nail-biting and work at an emotional level, and by today's standards Pitt is a refreshingly human-scaled movie hero, with no outsized strength, agility or superpowers to help him.

By contrast, *A Good Day To Die Hard* will be a letdown to the millions of Bruce Willis fans. Gone is the reluctant, vulnerable hero of the earlier films and in his place is a boring supercop. The hero travels to Russia to help his wayward son, unaware that he is a highly trained secret service operative, and gets caught up in the crossfire of a terrorist plot. Despite some good action sequences, much of the film is repetitive and cliché-ridden and the characterisation weak.

Whereas *World War Z* mixes crowd-pleasing fantasy with the serious issue of how governments around the world might respond if their populations were under threat, the Willis film has no depth to it at all.

Write a similar amount about each film.

Summarise your evaluation briefly.

Further practice

Your college newspaper has asked you to write a review of two magazines or newspapers (they can be online publications) that appeal to different kinds of readers. Say in what ways they are different **and** what makes them popular with their readers, giving your personal views about the publications.

Write your **review** in 220–260 words.

Linking devices

In a coherent piece of writing, all the ideas are relevant to the main point and are presented in a logical sequence. A cohesive piece of writing uses linking devices to signal the relationship between the ideas clearly and to avoid unnecessary repetition.

Logical links

1 Expressions which link ideas within a sentence (conjunctions)

- Addition: *and, as well as*
- Time: *after, as, as soon as, before, once, since, until, when, while*
- Contrast/change of direction: *although, but, despite, even if, even though, in spite of, while, whereas*
- Reason/result: *as, because, since, so*
- Purpose: *(in order) to, so that*

Note: *and, but, so* usually only go in the middle of the sentence. All the other conjunctions can go either in the middle or at the beginning of the sentence.

2 Expressions which link ideas across sentences (adverbials)

- Addition: *also, as well, besides, furthermore, in addition, moreover, too, what's more*
- Time: *afterwards, beforehand, eventually, finally, first, in the end, lastly, later, meanwhile, next, secondly*
- Example/Illustration: *for example, for instance*
- Contrast/Change of direction: *even so, however, nevertheless, nonetheless, on the other hand, still, yet*
- Reason/Result: *as a result, because of this, consequently, that's why, therefore*
- Conclusion: *in conclusion, in summary, last of all, to conclude*

Notes
1 *As well, too* go at the end of a sentence.
2 *Finally, later, eventually, also, therefore, consequently* usually go at the beginning of the sentence.
3 All the other adverbs normally go at the beginning of the sentence.

Grammatical reference links

1 Reference words

- Personal pronouns (*he, they, her, their, its,* etc.)
  I met your father. **He**'*s very young.*
- Articles (*the, a, an*)
  He's got two children. **The** *son is a doctor and* **the** *daughter is a teacher.*
- Determiners (*this, that, these, those*)
  That *idea was very original.*
- Relative pronouns (*who, which*)
  I met your father, **who** *is very young.*

2 Other substitutions

- *there, then*
  The Ritz is a good hotel. We stayed **there** *last July. It was very busy* **then**.
- *one, ones*
  We missed the bus so we got a later **one**.
  They will be the **ones** (= the people) *who will benefit.*
- auxiliary verbs (*do/does/did, have/had, can/could,* etc.)
  Tom likes fish and so **do** *I.* (= I like fish too.)
  'I couldn't go to the show.' 'Neither **could** *I.'*
  (= I couldn't go to the show either.)
- *so, such*
  She was very lively as a child and remained **so** *throughout her life.*
  He was very rude. **Such** *behaviour* (= behaviour like this) *is not acceptable.*
- *if so/if not*
  Do you eat meat? **If so** (= if you eat meat), *I'll cook chicken.* **If not** (= if you don't eat meat), *I'll do a vegetable stew.*
- Relative clauses
  I sat out in the sun without wearing sunscreen, **which** *was very stupid of me.* (which refers to the whole of the previous clause)

3 Omission

Sometimes, we can omit words altogether.
We could stay in, but I'd prefer not to ~~stay in~~.
He never offers to clean or ~~he never offers to~~ *wash the dishes.*
Sally likes tea but not (= she doesn't like) *coffee.*

Lexical reference links

Parallel expressions
Science fiction *is full of descriptions about how humans might look in the future. It may seem rather far-fetched to think we will have electronic arms and legs, laser vision or be able to fly, as* **the genre** (= science fiction) *would have us believe.*

Punctuation

1 Capital letters

- To begin a sentence: *We saw him yesterday.*
- For the pronoun *I*, names, titles, countries, nationalities, streets, cities, days of the week and months (not seasons) of the year:
  Mr Jones, the Welshman, Oxford Street, last Friday, last spring, in May

2 Full stops

- To mark the end of a sentence: *I'm very homesick.*
- For abbreviations: *Prof.* (= Professor), *a.m.* (= in the morning)
- With decimals, prices and time: *At 4.30 the price rose 3.3% to £4.99.*

Notes

1 Full stops are not used with abbreviations where the last letter of the abbreviation is also the last letter of the word: *Mr* for *Mister*, *Dr* for *Doctor*.
2 With some abbreviations, full stops are a matter of style and are sometimes omitted: *6 am, the UK*

3 Apostrophes

- To indicate possession: *my brother's house* (= one brother); *my brothers' house* (= more than one brother); *my parents' house*
- To indicate a contraction (a shorter form of a word or words): *haven't* is a contracted form of *have not*; *won't* is a contracted form of *will not*

Notes

1 When a word ends in *-s*, a second *-s* is not necessary:
  Mr Hughes' dog
2 The possessive pronoun *its* has no apostrophe:
  *The hotel has **its** own pool.*
  It's is a contraction of *it is* or *it has*:
  It's mine. Jack's got a new car.
3 Be careful not to use an apostrophe with numbers and abbreviations when the *s* is used to indicate a plural, not possession:
  the 1900s, CDs

4 Commas

- To separate items in a list:
  I bought apples, pears(,) and bananas.
- To separate an introductory word, phrase or clause:
  Happily, the weather was fine in the end.
  In my view, smoking should be banned.
  When it rains, I take an umbrella.
  If you're thirsty, have a drink of water!
  Being a nice person, he offered to help.
- Around inserted phrases and clauses:
  John, as we all know, is lazy.
  He is, however, very intelligent.
  Sue, who works in a bank, is a friend of mine.
  The woman, hungry after a long journey, started to eat.
- To separate some final elements such as question tags and participle clauses:
  You're tired, aren't you?
  I didn't go, not being interested in such things.
- In direct speech:
  'It's late,' he said. He said, 'It's late.'
- Optional before *and, or, but*:
  Tom tries hard(,) but Sue doesn't.

Note: the use of the comma before *and* in a list is much more common in American English than in British English.

5 Speech marks

- To separate direct speech from the rest of a sentence.

Notes

1 A comma is used to set off a direct quotation from the rest of the sentence, and a capital letter to start the quotation:
  John shouted, 'Come out of the water now!'
2 If a quoted sentence is split up, the second part does not begin with a capital:
  'That,' he said, 'is my house.'
3 Commas or full stops at the end of a quoted speech are inside the speech marks.

6 Other punctuation

- Colon (:)
  - to introduce a list:
    The hotel has everything: a gym, a sauna, …
  - before a phrase that gives more information or an example:
    He got poor marks: not surprising when you consider how little work he did.
  - to introduce a quotation.
    As Shakespeare said: 'All the world's a stage.'
- Semi-colon (;)
  - to separate two main clauses that are closely linked in meaning, so that a full stop would be too strong a break between them:
    He was once poor at English; now he's a Professor of English.
- Dash (–)
  - in informal writing, to separate a part of a sentence which adds extra information:
    The second man – Tom Jones – was well known to the police.
    I've been to Paris – in fact, I went there last year.

Spelling

Spelling changes

1 Words ending in -ch, -sh, -s, -ss, -x, -z, -zz

- Add -es instead of -s:
  bun**ches**, wash**es**, addres**ses**, coa**xes**, bu**zzes**

2 Words ending in consonant + -y

- Nouns/verbs change -y to -ie when a suffix is added:
  enquiry → enqui**ries**, fly → fl**ies**, tidy → tid**ier**
- But -y doesn't change before -ing:
  carry → carr**ied** → carr**ying**
- Change -y to -i for other suffixes:
  mystery → myster**ious**, pity → pit**iful**,
  busy → bus**ily**, heavy → heav**iness**

3 Words ending in vowel + -y

- Add -s: journ**eys**, pa**ys**
- But for past participles, change -y to -i and add -d:
  lay → la**id**
- Note these adverbs: day → da**ily**, gay → ga**ily**

4 Words ending in -f/-fe

- Add -s: gul**fs**, chie**fs**
- But note: thief → thie**ves**.
  Also: self, shelf, loaf, leaf, knife, wife, life, half

5 Words ending in vowel + -o

- Add -s: radi**os**, shamp**oos**

6 Words ending in consonant + -o

- Add -es: potat**oes**, tomat**oes**, her**oes**
- Note that loan words and abbreviations add -s:
  cell**os**, phot**os**

7 Words ending in -e

- Drop silent -e after a consonant and before a
  vowel: stride → strid**ing**, invite → invit**ation**
- But keep -e in words like like → lik**eable**,
  dye → dy**eing** and -ee words: s**eeing**, agr**eeable**

8 Words ending in -ie

- For -i suffixes, e.g. -ing, change -ie to -y:
  die → d**ying**, lie → l**ying**
- For -e suffixes, drop one -e: di**ed**, li**ed**

9 Words ending in -c

- To keep the /k/ sound, add -k panic → pani**cking**
- Add -al to -ic words for -ly words:
  frantic → franti**cally**

10 Words ending in a consonant

- For words ending in a vowel + a consonant, with
  the last syllable stressed, double the only or final
  consonant:
  fit → fi**tter**, prefer → pre**ferring**, occur → occu**rred**
- In British English, words ending in -l or -p
  normally double the consonant even if the stress is
  on other syllables (trave**lling**, handica**pped**)

- -s is sometimes doubled: focu**sed** or focu**ssed**
- Don't double the final consonant of
  – words with two vowels before the final
    consonant: plain → plain**er**
  – words with two final consonants: fast → fast**er**

Some useful rules

- -ise (verb)/-ice (noun): adv**ise**/adv**ice**
  Note the American English for some verbs: real**ize**,
  computer**ize**
- -ie when the sound is /iː/ except after -c: ach**ie**ve,
  n**ie**ce (but rec**ei**ve)
  Exceptions: s**ei**ze, prot**ei**n
- -ei for other sounds: n**ei**ghbour, l**ei**sure, th**ei**r, w**ei**ght,
  for**ei**gn
  Exception: fr**ie**nd

Hyphens

Hyphens are used to join words to form compound
nouns or adjectives and to add affixes. They are
important in

- numerical expressions: a five-star hotel, a thirty-minute
  wait
- compound adjectives which come before the noun:
  blue-eyed, up-and-coming
- affixes to help pronunciation (co-operate) or to avoid
  confusion: resent/re-sent.

Endings often misspelt

- Adjectives
  -ible/-able: vis**ible**, irresist**ible**, respons**ible**, lov**able**,
    valu**able**, advis**able**
  -ful: cheer**ful**, hand**ful**, success**ful**
  -ent/-ant: perman**ent**, confid**ent**, ignor**ant**, observ**ant**
  -ous/-eous/-ious: marvell**ous**, courag**eous**, anx**ious**
- Nouns
  -ence/-ance: influ**ence**, differ**ence**, correspond**ence**,
    assist**ance**, attend**ance**, appear**ance**
  -al/-le/-el: propos**al**, circ**le**, quarr**el**
  -er/-or/-ar: offic**er**, solicit**or**, fact**or**, burgl**ar**
  -ary/-ery/-ory/-ry: libr**ary**, robb**ery**, direct**ory**, fact**ory**,
    po**etry**
  -tion/-sion/-ssion: rela**tion**, occa**sion**, posse**ssion**
- Verbs
  -cede/-ceed: pre**cede**, re**cede**, ex**ceed**, pro**ceed**

Commonly misspelt words

accommodation, approximate, because, biscuit, building,
business, campaign, compare, desert/dessert, development,
different, disappoint, disguise, embarrass, exhaustion,
familiar, follow, frequent, guarantee, guilty, immediately,
immigrant, individual, interest, leisure, medicine,
mountaineer, necessary, occupation, pastime, pleasant,
professional, pronunciation, receipt, separate, scissors, similar,
surface, technical, through

Attitude clauses and phrases

Attitude, or comment, phrases are not an integral part of the sentence, but indicate the speaker's/writer's attitude to the action or event, or a comment on its truth.

1 Finite attitude clauses

As far as I know, she's coming next week.
As I said, we will need to leave very early.
John is leaving, *as you know*.
As we shall see, this decision was to cost him his life.
I can't help you, *I'm afraid*.
Believe it or not, he passed all his exams.
As it turns out, she didn't need to come.
You know, it might be a good idea to go by train.
I can't be the driver. *You see*, I don't know how to drive.
The truth is, nothing has changed since the election.

2 Non-finite attitude clauses

These include participle and *to*-infinitive phrases:

All things considered, we've done very well.
Considering (the problems we've had), we've done very well.
We've done very well, *considering* (the problems we've had).
Taking everything into consideration, I think we've earned a break.
Generally (speaking), women earn less than men.
To be honest, I didn't really like the book.
Judging by his recent performance, he should win the cup.
Speaking from memory, I'd say it's about ten miles from here.
Strictly speaking, we shouldn't be here.
To tell the truth, I'd forgotten all about it.
It's fairly risky. *Or to put it another way*, don't try this on your own.

3 Sentence adverbs

A Giving your opinion about/reaction to some event
annoyingly, funnily (enough), hopefully, luckily, naturally, oddly (enough), rightly, strangely, (not) surprisingly, understandably, worryingly

Hopefully, the government will change its mind.
Oddly enough, someone asked me the same question only yesterday.
There's a lot of talk, *quite rightly*, about the dangers of smoking.

B Commenting on the truth or likelihood of some event
actually, arguably, certainly, clearly, definitely, doubtless, evidently, obviously, presumably, really, surely, as a matter of fact, in fact, of course

Actually, what happened was that …
Doubtless he will be promoted before long.
Of course, his father is the managing director.
Surely you don't mean that?

C Emphasising what you have said
indeed, as a matter of fact, in fact

I don't mind at all. *Indeed*, I'm pleased to be asked.

D Admitting something is true
admittedly, granted

Her technique needs improving, *granted*, but she puts great feeling into her performance.

E Explaining how you are speaking
frankly, honestly, personally, seriously

Personally, I think it's a terrible idea.
I don't like him, *quite frankly*.

F Generalising
as a rule, by and large, in the main, on the whole

As a rule, I don't have breakfast at weekends.
By and large, the conference went very well.
In the main, the climate is very mild.
On the whole, things turned out for the best.

Sentence structure

1 The main sentence patterns of English

A Main clause: subject + verb (+ complement/object)

A sentence in English must have at least a subject + a verb.

The shop is closing. (S+V)
Coffee bars are a favourite with customers. (S+V+C)
Some stores employ a number of entertainment techniques. (S+V+O)

The subject always comes before the verb, except in questions and some special cases for style or emphasis.

➤ See Grammar reference pages 183 (cleft sentences) and 184 (fronting and inversion).

B Main clause + coordinating conjunction (*and, or, but, so*) + main clause

Shopping is something we all have to do(,) **but many people go shopping just for fun**.

Note: A comma is optional before a conjunction in British English.

C 1 Main clause + subordinate clause

I love going to parties **as I'm a very sociable person**.

2 Subordinate clause, + main clause

Although I enjoy lying on the beach doing nothing, *I couldn't do it for very long.*

Note: A comma is used when the subordinate clause comes first.

D Main clause + inserted information

Unfortunately, *there is not a lot to do in the evenings.*
To tell the truth, *most evenings I prefer to stay at home and read a book.*
Going to work, **believe it or not**, *is some people's idea of a good time.*
Not finding it easy to relax when I come home from work, *I usually watch TV.*
My father enjoys life to the full, **which is amazing for someone his age**.

E Main clause. Linking expression + main clause

I only enjoy myself when I'm with people I like.
That's why *I only go out with friends.*

Taking part in online auctions can be fun. **What's more**, *you can find some real bargains.*

The basic sentence patterns can be combined into complex sentences containing more than one clause.

Strolling through a town centre on a Saturday, the country's busiest shopping day, you might come across such things as drama workshops, a fairground ride or even a brass band raising money for charity, all of which are part of a campaign to encourage people to visit town.

2 Fragments

A group of words that does not contain a subject and verb and does not express a complete idea is a **fragment**.

She decided to study French. Because she loved the language so much. ✗

We can attach the fragment to the previous sentence:

She decided to study French because she loved the language so much. ✓
John promised to pay me back the money. Which he didn't do. ✗
John promised to pay me back the money, which he didn't do. ✓

We can add a subject to the second sentence:

John promised to pay me back the money. He didn't do so. ✓

3 Run-ons

When two complete, independent clauses are run together with no adequate punctuation to mark the break between them, this is a **run-on** sentence.

My job is very time-consuming, I have no time for a social life. ✗
A comma alone is not enough to join two independent clauses.

My job is very time-consuming. I have no time for a social life. ✓
Split the ideas into two separate sentences with a full stop.

My job is very time-consuming; I have no time for a social life. ✓
A semi-colon is also possible.

My job is very time-consuming and as a result, I have no time for a social life. ✓
Add a suitable linking expression.

Speaking material

Module 1B: Speaking (pages 16–17)

Exercise 5: Long turn

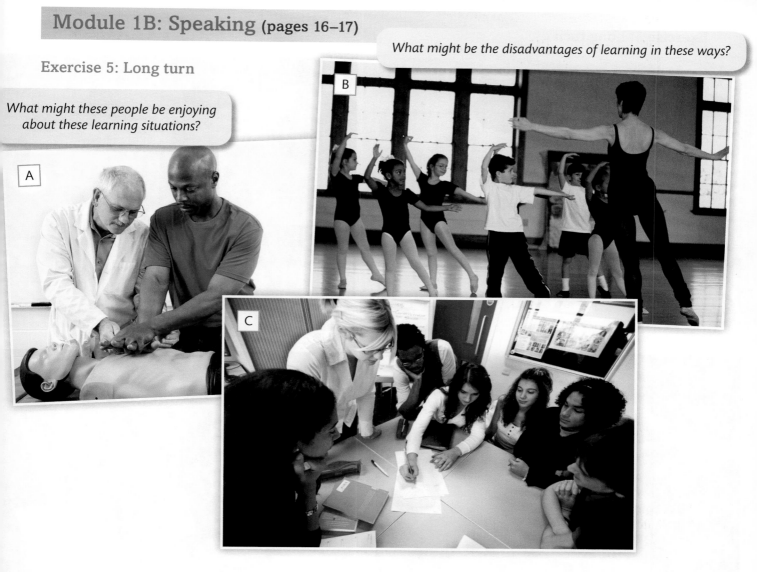

What might these people be enjoying about these learning situations?

What might be the disadvantages of learning in these ways?

Module 2B: Speaking (pages 32–33)

Exercise 4a: Social interaction

INTERLOCUTOR

First of all, we'd like to know something about you. (*Select one or two questions and ask candidates in turn.*)

- Where are you from?
- What do you do here/there?
- How long have you been studying English?
- What do you enjoy most about learning English?

Thank you. (*Select one or more questions from the following.*)

- How important do you think it is to speak more than one language? (Why?)
- Do you prefer to get your news from newspapers, television or the internet? (Why?)
- What has been your most interesting travel experience? (Why?)
- What do you hope to be doing in five years' time? (Why?)
- How do you like to spend time with your friends? (Why?)
- What interesting things have happened in your life recently? (Why?)
- If you could go anywhere you wanted on your holiday, where would it be?
- If you had the opportunity to try a new activity, what would it be?

Module 4B: Speaking (pages 64–65)

Exercise 5: Long turn

Module 6B: Speaking (pages 96–97)

Exercise 5: Long turn (Task 2)

Why might the people be making a decision in this situation?

Why might the decision be difficult?

Module 8A: Lead-in (page 119)

Exercise 1a: Key

1a   All true – except 8 (The euro was introduced in 1999) and 10 (The pound sterling is the oldest currency in the world.)

Module 8B: Speaking (pages 128–129)

Exercise 4c: Long turn

> Why may people have chosen to raise money in this way?

> How difficult might it be for them to raise money?

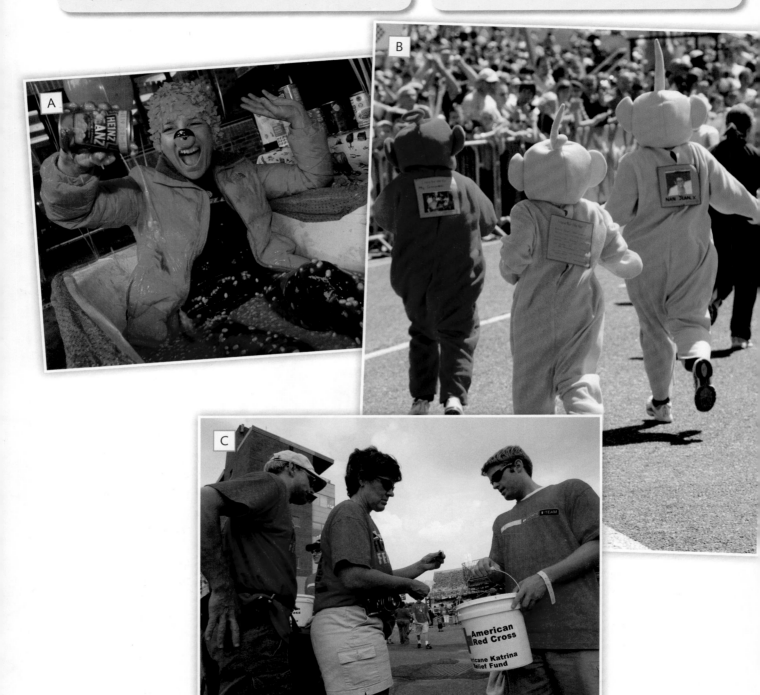

Module 9A: Lead-in (page 135)

Exercise 1a: Science quiz answers

1 B   2 B   3 C   4 A   5 C   6 B   7 A   8 B

Module 10: Speaking (pages 160–161)

Part 1: Social interaction

INTERLOCUTOR

(*Select one or two of the questions and ask candidates in turn, as appropriate.*)

First of all, we'd like to know something about you.
- Where are you from?
- What do you do here/there?
- How long have you been studying English?
- What do you enjoy most about learning English?

Thank you. (*Select one or more questions from the following, as appropriate.*)
- What free-time activity do you most enjoy? (Why?)
- What sort of work would you like to do in the future? (Why?)
- Do you think you spend too much time working or studying? (Why?/Why not?)
- Do you like using the internet to keep in touch with people?
- Have you celebrated anything recently? (How?)
- If you could travel to one country in the world, where would you go? (Why?)
- How important is it to you to spend time with your family? (Why?/Why not?)
- Who do you think has had the greatest influence on your life? (Why?)

(*Stop the discussion after two minutes.*)

Thank you.

Part 2: Long turn

INTERLOCUTOR

In this part of the test, I'm going to give each of you three pictures. I'd like you to talk about two of them on your own for about a minute, and also to answer a question briefly about your partner's pictures. (*Candidate A*), it's your turn first. Here are your pictures. They show people doing things in their spare time. I'd like you to compare two of the pictures and say why the people might have chosen to do these things, and how relaxing the activities might be. All right?

(*Stop the candidate after one minute.*)

Thank you. (*Candidate B*), which activity is the most difficult? (Why?)

(*Candidate B gives a short answer – about 30 seconds.*)

Thank you. Now, (*Candidate B*), here are your pictures. They show people taking part in different physical activities. I'd like you to compare two of the pictures, and say how the people might benefit from these activities, and how the people might be feeling. All right?

(*Stop the candidate after one minute.*)

Thank you. (Candidate A), which activity do you think benefits people the most? (Why?)

(*Candidate A gives a short answer – about 30 seconds.*)

Thank you.

Part 3: Collaborative task

INTERLOCUTOR

Now I'd like you to talk about something together for about two minutes. Here are some activities that some people find increase their sense of well-being and a question for you to discuss. First you have some time to look at the task.

(*Pause for 15 seconds.*)

Now, talk to each other about how these activities might contribute to someone's sense of well-being.

All right? Could you start now, please?

(*Stop candidates after two minutes.*)

Thank you.

(*Address both candidates.*)

Now you have about a minute to decide which experience would give the greatest satisfaction in the long run.

(*Stop the candidates after one minute.*)

Thank you.

Part 4: Extending the discussion

INTERLOCUTOR

Use the following questions in order, as appropriate. Stop the discussion after five minutes.
- How important is it for people to have a hobby? (Why?)
- Some people prefer to spend their spare time doing things on their own. Why do you think this is?
- Do you think that parents should decide how childre spend their spare time (get involved in their childre spare-time activities)? (Why?/Why not?)
- Some people find it difficult to choose a spare-tim activity. Why do you think this is?
- Which do you think is more important in your spa time – relaxing or getting exercise?
- Some people say that people nowadays spend to much time working and not enough time enjoyin themselves. What do you think?

Pearson Education Limited
Edinburgh Gate
Harlow
Essex CM20 2JE
England
and Associated Companies throughout the world.

www.pearsonELT.com

© Pearson Education Limited 2014

The right of Jan Bell and Roger Gower to be identified as author of this
Work has been asserted by him in accordance with the Copyright,
Designs and Patents Act 1988.

First published 2014
Second impression 2014

ISBN: 978-1-4479-6198-7

Set in Amasis and Mundo Sans
Printed in Slovakia by Neografia

Author Acknowledgements

Special thanks go to Nick Kenny, whose input and expertise was
invaluable, and to Liz Gardiner, the development editor. The authors
(Jan Bell and Roger Gower) would also like to thank all the staff at Pearson
who worked on the book in a range of professional capacities.

Acknowledgements

The publishers and author(s) would like to thank the following people and
institutions for their feedback and comments during the development of
the material: Rachel Buttery-Graciano,Teresita Curbelo (Instituto Cultural
Anglo Uruguayo),Krzysztof Lukaszewicz, John Schafer and Daniel Vincent.

Extract 1.a adapted from "The secret of my success: How five high-flying
women made it", The Independent, 27/08/2011 (Holly Williams),
copyright © The Independent, www.independent.co.uk; Extract 1.a
adapted from "Workspace design: How office space is becoming fun
again", The Guardian, 17/02/2012 (Tim Smedley), copyright © Guardian
News & Media Ltd 2012; Extract 1.a adapted from "Time out, not time
off for year projects", The Guardian, 19/08/2011 (Phoebe Kirk, Hal
Watts and Siraj Datoo), copyright © Guardian News & Media Ltd 2011;
Extract 2.a adapted from "Why Dudamel and the Simon Bolivar
Youth Orchestra have got a lot to prove", The Guardian, 22/06/2012
(Tom Silden), copyright © Guardian News & Media Ltd 2012;
Extract 2.a adapted from "Johann Hari: What I've got in common with
my teacher's kids", The Independent, 22/03/2011 (Johann Hari),
copyright © The Independent, www.independent.co.uk; Extract 2.b
adapted from Sentenced to dance (Angela Neustatter 2009) pp.66–72,
reproduced by permission of Reader's Digest Association Inc.; Extract 2.b
adapted from "Richard Branson champions employment of ex-offenders",
The Guardian, 15/11/2011 (Erwin James), copyright © Guardian News &
Media Ltd 2011; Extract 3.a adapted from "Foley artists: heard any good
films lately?", The Telegraph, 30/10/2011 (Richard Johnson), http://www.
telegraph.co.uk/culture/film/filmmakersonfilm/8853473/Foley-artists-
heard-any-good-films-lately.html, copyright © Telegraph Media Group
Limited; Extract 4.a adapted from "Slumber's unexplored landscape",
New Scientist, vol.156, no. 13, p.205 adapted with permission from
New Scientist; Extract 5.a adapted from "Britain's problem with pets:
how bad is it for the planet", The Guardian, 13/11/2009 (Leo Hickman),
copyright © Guardian News & Media Ltd 2009; Extract 5.a adapted from
"Can animals predict tsunamis?", The Guardian, 15/04/2012 (Philip Hoare),
copyright © Guardian News & Media Ltd 2012; Extract 6.a from You've
been framed, Intelligent Life Magazine, Winter 2010, http://
moreintelligentlife.com/content/ideas/anthony-gardner/youve-been-
framed by Anthony Gardner; Extract 7.a adapted from "Why we're living in a
tent culture", The Guardian, 11/02/2012 (Patrick Barkham), copyright
© Guardian News & Media Ltd 2012; Extract 8.a adapted from "Two's
company couples who work together", The Telegraph, 16/03/2012
(Angela Neystatter), http://www.telegraph.co.uk/family/9146563/
Twos-company-couples-who-work-together.html, copyright © Telegraph
Media Group Limited; Extract 8.a adapted from Two's company, Director
magazine (Sarah Nicolas), 2011, www.director.co.uk, copyright © Director
Publications; Extract 9.a adapted from "Eureka: Delia Strand Charging
ahead", The Times, p.50, October 2011, Issue 25, copyright © News
International Syndication Ltd; Extract 10.a after "Charging ahead", The Red
Bulletin, 01/03/2011, http://www.redbull.com, Reproduced with
permission

In some instances we have been unable to trace the owners of copyright
material, and we would appreciate any information that would enable us
to do so.